Lecture Notes
in Business Information Processing

264

Series Editors

Wil M.P. van der Aalst
Eindhoven Technical University, Eindhoven, The Netherlands
John Mylopoulos
University of Trento, Trento, Italy
Michael Rosemann
Queensland University of Technology, Brisbane, QLD, Australia
Michael J. Shaw
University of Illinois, Urbana-Champaign, IL, USA
Clemens Szyperski
Microsoft Research, Redmond, WA, USA

More information about this series at http://www.springer.com/series/7911

Stanislaw Wrycza (Ed.)

Information Systems: Development, Research, Applications, Education

9th SIGSAND/PLAIS EuroSymposium 2016
Gdansk, Poland, September 29, 2016
Proceedings

 Springer

Editor
Stanislaw Wrycza
Department of Business Informatics
University of Gdansk
Sopot
Poland

ISSN 1865-1348   ISSN 1865-1356   (electronic)
Lecture Notes in Business Information Processing
ISBN 978-3-319-46641-5   ISBN 978-3-319-46642-2   (eBook)
DOI 10.1007/978-3-319-46642-2

Library of Congress Control Number: 2016951708

Printed on acid-free paper

This Springer imprint is published by Springer Nature
The registered company is Springer International Publishing AG
The registered company address is: Gewerbestrasse 11, 6330 Cham, Switzerland

Preface

Systems analysis and design (SAND) is the classic field of research and education in the area of management information systems (MIS) or, as it is called more frequently in Europe – business informatics, almost from its origins. SAND continuously attracts the attention of both academia and business. The rapid and natural progress of ICT has generated the requirements for the new generation of methods, techniques, and tools of SAND, adequate for modern IS challenges. Therefore, international thematic conferences and symposia have become widely accepted forums for the exchange of concepts, solutions, and experiences in SAND. In particular, the Association for Information Systems (AIS) is undertaking the initiatives towards SAND's international development.

The objective of the EuroSymposium on Systems Analysis and Design is to promote and develop high-quality research on all issues related to SAND. It provides a forum for SAND researchers and practitioners in Europe and beyond to interact, collaborate, and develop their field. The Eurosymposia were initiated by Prof. Keng Siau as the SIGSAND – Europe Initiative. Previous EuroSymposia were held at:

- University of Galway, Ireland – 2006
- University of Gdansk, Poland – 2007
- University of Marburg, Germany – 2008
- University of Gdansk, Poland – 2011
- University of Gdansk, Poland – 2012
- University of Gdansk, Poland – 2013
- University of Gdansk, Poland – 2014
- University of Gdansk, Poland – 2015

The accepted papers of Gdansk EuroSymposia were published in:

- 2nd EuroSymposium 2007: A. Bajaj, S. Wrycza (eds), Systems Analysis and Design for Advanced Modeling Methods: Best Practises, Information Science Reference, IGI Global, Hershey, New York, 2009
- 4th EuroSymposium 2011: S. Wrycza (ed) 2011, Research in Systems Analysis and Design: Models and Methods, series: LNBIP 93, Springer, Berlin 2011
- Joint Working Conferences EMMSAD/EuroSymposium 2012 held at CAiSE'12: I. Bider, T. Halpin, J. Krogstie, S. Nurcan, E. Proper, R. Schmidt, P. Soffer, S. Wrycza (eds.) 2012, Enterprise, Business-Process and Information Systems Modeling, series: LNBIP 113, Springer, Berlin 2012
- 6th SIGSAND/PLAIS EuroSymposium 2013: S. Wrycza (ed.), Information Systems: Development, Learning, Security, Series: Lecture Notes in Business Information Processing 161, Springer, Berlin 2013
- 7th SIGSAND/PLAIS EuroSymposium 2014: S. Wrycza (ed.), Information Systems: Education, Applications, Research, Series: Lecture Notes in Business Information Processing 193, Springer, Berlin 2014

- 8th SIGSAND/PLAIS EuroSymposium 2015: S. Wrycza (ed.), Information Systems: Development, Applications, Education, Series: Lecture Notes in Business Information Processing 232, Springer, Berlin 2015

There were three organizers of the 9th EuroSymposium on Systems Analysis and Design:

- SIGSAND – Special Interest Group on Systems Analysis and Design of AIS
- PLAIS – Polish Chapter of AIS
- Department of Business Informatics of University of Gdansk, Poland

SIGSAND is one of the most active SIGs with a substantial record of contributions for AIS. It provides services such as annual American and European Symposia on SIGSAND, research and teaching tracks at major IS conferences, listserv, and special issues in journals.

The Polish Chapter of the Association for Information Systems (PLAIS) was established in 2006 as the joint initiative of Prof. Claudia Loebbecke, former president of AIS and Prof. Stanislaw Wrycza, University of Gdansk, Poland. PLAIS co-organizes international and domestic IS conferences.

The Department of Business Informatics of the University of Gdansk conducts intensive teaching and research activities. Some of its academic manuals are bestsellers in Poland and the department is active internationally. The most significant conferences organized by the department were: the Xth European Conference on Information Systems ECIS 2002 and the International Conference on Business Informatics Research, BIR 2008. The department is a partner of the ERCIS consortium – European Research Center for Information Systems.

EuroSymposium 2016 had an acceptance rate of 40 %, with submissions divided into the following three groups:

- Information Systems Development
- Information Systems Management
- Information Systems Learning

The accepted papers reflect the current trends in the field of systems analysis and design.

I would like to express my thanks to all authors, reviewers, advisory board, international Program Committee, and Organizing Committee members for their support, efforts, and time. They made possible the successful accomplishment of EuroSymposium 2016.

August 2016   Stanislaw Wrycza
                                                          General Chair

Organization

General Chair

Stanislaw Wrycza   University of Gdansk, Poland

Program Chairs

Stanislaw Wrycza   University of Gdansk, Poland

Advisory Board

Wil van der Aalst	Eindhoven University of Technology, The Netherlands
David Avison	ESSEC Business School, France
Joerg Becker	University of Muenster, Germany
Jane Fedorowicz	Bentley University, USA
Dimitris Karagiannis	University of Vienna, Austria
Julie Kendall	Rutgers University, USA
Helmut Krcmar	Technische Universität Muenchen, Germany
Claudia Loebbecke	University of Cologne, Germany
Keng Siau	Missouri University of Science and Technology, USA

International Program Committee

Stanisław Wrycza	University of Gdansk, Poland - chairman
Eduard Babkin	Higher School of Economics, Moscow, Russia
Akhilesh Bajaj	University of Tulsa, USA
Palash Bera	Saint Louis University, USA
Patrick Y.K. Chau	The University of Hong Kong, China
Petr Doucek	University of Economics, Prague, Czech Republic
Rolf Granow	Luebeck University of Applied Sciences, Germany
Bjoern Johansson	Lund University, Sweden
Kalinka Kaloyanova	Sofia University, Bulgaria
Vijay Khatri	Indiana University Bloomington, USA
Marite Kirikova	Riga Technical University, Latvia
Jolanta Kowal	University of Wroclaw, Poland
Tuomo Lindholm	Lapland University of Applied Sciences, Finland
Tim Majchrzak	University of Agder, Norway
Yannis Manolopoulos	University of Thessaloniki, Greece
Nikolaus Obwegeser	Aarhus University, Denmark
Jinsoo Park	Seoul National University, Korea
Nava Pliskin	Ben-Gurion University of the Negev, Israel

Jolita Ralyte   University of Geneva, Switzerland
Michael Rosemann   Queensland University of Technology, Australia
Isabel Ramos   The University of Minho, Portugal
Kurt Sandkuhl   The University of Rostock, Germany
Thomas Schuster   Forschungszentrum Informatik, Karlsruhe, Germany
Marcin Sikorski   Gdansk University of Technology, Poland
Piotr Soja   Cracow University of Economics, Poland
Angelos Stefanidis   University of Glamorgan, UK
Reima Suomi   University of Turku, Finland
Janice C. Sipior   Villanova University, USA
Pere Tumbas   University of Novi Sad, Serbia
Yinglin Wang   Shanghai University of Finance and Economics, China
H. Roland Weistroffer   Virginia Commonwealth University, USA
Carson Woo   Sauder School of Business, Canada
Jelena Zdravkovic   Stockholm University, Sweden
Iryna Zolotaryova   Kharkiv National University of Economics, Ukraine
Joze Zupancic   University of Maribor, Slovenia

Organizing Committee

Anna Studzińska   University of Gdansk, Poland
Dorota Buchnowska   University of Gdansk, Poland
Bartłomiej Gawin   University of Gdansk, Poland
Bartosz Marcinkowski   University of Gdansk, Poland
Jacek Maślankowski   University of Gdansk, Poland
Przemysław Jatkiewicz   University of Gdansk, Poland
Michał, Kuciapski   University of Gdansk, Poland

Contents

Information Systems Learning

Information Systems Development

Contractual Specification of Communication Tools in Outsourced ISD Projects

Sonia Gantman[1]([⊠]) and Jane Fedorowicz[2]

[1] Providence College, Providence, RI, USA
sgantman@providence.edu
[2] Bentley University, Waltham, MA, USA
jfedorowicz@bentley.edu

Abstract. Technical and organizational complexity of outsourced information systems development (ISD) projects calls for increased attention to communication, governance and control. Contract management and client-vendor relationships are both well studied but rarely analyzed together. Earlier studies suggest combining formal (i.e., agreed upon upfront and contractually specified) and informal (i.e., voluntary and emerging during the project) communication mechanisms for best results.

This study investigates "formalization" of communication by comparing the usefulness of communication tools specified in outsourcing contracts and tools selected by other means. Using survey responses from 389 IT project managers, we analyze communication mechanisms' effectiveness across four categories of contract provisions, and compare the perceptions of project participants regarding contractually specified vs. emergent communication tools.

Our results confirm that specifying communication tools in the outsourcing contract for complex knowledge intensive projects supports the main contract provisions, and, in turn, leads to better project outcomes.

Keywords: IT project management · Outsourcing · Contracts · Communication · Knowledge management

1 Introduction

Information systems development (ISD) projects, especially those outsourced to an external vendor, pose a significant challenge to project managers. The technical and organizational complexity of these projects leads to high uncertainty and interdependency, and, subsequently, calls for increased attention to communication practices and control mechanisms [6].

Contemporary literature on outsourcing and project management, both academic and practitioner-oriented, pays significant attention to communication in IT projects, client-vendor relationships, effective knowledge management, governance and control [5, 8, 12].

Contract management and client-vendor relationships are both critical components of IT outsourcing arrangements. However, they are addressed by two separate streams of research (e.g., [12]), and are rarely analyzed together. Earlier studies on communication

© Springer International Publishing AG 2016
S. Wrycza (Ed.): SIGSAND/PLAIS 2016, LNBIP 264, pp. 3–17, 2016.
DOI: 10.1007/978-3-319-46642-2_1

mechanisms in complex IT projects suggest that most successful systems of communication in knowledge intensive projects combine formal (i.e., agreed upon upfront and contractually specified) and informal (i.e., voluntary and emerging during the project) mechanisms.

In this study, we investigate the results of "formalization" of project related communication, by comparing the usefulness of communication tools specified in outsourcing contracts and tools selected by other means. We investigate the effect of formalization of communication mechanisms enabled by specifying communication tools in the outsourcing contract. Using survey responses from 389 project managers of complex outsourced IT projects, we analyze communication mechanisms' effectiveness across four categories of contract provisions uncovered in prior research on IT outsourcing contracts, and compare the perceptions of project participants regarding contractually specified vs. emergent communication tools.

Our results confirm that specifying communication tools in the outsourcing contract for complex knowledge intensive projects supports the main contract provisions of these contracts, and, in turn, leads to better project outcomes.

The paper is structured as follows. The next section provides an overview of the existing literature on the structure of IT outsourcing contracts, and presents the research questions/hypotheses to be addressed. The study methodology and data collection are discussed next. The paper concludes with a discussion of findings and suggestions for future research.

2   Background

Communication and knowledge management in complex knowledge intensive environments, such as outsourced Information systems development (ISD) projects, has attracted the attention of scholars from several social science and business disciplines, including Information Systems (IS) [5, 8, 12]. IS researchers approach ISD projects from pragmatic, economic, legal and behavioral perspectives (e.g., [15, 16]). We briefly discuss prior IS work related to the contract structures that accompany ISD projects, relating it to the nature and extent of communications guidance they embody.

Traditionally, explicit definitions of formal mechanisms of client-vendor relationship governance and control have been recommended for inclusion in contracts. The literature suggests that including governance mechanisms in an outsourcing contract significantly improves the quality of project control and positively affects the project's outcomes (e.g., [17]). However, in complex knowledge intensive environments tight formal control was found to impede creativity, and therefore should be complemented by informal governance mechanisms [1, 4, 13]. It is argued that well-managed complex projects allow for adjustments to communication practices during the project [14], as well as for introduction of new communication methods [3]. In the most successful projects part of the communications mechanisms are defined at the early stages as would be the case with those stipulated by contract [3, 11].

2.1   Types of Contracts

There are two main types of outsourcing contracts – "Time and materials" (TM) and "Fixed price" (FP). "Fixed price" contracts are focused on the outcomes more than on the process; "time and material" contracts are more likely to include procedures for behavior based control, such as those embedded in communication [3].

Although TM contracts are considered to be more flexible and lead to better outcomes, FP contracts still dominate the industry due to client companies' fear of losing control over the project. This fear may lead to specifying more communications mechanisms in the contract compared to TM projects, including the prescribed use of specific communication tools [3]. FP contracts, therefore, would be expected to include fewer communications requirements compared to TM contracts, due to their focus on the outcomes rather than on the process. At the same time, FP contracts are expected to include more control mechanisms in general, including control mechanisms inherent in communication media requirements [3]. As there is no evidence indicating which of these two inclinations would be stronger in practice, we propose a first hypothesis that contends that they will cancel each other out, and that communications-related stipulations would be found equally in the two types of contracts.

Hypothesis 1: There is no difference in the number of contractually specified communication tools between TM and FP projects.

Some studies of outsourcing contract structure provide a deeper insight into the specifics of contractual stipulations. For example, Poppo and Zenger [18] found that parties involved in customized technology development anticipate a greater likelihood of disputes and are more likely to include provisions on conflict resolution in the contract.

Contracts are very complex legal documents. While there are standard sections and clauses in those contracts initiating ISD projects, there are differences as well. One difference pertains to the language around the governance of the client-vendor relationship. The governance of day-to-day operations must be augmented by instruction concerning problems that arise and methods for resolving problems. Chen and Bharadwaj [2] classify ISD outsourcing contracts clauses into four major dimensions: *monitoring provisions* (timing and content of reviews), *dispute resolution* (procedures and conditions for escalation), *property rights allocation/protection* (including early agreement between the parties on the knowledge management procedures during the project), **and** *contingency provisions* (negotiation of changes in requirements). Each of these four dimensions provide opportunity for stipulating communication activity and means. Whether or not their inclusion will improve the governing ability of the project team is an open question not addressed by Chen and Bharadwaj [2]. Our next hypothesis therefore considers whether the inclusion of communication tools in an outsourcing contract improves their ability to support each of the four dimensions. We compare their usefulness to those selected by other means, for example, proposed by the management or emerged during the project.

Hypothesis 2. Specification of communication tools in the project contract makes them more useful for managing the project compared to tools chosen by other means.

H2a: *Specification of communication tools in the project contract makes them more useful for monitoring progress compared to the tools chosen by other means.*

H2b: *Specification of communication tools in the project contract makes them more useful for dispute resolution compared to the tools chosen by other means.*

H2c: *Specification of communication tools in the project contract makes them more useful for early agreement on knowledge management and property rights protection compared to the tools chosen by other means.*

H2d: *Specification of communication tools in the project contract makes them more useful for negotiating changes compared to the tools chosen by other means.*

Finally, the ultimate goal of studying any managerial practices in outsourced projects is to understand if the practice in question will result in better project outcomes. In the case of ISD projects, these usually combine both processual (budgetary and schedule) and product (quality and functionality) outcomes [6].

Hypothesis 3. Specification of communication tools in the project contract leads to better project outcomes.

3   Research Methodology

Post-hoc perceptual field data were collected from project managers of recently completed or close to completion outsourced ISD projects through an online cross sectional survey implemented with Qualtrics software. The study reported here uses part of the data collected in that survey. (Also see [6]).

The list of communication tools offered to survey participants was developed based on academic literature and interviews of field experts. The survey instrument was first pre-tested on two experienced project managers using the cognitive interviewing technique [19], and subsequently edited. This was followed by a pilot survey on a convenience sample of 26 project managers, leading to additional revisions to the questions and the list of tools commonly used for communication in IS development projects, assuring that the tool list reflected current project management practice.

The collected data cover use of various tools in client-vendor communication, details on the contract, the perceived usefulness of these tools for achieving various control objectives, client's perception of communication quality and satisfaction with the project outcomes. We also collected demographic information on respondents, projects and client organizations. All variables and calculated indices are listed in Table 1 and explained in the following sections.

3.1   Communication Tools Used in the Project

Study participants were asked to focus on their most recent project, whether completed, close to completion or ongoing, and indicate which tools they used for client-vendor

Table 1. Variables used in the study

Variable	Description	Scale
The use of communication tools in the project		
VisUML	Visuals: Flowcharts, diagrams	Dichotomous
VisCAD	Visuals: Engineering charts	1 - Yes,
Track	Issue tracking systems	0 - No
PM	Project Management tools	
Beta	Prototypes and beta versions	
WebShDocs	Web tools: Shared documents	
WebBlog	Web tools: Blogs, Wikis, Forums	
WebNet	Web tools: Virtual social networks	
Inclusion of communication tools in contract		
TC_Vis	Visual aids are specified in the contract	Dichotomous
TC_Track	Issue tracking systems are specified in the contract	1 - Yes,
TC_PM	Project Management tools are specified in the contract	0 - No
TC_Beta	Prototypes and beta versions are specified in the contract	
TC_Web	Web tools are specified in the contract	
Usefulness of communication tools for four dimensions of contract clauses		
"How useful are these tools for monitoring project progress?" (Monitoring provisions)		
Mon_Vis	Contribution of Visualizations to monitoring performance	3 - very
Mon_TR	Contribution of Issue Tracking tools to monitoring performance	useful; 2 - useful;
Mon_PM	Contribution of Project Management tools to monitoring performance	1 - somewhat useful;
Mon_Beta	Contribution of Prototypes and beta versions to monitoring performance	0 - not useful
Mon_Web	Contribution of Web based tools to monitoring performance	
"How useful are these tools for resolving conflict situations and misunderstandings between your company and the vendor?" (Dispute resolutions)		
Cnfl_Vis	Contribution of Visualizations to dispute resolution	3 - very
Cnfl_TR	Contribution of Issue Tracking tools to dispute resolution	useful;
Cnfl_PM	Contribution of Project Management tools to dispute resolution	2 - useful; 1 - somewhat
Cnfl_Beta	Contribution of Prototypes and beta versions to dispute resolution	useful; 0 - not useful
Cnfl_Web	Contribution of Web based tools to dispute resolution	

(*Continued*)

Table 1. (*Continued*)

Variable	Description	Scale
\"How useful are these tools for communicating your company's strategic goals and directions to the vendor?\" (Property rights allocation and protection)		
PrR_Vis	Contribution of Visualizations to property rights protection	3 - very useful;
PrR_TR	Contribution of Issue Tracking tools to property rights protection	2 - useful;
PrR_PM	Contribution of Project Management tools to property rights protection	1 - somewhat useful;
PrR_Beta	Contribution of Prototypes and beta versions to property rights protection	0 - not useful
PrR_Web	Contribution of Web based tools to property rights protection	
\"How useful are these tools for introducing and re-negotiating changes in requirements and procedures?\" (Contingency provisions)		
Cont_Vis	Contribution of Visualizations to supporting contingencies	3 - very useful;
Cont_TR	Contribution of Issue Tracking tools to supporting contingencies	2 - useful;
Cont_PM	Contribution of Project Management tools to supporting contingencies	1 - somewhat useful;
Cont_Beta	Contribution of Prototypes and beta versions to supporting contingencies	0 - not useful
Cont_Web	Contribution of Web based tools to supporting contingencies	
Cont_Vis	Contribution of Visualizations to supporting contingencies	
Contract Type		
Contract Type	Fixed Price (FP), Time and Material (TM) or a mix of the two types (at least 25 % is FP and at least 25 % is TM)	
Project Outcomes		
Budget	The project is within budget	7-point Likert scale
Schedule	The project is within the planned schedule	(1 - \"Much worse\",
Quality	The expectations for product quality have been met to date	4 - \"As expected\",
Functionality	The expectations for product functionality have been met to date	7 - \"Much better\")
Overall	Overall satisfaction with the project	

communication in it, using a pre-defined list of tools. Five categories of communication tools are used for data analysis (Table 2). For each type of communication tool identified by a survey respondent, we asked if this type of tool is included in the contract.

Table 2. Five categories of communication tools

Category	Subcategories, where applicable
Visualizations	Flowcharts and diagrams (for example, UML)
	Engineering charts
Issue tracking systems	
Project management tools	
Prototypes and beta versions	
Web 2.0 and groupware	Shared documents
	Wikis, forums, blogs
	Virtual social networks

3.2 Project Type and Specification of Communication Tools

We captured the type of contract as falling into one of three buckets: FP, TM and "mixed" projects, where "mixed" contract includes at least 25 % of TM and FP component. If study participants were not aware of the structure of their project contract, we omitted their responses from our data analysis.

3.3 The Effectiveness of Communication Tools

The effectiveness of communication tools was captured with four variables representing the four major dimensions identified in outsourcing contracts by Chen and Bharadwaj [3]: monitoring provisions, dispute resolution, property rights allocation and protection, and contingency provisions. Allocation of property rights should be communicated at the early stage of the project, together with strategic and tactical goals, which are at the core of the client-vendor relationship.

Table 3. Survey questions corresponding to the four contract provisions identified by Chen and Bharadwaj [3]

Survey question	Contract provisions
How useful are these tools for monitoring project progress?	Monitoring provisions
How useful are these tools for resolving conflict situations and misunderstandings between your company and the vendor?	Dispute resolution
How useful are these tools for communicating your company's strategic goals and directions to the vendor?	Property rights allocation/protection
How useful are these tools for introducing and re-negotiating changes in requirements and procedures?	Contingency provisions

For each category where at least one communication tool was selected, respondents assessed the usefulness of the tool category during the project for fulfilling each of the four contract provisions from Table 3. These twenty variables (five categories of tools across four contract dimensions) were measured on a 4-point Likert scale, with 3 meaning "very useful", 2 – "useful", 1 – "somewhat useful" and 0 – "not useful at all or counterproductive".

3.4   Satisfaction with the Project's Outcomes

Prior literature offers several theoretically supported and empirically tested frameworks for measuring the success of outsourcing arrangements (e.g., [10]). We adopted a scale used by several previous studies (e.g., [7]). Two items capture satisfaction with the final result (the quality and functionality of the implemented information system), two more items are concerned with the efficiency of the process (adherence to project's schedule and budget). An additional item captures overall satisfaction with the project results. All of these items are measured on a 7-point Likert scale, with 4 meaning that the project matches the expectations, and 1 and 7 indicating much worse and much better than expected respectively.

4   Findings

Most data analyses in this study are based on means comparisons and correlations. These methods are appropriate for our purposes, since the study is exploratory in nature.

4.1   The Sample

432 project managers of recently completed or close to completion outsourced ISD projects provided full valid responses to the survey. After eliminating 43 responses from project managers who were unfamiliar with their contract details, 389 responses remained. Examples of projects include ERP implementations, integrations of new modules, migrations of data or major software and infrastructure upgrades. The majority of study participants were recruited through the IS Community of Practice (IS CoP) of the Project Management Institute (PMI), the world's leading non-profit membership association for the project management profession.

The sample is well balanced in terms of respondents age, education and gender (Tables 4a, b and c), as well as in terms of industries represented by the client organizations (Table 5).

Table 4a. Age of study participants

Age	N	% of total 382
<35	73	19.1 %
35–45	134	35.1 %
45–55	111	29.1 %
55 +	57	14.9 %

Table 4b. Education of study participants

Highest completed degree	N	% of total 383
B.S.	187	48.8 %
M.S.	84	21.9 %
MBA	97	25.3 %
Ph.D.	4	1 %

Table 4c. Gender of study participants.

Gender	N	% of total 383
Female	104	27.2 %
Male	273	71.3 %

Table 5. Industries of client companies represented in the study

Industry	N	% of total 383
Finance	86	22.5 %
Manufacturing and Construction	45	11.7 %
Hi tech and Bio tech	36	9.4 %
Healthcare	37	9.7 %
Transport and Energy	36	9.4 %
Communication and Media	33	8.6 %
Public Services	32	8.4 %
Wholesale and Retail	25	6.5 %
Professional Services	21	5.5 %
Education	5	1.3 %
Tourism and Entertainment	5	1.3 %
Other	37	9.7 %

4.2 Communication Tools, Their Contractual Specification, and the Role of Contract Type

The data suggest that a variety of different tools are used for communication in outsourced ISD projects. The reported use of various tools for communication and their specification in the contracts are summarized in Table 6.

A comparison of Fixed Price (FP) and Time and Materials (TM) contracts does not reveal any differences neither in the number of tools used nor in their specification in the contract. Hypothesis 1, therefore, is supported (Table 7).

4.3 Usefulness of Contractually Specified Tools

Following this overall assessment, we next compare project managers' perception of tools' usefulness between tools specified in the contracts and tools selected by other means. Tables 8, 9 and 10 summarize pairwise comparisons between contractually

Table 6. Categories of tools used for communication in outsourced projects

	Projects where these tools are used		Projects where the use of these tools is specified in the contract		
	N	% of total 389 observations	N	% of total 389 observations	% of projects where this tools is used
Visual aids	291	74.8 %	120	30.8 %	41.2 %
Issue tracking tools	305	78.4 %	202	51.9 %	66.2 %
Project management tools	315	81.0 %	211	54.2 %	67.0 %
Beta versions and prototypes	171	44.0 %	89	22.9 %	52.0 %
Web based tools	245	63.0 %	60	15.4 %	24.5 %

Table 7. Average number of communication tools in contracts of different types

	FP (N = 171)		TM (N = 98)		Mixed (N = 93)		F	Sig. (2-tailed)
	Mean	St. Dev.	Mean	St. Dev.	Mean	St. Dev.		
Total of tools used	3.29	1.240	3.42	1.175	3.38	1.160	.376	.687
Tools specified in contract	1.68	1.493	1.71	1.400	1.75	1.349	.069	.933

specified and emergent communication tools. In most cases, the specification of a communication tool in the contract increases its contribution to the four contract provisions. Examining the average indices for each domain and each tool, all differences are statistically significant at 0.01 level. This provides strong support to Hypothesis 2 and all four sub-hypotheses.

4.4   Project Outcomes and Communication Tools

Survey respondents assessed their projects' performance with respect to five project outcomes. Their assessments are summarized in Table 11. The relatively low satisfaction (all average metrics are lower than 4 ("as expected")) are consistent with other studies (e.g., [9]).

Correlations between project outcome metrics and average usefulness of communication tools show some differences between communication tools specified in the contract and tools selected by other means (Table 12). There is no connection between process-based metrics of project success and the use of communication tools regardless of their specification in the contract. The outcome-based metrics, however, are correlated with the usefulness of communication tools in all areas except for managing

Table 8. Perceived usefulness of contractually specified and emerging communication tools

	Not in contract			In contract			t	Sig. (2-tailed)
	N	Mean	St. Dev.	N	Mean	St. Dev.		
Mon_Vis	170	1.78	0.959	119	1.90	0.906	−1.10	0.275
Cnfl_Vis	170	1.73	1.019	119	2.10	0.906	−3.26	0.001
PrR_Vis	169	1.91	1.034	119	2.06	0.886	−1.30	0.195
Cont_Vis	170	1.92	1.011	119	2.19	0.823	−2.47	0.014
Mon_Trk	108	2.19	0.084	197	2.45	0.053	−2.66	0.008
Cnfl_Trk	108	1.97	0.085	196	2.20	0.063	−2.19	0.029
PrR_Trk	107	1.09	0.108	197	1.62	0.082	−3.88	0.000
Cont_Trk	108	1.89	0.091	196	2.20	0.059	−3.04	0.003
Mon_PM	110	2.41	0.816	206	2.53	0.659	−1.36	0.177
Cnfl_PM	110	1.71	0.952	206	1.94	0.904	−2.12	0.035
PrR_PM	109	1.33	1.010	206	1.74	1.043	−3.32	0.001
Cont_PM	110	1.83	0.957	206	2.04	0.894	−1.98	0.049
Mon_Beta	83	1.45	1.027	86	1.80	1.027	−2.26	0.025
Cnfl_Beta	83	1.80	1.068	87	2.10	1.012	−1.93	0.055
PrR_Beta	83	1.51	1.056	87	1.84	1.098	−1.98	0.050
Cont_Beta	83	1.91	0.997	87	2.18	0.896	−1.89	0.061
Mon_Web	157	1.25	0.970	55	1.58	1.066	−2.16	0.032
Cnfl_Web	158	1.17	0.976	55	1.49	1.052	−2.03	0.043
PrR_Web	158	1.01	0.932	55	1.71	1.012	−4.69	0.000
Cont_Web	159	1.22	0.982	55	1.71	0.896	−3.23	0.001

Table 9. Average perceived usefulness of contractually specified and emerging communication tools for four contract dimensions.

	Not in contract			In contract			t	Sig. (2-tailed)
	N	Mean	St. Dev.	N	Mean	St. Dev.		
Avg. Mon	188	1.56	.907	188	2.28	.720	10.28	.000
Avg. Cnfl	188	1.48	.915	188	1.94	.848	6.16	.000
Avg. PrR	187	1.40	.941	187	1.65	.965	3.46	.001
Avg. Cont	188	1.55	.899	188	2.07	.763	7.34	.000

contingencies. Support for managing property rights and conflict situations provided by contractually specified tools leads to higher satisfaction with the final product, which in turn affects general satisfaction with the project. Interestingly, for the dimension of monitoring progress, higher satisfaction with the final product is associated more with the emergent tools rather than with the tools specified in the contract. This reinforces the findings in previous literature that formal control achieved via formally prescribed communications mechanisms (i.e., those specified in the contract) should be augmented by less formal control mechanisms that emerge during the project for best results.

Table 10. Average perceived usefulness of contractually specified and emerging communication tools for five tool types.

	Not in contract			In contract			t	Sig. (2-tailed)
	N	Mean	St. Dev.	N	Mean	St. Dev.		
VIS	170	1.83	.776	119	2.06	.639	−2.617	0.009
TRK	108	1.79	.703	197	2.12	.638	−4.179	0.000
PM	110	1.82	.715	206	2.06	.666	−2.992	0.003
BETA	83	1.67	.756	87	1.98	.751	−2.734	0.007
WEB	159	1.16	.803	55	1.62	.867	−3.629	0.000

Table 11. Metrics of project success

	Mean	Median	Std. Dev.
Budget	3.71	4	1.25
Schedule	3.34	3	1.33
Quality	3.87	4	1.31
Functionality	3.88	4	1.3
Overall	3.94	4	1.4

Table 12. Correlations between tools usefulness and project outcomes

		Monitoring provisions		Dispute resolution		Property rights and strategic goals		Contingency provisions	
		In contract	Not in contract	In contract	Not in contract	In contract	Not in contract	In contract	Not in contract
Budget	Corr.	.068	.048	.111	.021	.138	.045	.113	−.041
	Sig.	.253	.419	.062	.717	.021	.449	.057	.483
Schedule	Corr.	.032	.068	.114	.024	.116	.026	.086	−.043
	Sig.	.595	.246	.054	.683	.051	.665	.149	.464
Quality	Corr.	.072	.135	.168	.097	.184	.053	.083	.041
	Sig.	.230	.022	.005	.100	.002	.370	.163	.483
Functio-nality	Corr.	.078	.167	.171	.109	.211	.094	.119	.086
	Sig.	.189	.004	.004	.065	.000	.113	.046	.147
Overall	Corr.	.060	.093	.163	.097	.183	.059	.076	.015
	Sig.	.312	.116	.006	.099	.002	.318	.200	.805

5   Discussion

Analysis of 389 surveys on communication in outsourced IS development projects provides strong support to the initial proposition of this study that specification of communication tools in the outsourcing contract improves their perceived usefulness in all four major contractual control domains.

As expected, we did not find any notable differences related to contract type in tools use and specification between the two types of outsourcing contracts, fixed price vs. time and materials. We hypothesized that there are competing reasons for specifying (or not specifying) tools that lie beyond the payment terms that distinguish these two types. Although we were not positioned to predict why there is no significant difference, this does help to emphasize the contribution of the findings in the remaining hypotheses, as it eliminates an alternative explanation for differences among contracts.

Our next set of findings suggest that specifying communication tools in the outsourcing contract increases their ability to support control activities in all four major dimensions typically addressed by outsourcing contracts: *monitoring provisions, dispute resolution, property rights allocation/protection, and contingency provisions.* While different types of communications tools support each of the four control dimensions to a different extent, overall the practice of specifying communication mechanisms in the outsourcing contract proves to be beneficial for project managers.

Finally, we analyzed the relationship between the tools' usefulness and the project outcomes, comparing contractually specified and emergent tools. The use of contractually specified tools for communicating strategic goals and property rights and dispute resolutions is associated with higher quality of the final product; this is not true for tools that are not contractually specified. However, the use of tools that are not contractually specified for monitoring progress is associated with higher quality of the final product, while contractually specified tools do not contribute to the project outcomes in this dimension. This finding is in line with previous studies that recommend a combination of formal and informal governance and control mechanisms for the best outcomes in complex knowledge intensive projects.

6 Conclusion

This study contributes to our knowledge of best practices to support IS development projects. We show the value of requiring the adoption of specific communication tools within the contract that governs the client-vendor relationship. By examining the role of communication tools with respect to the type of contract and the structure of the contract, we provide evidence of their value in supporting project control and governance. Our evidence about the interplay between formal and informal control shows that specifying a communication tool in the outsourcing contract formalizes an informal control by making it more "formal", while preserving most of its flexibility. This is critically important in communication-intensive creative environments, which benefit from a combination of formality and flexibility in their governance mechanisms. Going forward, we suggest that further studies address other aspects of contractual vs. emergent communication mechanisms.

The findings of this study are also of immediate value for practitioners. Conscious selection of communication practices at the preliminary stages of the project and subsequent inclusion of these practices in the contract can, according to our findings, improve the effectiveness of project management and contribute to higher quality of the final product regardless of contract type. In contrast, we did not observe any effect on process-based project success metrics (i.e., adherence to budget and schedule). The findings also support a recommendation for project managers to support the emergence communication tools beyond those mandated contractually, especially those related to monitoring performance.

Communication is a complex process, and communication practices are highly situational. Survey-based data collection for quantitative analysis inevitable reduces the richness of data. In our planning conversations with practitioners, we learned that project managers are often not privy to contract details and would not be a reliable source of detailed information about their content. This constraint naturally limits the scope of the contract-related data that we could collect for this study.

This research provides an initial foundation for a further investigation of the role of contractual specification of communication practices in the quality of communication, control mechanisms, and ultimately project outcomes. A more focused inquiry into the role of specific tools and different control dimensions would make another valuable contribution to research and practice. In particular, a more intensive qualitative inquiry into specific contractual provisions and specific types of communication tools would allow for developing guidelines for practitioners to assist in adopting optimal communication and governance practices for complex projects.

References

1. Adler, P., Chen, C.: Combining creativity and control: understanding individual motivation in large-scale collaborative creativity. Account. Organ. Soc. **36**(2), 63–85 (2011)
2. Chen, Y., Bharadwaj, A.: An empirical analysis of contract structures in IT outsourcing. Inf. Syst. Res. **20**(4), 484–506 (2009)
3. Choudhury, V., Sabherwal, R.: Portfolios of control in outsourced software development projects. Inf. Syst. Res. **14**(3), 291–314 (2003)
4. Clegg, S., Kornberger, M., Rhodes, C.: Noise, parasites and translation: theory and practice in management consulting. Manag. Learn. **35**(1), 31 (2004)
5. Cram, A.: Success factors for information systems outsourcing: a meta-analysis. In: Proceedings of the 15th Americas Conference on Information Systems, p. 554, San Francisco, CA (2009)
6. Gantman, S., Fedorowicz, J.: Communication and control in outsourced IS development projects: mapping to COBIT domains. Int. J. Account. Inf. Syst. **21**, 63–83 (2016)
7. Gopal, A., Gosain, S.: The role of organizational controls and boundary spanning in software development outsourcing: implications for project performance. Inf. Syst. Res. **21**(4), 960–982 (2010)
8. Hätönen, J., Eriksson, T.: 30+ years of research and practice of outsourcing–exploring the past and anticipating the future. J. Int. Manag. **15**(2), 142–155 (2009)
9. Kappelman, L., McKeeman, R., Zhang, L.: Early warning signs of IT project failure: the dominant dozen. Inf. Syst. Manag. **23**(4), 31–36 (2006)
10. Kim, S., Chung, Y.: Critical success factors for IS outsourcing implementation from an interorganizational relationship perspective. J. Comput. Inf. Syst. **43**(4), 81–90 (2003)
11. Kirsch, L.: Portfolios of control modes and IS project management. Inf. Syst. Res. **8**(3), 215 (1997)
12. Lacity, M., Khan, S., Willcocks, L.: A review of the IT outsourcing literature: insights for practice. J. Strateg. Inf. Syst. **18**(3), 130–146 (2009)

13. Levina, N., Ross, J.: From the Vendor's perspective: exploring the value proposition in IT outsourcing. MIS Q. **27**(3), 331–364 (2003)
14. Levina, N., Vaast, E.: The emergence of boundary spanning competence in practice: implications for implementation and use of information systems. MIS Q. **29**(2), 335–363 (2005)
15. Lim, W., Sia, S., Yeow, A.: Managing risks in a failing IT project: a social constructionist view. J. Assoc. Inf. Syst. **12**(6), 2 (2011)
16. Mastrogiacomo, S., Missonier, S., Bonazzi, R.: Talk before it's too late: reconsidering the role of conversation in information systems project management. J. Manag. Inf. Syst. **31**(1), 47–78 (2014)
17. Ngwenyama, O., Sullivan, W.E.: Outsourcing contracts as instruments of risk management. J. Enterp. Inf. Manag. **20**(6), 615 (2007)
18. Poppo, L., Zenger, T.: Do formal contracts and relational governance function as substitutes or complements? Strateg. Manag. J. **23**(8), 707–725 (2002)
19. Willis, G.: Cognitive Interviewing: A Tool for Improving Questionnaire Design. Sage Publications, Thousand Oaks (2005)

Weighted Evaluation Framework for Cross-Platform App Development Approaches

Christoph Rieger[1] and Tim A. Majchrzak[2](✉)

[1] ERCIS, University of Münster, Münster, Germany
christoph.rieger@ercis.de
[2] ERCIS, University of Agder, Kristiansand, Norway
tima@ercis.de

Abstract. Cross-platform app development is very challenging, although only two platforms with significant market share (iOS and Android) remain. While device fragmentation – multiple, only partly compatible versions of a platform – has been complicating matters already, the need to target different device classes is a new emergence. Smartphones and tablets are relatively similar but app-enabled devices such as TVs and even cars typically have differing capabilities. To facilitate usage of cross-platform app development approaches, we present work on an evaluation framework. Our framework provides a set of up-to-date evaluation criteria. Unlike prior work on this topic, it offers weighted assessment to cater for varieties in targeted device classes. Besides motivating and explaining the evaluation criteria, we present an exemplary application for one development approach and, as benchmarks, for native apps and Webapps. Our findings suggest that the proliferation of app-enabled devices amplifies the need for improved development support.

Keywords: App · Mobile computing · Mobile application · Cross-platform · Multi-platform · Evaluation

1 Introduction

Only two platforms for smartphone and tablet devices with significant market share remain [67]. Even developing applications *only* for Apple's iOS and Google's Android is challenging (cf. e.g. [41]). Essentially, apps need to be realized separately for both, doubling the effort and prolonging the time-to-market [29]. Moreover, device fragmentation – the parallel usage of several versions and possibly vendor-specific additions – complicates development, particularly for Android [17]. Cross-platform development frameworks promise to relieve developers from the hardships of considering idiosyncrasies of several platforms and versions by providing uniform development interfaces [28].

As an additional challenge for developers, an increasing number of devices is *app-enabled*. Arguably, most apps in today's sense target the smartphone but

© Springer International Publishing AG 2016
S. Wrycza (Ed.): SIGSAND/PLAIS 2016, LNBIP 264, pp. 18–39, 2016.
DOI: 10.1007/978-3-319-46642-2_2

soon they will be routinely used on a much wider variety of platforms. Modern entertainment technology such as TVs, BluRay players and game consoles are capable of *running* apps. Cars are seen as a major target of tomorrow's apps [66]. Wearable devices such as smartwatches and augmented reality glasses introduce novel usage scenarios [39]. Although it can be rightfully doubted that a fridge will be the main unit to install new apps on, it is likely that with the advent of the Internet of Things (IoT) many more devices will run apps. In consequence, catering for *all* device-specific particularities will become much harder.

Extending the already well-understood general requirements for cross-platform app development, we suggest taking into account the multitude of potential devices. Heitkötter, Hanschke and Majchrzak have proposed an evaluation framework for cross-platform approaches in 2012 [27]. The extension [28] is still very useful and routinely cited in current papers on cross-platform development. However, even though the set of criteria they proposed is based on a thorough foundation, the rapid proliferation of the field mandates an overhaul. In addition, the former focus on smartphone and tablet devices ignores the plethora of novel devices reaching the consumer market.

We build on the existing work on cross-platform technology. In particularly, we use the existing set of criteria [28] as the foundation to provide an extended, revised catalogue of them. This allows matching the criteria with the status quo of mobile computing. An approach that is best suited for smartphone apps might fail if apps also target entertainment systems. However, selecting a "catch-all" solution might be inferior to a specific one if only handheld devices should be supported. Therefore, we not only extend criteria but also embed them in a framework that includes a *weighting scheme*. The assessment of platforms can thereby be employed to make a per-scenario choice.

This paper makes several contributions. Firstly, it provides an evaluation framework for cross-platform development frameworks in the domain of mobile consumer devices. Evaluation criteria are explained in detail and the rationale for employing them is highlighted. Secondly, we provide the means to use our framework in an individual – particularly in a device-class specific – way by proposing the integration of balanced weights. Thirdly, we demonstrate the feasibility of our work with an exemplary evaluation. Accordingly, in Sect. 2 we discuss related work and in Sect. 3 we give the necessary background. Based on this foundation, Sect. 4 provides our catalogue of evaluation criteria. The exemplary use of the criteria for evaluation follows in Sect. 5. The findings are then discussed in Sect. 6, which leads to a conclusion in Sect. 7.

2 Related Work

Since cross-platform development of apps has been a topic for a few years now, there is plenty of scientific work on the topic in general. However, most papers tackle single frameworks or have an experimental nature. Consequently, there are relatively few papers that provide an overview, and even less than offer an evaluation. A comprehensive summary of related literature regarding covered

Table 1. Literature on cross-platform app development tool evaluations

Paper	Year	Evaluated tools	Main categories (number of criteria)	Focal areas
[47]	2012	RhoMobile, PhoneGap, DragonRad, MoSync	Platform compatibility (2), development features (4), general features (4), device APIs (17)	Qualitative tool comparison
[13]	2013	PhoneGap, jQuery Mobile, Sencha Touch, Titanium	Platform support, rich user interface, back-end communication, security, app extensions, power consumption, device features, open-source	Performance evaluation (memory, CPU, power consumption)
[61]	2013	Titanium, Rhodes, PhoneGap, Sencha Touch	Functionality (8), usability (6), developer support (4), reliability/performance (4), deployment (8)	Criteria definition and qualitative tool comparison
[68]	2013	*none* (cross-platform approaches in general)	Distribution, programming languages, hardware & data access, user interface, perceived performance	Criteria definition
[11]	2014	MoSync, Titanium, jQuery Mobile, PhoneGap	License, community, API, tutorials, complexity, IDE, devices, GUI, knowledge	Qualitative tool comparison and apps with animations
[10]	2015	PhoneGap, Titanium	Battery consumption, device resource usage	Evaluation of battery consumption
[16]	2015	PhoneGap, Titanium, Adobe Air, MoSync	Tool capabilities (9), performance (5), developer support (2)	Performance benchmarks and development experience discussion
[32]	2015	AngularJS, jQuery Mobile, HTML5/JS, RhoMobile, PhoneGap, Sencha Touch	Platform support (4), development support (7), deployment factors (6)	Criteria definition and qualitative tool comparison

tools, criteria and focal areas of comparison is given in Table 1. In the following, we only comment on particularly notable details.

The papers by Heitkötter et al. [27,28] have been used as basis for further research on apps. Examples include the definition of quality criteria for HTML5 frameworks [60], quantitative performance evaluations [65], and the creation of the cross-platform development frameworks ICPMD [21] and MD^2 [31].

Early papers have typically taken into account few criteria only (if at all [7, 57]) – e.g. only seven [47], and only from a developer's perspective [11]. Few works take a rather comprehensive approach. For example, Ohrt and Turau [46] have analysed nine tools with taking a developer focus and assessing user expectations. They e.g. have had a look at programming language, compilation without SDK, code completion, GUI designer, debugger, emulator, and extensibility with native code, as well as launch time, app package size, and memory usage.

Many papers focus on particular aspects, e.g. animations [11], performance [13], and energy consumption [10]. Nonetheless, most authors at least provide criteria grouped into common categories [32,46,61,68]. One problem typically found is a shortage of explanations (c.f. e.g. [32]).

It can be summed up that many authors set out to conquer the field of cross-platform app development systematically. Without doubt, the papers shown in Table 1 provide substantial contributions. However, the rapid proliferation of the field and the only slowly emerging theory-building mandate further work. This is also illustrated by many papers being published recently that – more or less isolated – address issues also discussed in this article. To conclude the study of related work, we highlight such works that address novel mobile devices.

Several papers address *smart TVs*. Typically, a combination of HTML5 and JavaScript is proposed to enable cross-platform development. Sub-topics are interactive ads [48], serious games [55], and 3D content [49]. Work on *wearables* is more scarce [34]. Some authors have proposed middleware approaches to achieve a broader device-span [9], in one case even on the hardware layer [70]. Despite much blurriness, *smart homes* could be a future area of cross-platform research [33].

Contrasting the hype around multimedia novelties for cars, few scientific papers tackle *in-vehicle apps*. Current discussions revolve around general challenges and potential applications [66], the integration of non-automotive applications into the automotive environment [54], and usability [51]. A few papers provide experimental implementations of novel concepts such as a route planning app for head-up (HUD) displays [45], an *Open Service Cloud* for cars [15], and "remote" human machine interfaces (HMI) [20]. While these papers help to understand the possibilities of cars as a potential target of apps, they are far away from actually discussing cross-platform challenges and chances.

3   Background

As a prerequisite for a differentiated evaluation of mobile platforms, we need to categorize the variety of devices. From our understanding, *mobile consumer devices* are designed to be used in absence of *stationary* workstation hardware by non-business users. While formerly it was possible to categorise by operation system, this is not feasible anymore: e.g. Windows 10 spans device classes. As no such classification exists in scientific literature, we propose a simple subdivision.

This list is not meant as a *proven* categorisation but as a working scheme for this paper. Thus, we refrain from an elaborated explanation. Within each of these device classes, a multitude of devices based on different platforms has emerged. Whereas Android and iOS have divided most of the market share of

Traditional general-purpose devices	Novel mobile devices
Smartphone	Smart TVs and entertainment devices[a]
Tablets, including hybrids such as netbooks and (so called) ultrabooks	Wearables
	Smart watches, e.g. iWatch, Pebble, Samsung Gear
	Sensing devices, e.g. fitness trackers, GPS watches
	Smart glasses for augmented reality, e.g. Google glass, MS Hololens
	Vehicles, e.g. from BMW, Tesla, Ford
	Smart home applications[b]

[a] While such devises impose themselves as being included in a categorisation as such, they arguably are not *mobile* in the sense of all other devices named here.

[b] This field is still very fuzzy but rapid proliferation mandates naming it here already.

smartphone platforms amongst themselves [67], competition among the novel mobile device platforms is high and no clear winners are foreseeable. A short overview of this field is provided next.

App-enabled smart TVs are already present in 35 % of U.S. households [62] and two approaches of development exist: middleware and frameworks. Over 90 % of connected TVs sold in Germany support the HTML5-based HbbTV standard that has evolved from previous approaches such as CE-HTML and Open IPTV [26,62]. In addition, many individual frameworks emerged, for example the open-source media centre Kodi/XBMC with various forks, Android TV, Tizen OS for TV, and webOS [2,38,63,69].

With smartwatches, Google and Apple again compete for dominance with their respective Android Wear and watchOS platforms. Pebble OS, Tizen OS, and webOS are further players in this domain [6]. Whereas several vendors open-sourced their operating system, few vendor-agnostic platforms exist such as AsteroidOS [53]. Other wearable devices such as fitness trackers usually ship with proprietary platforms, e.g. Microsoft Band and Firefox OS for Wearables. Those devices often support pairing with smartphones of multiple platforms; however app development is still limited. Vendors such as Fitbit and Garmin do not even produce devices with modifiable operating system [6].

Concerning the upcoming connected cars, there are four approaches for developing in-vehicle apps [59]. First, Android Auto, Blackberry QNX, and Windows Embedded are technologies that are rebranded by car manufacturers and run native apps on the car's head unit. Second, some cars allow access and control of features such as door locks through a remote API. Examples include General Motors, Airbiquity, and an unofficial API for Tesla cars [18]. Third, platforms including Apple CarPlay and the MirrorLink alliance use screen mirroring of apps running on the smartphone and displayed on the car's screen [20]. This approach honours security concerns by car manufacturers. Fourth, Dash Labs, Mojio, Carvoyant, or Automatic connect to the on-board diagnostics port to interact with the car. Although this requires a Bluetooth dongle as additional hardware, many cars can be supported that are not designed to be app-enabled in the first place. In addition to this variety of approaches, distribution of apps is a challenge because of the underlying fight for dominance between car manufacturers "owning" the car platform [59].

This overview of technologies shows similar characteristics of fragmentation as the smartphone market several years ago [28]. However, few cross-platform approaches currently exist in the domain of novel mobile consumer devices. Interestingly from a cross-platform perspective, many smart TV platforms natively support app development using Web technologies such as HTML5 and JavaScript, thus being well-suited for cross-platform approaches. Some platforms such as Android and Tizen have branches that run on multiple devices from TVs to smartwatches, potentially allowing for a future development across device class borders. Samsung TOAST is an early initiative to simultaneously develop for Samsung Smart TV, the new Tizen platform and browsers, based on the established Apache Cordova framework [56].

The other way around, smartwatches can be paired with more than one platform [19]. Such apps that act as a (smartphone) device extension are current practice and thus cross-platform development approaches must consider and support each combination of host and watch platform. However, some smartwatch platforms are announcing stand-alone capabilities [25].

Several platforms claim to be the adequate open platforms for smart home and IoT applications. Qualcomm's AllJoyn, Intel's IoTivity, Apple HomeKit, and Google Brillo are the most important players that try to establish their middleware as comprehensive solution [8].

Finally, for in-vehicle apps, no widespread cross-platform frameworks exist due to the novelty of devices and a lack of platform accessibility. Potentially, a middleware approach [15] might be an option to provide an open ground for developers and at the same time guarantee security.

4   Criteria

In the following, we propose our categorisation framework. We start by discussing methodological considerations before explaining the criteria.

4.1   General Considerations

As argued in Sect. 2, we have been inspired by existing evaluation frameworks. Facilitating the requirements arising from the broad scope intended for our framework and catering for the progress in the field in the meantime, we propose numerous extensions and revisions. Most notably, we do not distinguish criteria by two perspectives (*infrastructure* and *development* originally [28]) but by four.

The *infrastructure* perspective describes the general background and prospect of a cross-platform development approach. The *development* perspective takes into account aspects of using an approach for carrying out the actual programming activities. In addition to these, we introduce the *app* perspective and the *usage* perspective. The former offers an assessment of the capabilities of apps that can be realized with a given approach. This not only leads to more clarity with regard to the distinction of actual development activities and the outcome of development but also has multi-device class support in mind. While development might not differ much for different classes of devices, the capabilities of an app might vary significantly. The usage perspective considers usability, ergonomic, and performance aspects that are essential factors for user acceptance.

The categorisation into four perspective allows focussing on relevant aspects for particular needs. These needs might arise from the targeted device class(es) but may as well come from other sources. An example could be a specific focus on business apps [43]. In the following, we provide the rationale for each of our criteria following the above proposed categorisation. Besides referencing sources already discussed, we provide additional evidence where appropriate[1].

4.2   Infrastructure Perspective

(I1) **License:** The license under which a framework is published is essential for the type of product to develop. It needs to be assessed whether a developer is free to create commercial apps, for example when using open source software [11,13,47]. In addition, the pricing model needs to be considered. A framework could be freely distributed, or require one-time or regular license payments with regard to the number of developers, projects, or as a flat fee [32,61].

(I2) **Supported Target Platforms:** The number and importance of supported mobile platforms within a device class is a major concern for choosing a cross-platform approach [11,47]. Furthermore, support varies regarding different versions of each mobile operating system. The most recent version provides the newest features and its support is important to reach early adopters of a new technology [5]. However, the majority of users will use an old version of the system due to hardware limitations or slow update behaviour by users or vendors [17]. Finally, it needs to be considered whether multiple device classes have to be bridged, for example a combination of smart TV and tablet application.

(I3) **Supported Development Platforms:** Flexibility regarding supported development platforms is beneficial for heterogeneous teams in which developers are accustomed to specific hardware and software such as an development environment [47] (see also criterion D1). Moreover, the role within a team such as UI or UX design may require the approach to support multiple platforms.

(I4) **Distribution Channels:** With proprietary platform- or vendor-specific app stores typical for publication, the number of users who can be reached is critical. It needs to be weighted against fixed and variable costs of app store accounts and app publishing. The ease of the publication process itself also

---

[1] However, we do *not* cite [28] for each single criterion originating from this work.

needs to be considered, regarding e.g. the average duration for initial app place-
ment and update distribution as well as the strictness and detailedness of the
review process [68]. Cross-platform frameworks vary by the degree of compatibility with app store restrictions and submission guidelines [16,61]. Further app
store integrations include app rating to reach a better app store ranking as well
as automatic update notifications within the app for rolling out updates fast [32].

(I5) Monetisation: From a business perspective, the possibility and the
complexity of selling the app itself and subsequent in-app purchases need to be
considered as well as the availability of advertisement [16]. These features need
to be traded off against direct costs and commissions to the app store operator. Again, cross-platform development frameworks can support this aspect, for
example by providing interfaces to payment providers or advertising networks.

(I6) Global App Distribution: Typically, a global distribution of apps
is desired – unless specific reasons for restrictions exist. Approaches can offer
built-in support for internalisation and localisation to create and distribute app
versions targeted (and potentially restricted) to specific geographic regions. In
addition, translation capabilities allow for easy delivery of multi-language content and provide format conversions for dates, currencies and location particularities [61].

(I7) Long-term Feasibility: Choosing an approach might be an important strategic decision considering the significant initial investment for training
or hiring developers as well as the risk of technology lock-in, particularly for
smaller companies. The maturity and stability of a framework can be evaluated
concerning the historical and expected backwards incompatible changes of major
releases. Other indicators are short update cycles, regular bug-fixes, and security
updates. In an active community, developers exchange knowledge to solve issues.
Ideally, several commercial supporters back the project with financial resources
and steady contribution. Costs for professional support inquiries need also be
considered, potentially increasing the attractiveness of a promising open-source
project while safeguarding efficient solutions to development issues [32,61].

4.3   Development Perspective

(D1) Development Environment: The maturity and features of an integrated development environment (IDE) heavily influence development productivity and speed. Tool support includes functionalities of the IDE such as auto-
completion, debugging tools, and an emulator to enable rapid app development
cycles [11,16,32,47,61]. In addition to the IDE typically associated with the
cross-platform approach, the freedom to use accustomed workflows, e.g. choose
a preferred IDE, lowers the initial set-up effort for additional dependencies such
as runtime environments or software development kits (SDK) [61].

(D2) Preparation Time: The learning curve, i.e. the subjective progress of
a developer while exploring the capabilities and best practices of the approach,
should foster rapid initial progress. To lower the entry barrier, the number and
type of required technology stack and programming languages need to be considered [11,47,61,68], e.g. using known paradigms to further reduce the initial

learning efforts [11]. With unique benefits and characteristics, the quality of API documentation is also of major importance. "Getting started" guides, tutorials, and code examples initially clarify the framework's features and structure, whereas a corpus of best practices, user-comments, and technical specifications support in solving issues over the course of development [16,61].

(D3) Scalability: Scalability refers to the modularisation capabilities of the framework and generated apps in larg-scale development projects. Partitioning code in subcomponents and architectural design decisions such as the well-known Model-View-Controller pattern has implications on the app structure. Thus, the number of developers can be increased while extending the app's functionality [32,47]. However, a modular framework itself can guide and support this division of labour. With specified interfaces and interactions between the components, developers can specialize themselves on few relevant components.

(D4) Development Process Fit: Departing from the traditional approach of implementing software from a fixed and comprehensive specification, a variety of methods with agile characteristic exist today. For such projects, the cross-platform approach can be evaluated regarding the effort to create the *minimum viable product*, e.g. the amount of boilerplate code and initial configuration, as well as the effort to subsequently modify its scope. This criterion also relates to the organisational aspect of scalability in terms of developer specialisation. In contrast to full-stack developers in small projects, modularizing development using roles can be supported through tailored views or specialized tools [64].

(D5) UI Design Approach: UI development is a major concern for cross-platform approaches. Graphical user interfaces are highly platform-specific and often just covered by a default appearance defined by the framework [29]. In addition, a separate WYSIWYG editor to develop appealing interfaces for multiple devices can be beneficial and increases the speed of development compared to constantly deploying the full app to a device or an emulator.

(D6) Testing Support: App logic and user interfaces need to be tested with established concepts such as system and unit tests [32,61]. To test context-sensitive mobile scenarios more authentically, external influences (such as *bad* connectivity) may be simulated [42]. Furthermore, possibilities of monitoring the app at runtime improve the testability, e.g. providing a developer console, meaningful error reporting, and logging functionalities for app-specific and system events. Tool support may also include remote debugging on a connected device rather than emulator environments, test coverage visualisation and metrics [32].

(D7) Deployment Support: Build toolchain support immensely simplifies the deployment process, i.e. generating individual packages for all targeted platforms. Approaches vary from requiring all native SDKs to external build services and cloud-based techniques [32,61]. Sophisticated projects additionally use *continuous integration* platforms to automate testing. Frameworks can be explicitly designed to integrate with such toolchains. Regarding production, the framework might also offer optimised build options (e.g. *minified* code) and app store integrations to automatically publish updates [32].

(D8) Maintainability: In contrast to (I7), maintainability deals with the evolution of a code base over time [61] and difficult to quantify. Lines of code (LOC) for a specified reference app may be used for comparison with the assumption that less LOC are easier to support regarding readability of source code, amount of training and familiarisation, etc. This concept is similar to programming languages themselves, where so-called *gearing factors* try to compare the amount of code per unit of functionality [23]. Advanced maintainability metrics are hard to apply due to the heterogeneity and varying complexity of frameworks, especially in case of apps composed of different programming languages. Furthermore, the reusability of source code across development projects can be evaluated, for instance concerning the portability to other software projects [61].

(D9) Extensibility: Special requirements may introduce the need for features that go beyond the core of the framework. These might not be put into practice with high priority. Therefore, the possibility to extend the framework with custom components and third-party libraries should be evaluated. Examples for such extensions include additional UI elements, functionalities to access device features, and solutions to common challenges such as data transfer [32,47].

(D10) Integrating Native Code: For some applications, running native code within the application is a requirement. This seemingly invalidates the idea of cross-platform development; nonetheless, it *can* be beneficial: Previously existing code can be reused, e.g. when migrating apps to a cross-platform development approach and replacing platform-specific code over time. Also, native platform APIs might enable access to platform functionalities and device features currently not available on the framework's level of abstraction [47,61].

(D11) Speed of Development: Rapid development is influenced by the amount of boilerplate code necessary for functional app skeletons (cf. [30]) and the availability of typical app functions such as user authentication. Assuming salaries to be independent of programming language proficiency, development speed directly influences the variable costs and ultimately the return-on-investment.

4.4 App Perspective

(A1) Access to Device-specific Hardware: For cross-platform approaches, the coverage of platform- and device-specific hardware is of supreme importance [11,13,16,32,61]. Especially regarding the capabilities of novel mobile devices, a plethora of device hardware is present today. This includes sensors such as camera, microphone, GPS, accelerometer, gyroscope, magnetometer, temperature sensor, and heart rate monitor. In addition, cyberphysical systems enable bidirectional interaction that can modify the environment through actuators. The set of individual features is evaluated according to the framework's documentation.

(A2) Access to Platform-specific Functionality: Regarding the software side of the various mobile platforms, functionalities include a persistence layer such as the file system and access to a database on the device, contact lists, information on the network connection, and battery status [16,32]. In addition, in-app browser support may be desirable for fetching additional content from the Internet without leaving the app [32]. Advanced features like monitoring or push notifications can be realised using background services [61].

(A3) Support for Connected Devices: Current wearable devices and also sensor/actuator networks of cyberphysical systems often require to be coupled to a respective master device (e.g. a smartphone). This trend of "device extensions" needs to be evaluated regarding viable device combinations. More specific this includes the level of access to coupled device data and sensors as well as additional user interfaces. This may be trivial if the platform provides a layer of abstraction that exposes the coupled device similar to other device components. Yet, in many cases the cross-platform approach needs to take care of this additional complexity.

(A4) Input Device Heterogeneity: The input device criterion evaluates the support of the approach with regard to the variety of input devices that can be used to interact with the app. This includes traditional devices such as keyboard and mouse as well as (multi-) touch screens, voice recognition, remote controls, hardware buttons and more. Each of these devices can process many interaction mechanisms, for example multi-touch screens reacting to gestures such as different types of taps, swipes, pinches, pressure, orientation changes etc., all of which the cross-platform tool needs to make available to the app developer.

(A5) Output Device Heterogeneity: Mobile devices provide a huge variety of different output devices differing in device size, resolution, format (e.g. *round* smartwatches), colour palette, frame rate (e.g. E-Ink screens), and opacity (e.g. augmented reality projections). This poses challenges as adaptability is already a major challenge for traditional devices [1]. In addition, the app has to adapt to device class-specific context changes, thereby realizing well-understood design ideals [58] such as day/night-mode appearances for in-vehicle apps.

(A6) Application Life Cycle: This criterion refers to how far a framework supports the life-cycle inherent to an app. Platforms may differ in starting, pausing, continuing, and exiting an app [61]. Additional differences arise from the life cycle of individual views and view elements.

(A7) Business Integration: To integrate with the overall business, support for data exchange protocols, serialisation, and multiple data formats are often required [13]. Apps may communicate with existing Web service back-ends for data storage and processing, or initiate inter-app communication. E.g., business processes often require collaboration of different user roles. Business integration also refers to customizability, e.g. being adaptable to a *corporate identity* [61].

(A8) Security: Frameworks can support the development of secure apps on several levels. First, mobile platforms are usually restrictive regarding access permissions. Requesting permissions on demand increases not only the perceived security of an app. Second, data loss can be avoided by using data encryption mechanisms on the device as well as secure data transfer protocols against eavesdropping [13,32]. Third, the framework may provide user input validation and prevent cross-site forgery and code injection [32].

(A9) Fallback Handling: Considering the device and platform heterogeneity of (A1)–(A5), intelligent fallback mechanisms aid in case individual features are unsupported or restricted. As a naïve approach, the user may be redirected to a Web page. Sophisticated actions include *graceful degradation* techniques with simpler representations [22], or alternative functions to fulfil the user's task.

4.5   Usage Perspective

(U1) Look and Feel: This criterion considers whether available UI elements have a native look & feel or rather behave like a Web site [61]. The set of elements can be evaluated according to the human interface guidelines of the respective platform. Particularly, rich user interfaces with 2D/3D animation and multimedia features are challenging for cross-platform tools [13]. In addition, it should be considered to which degree a framework supports the platform-specific usage philosophy, e.g. the position of navigation bars, scrolling, and gestures [61].

(U2) Performance: Application speed, stability, and responsiveness of the app on user interaction are essential performance aspects. Apart from the subjective user experience, the speed at start-up, after interruptions and for shut-down can be measured [16]. Moreover, resource usage can be assessed, e.g. CPU, RAM and battery utilisation at runtime, or download size [10,11,13,61].

(U3) Usage Patterns: Apps are frequently used for a short amount of time and are likely to be interrupted. Users want an "instant on" experience and continue where they left the app. To match usage patterns, apps have to integrate into personal workflows for information processing such as sharing with other apps or saving to persistent storage, and community interactions such as messaging, e-mail, and social media. For some use cases, support for synchronisation of app data across multiple devices of the user for seamless context switching is beneficial. In addition, notification centres of the platform are gaining importance for app interaction.

(U4) User Management: Cross-platform frameworks may support different types of user handling, reaching from purely local apps to user accounts across multiple devices and role-based authentication. Authentication may therefore be performed in-app or server-based, and potentially connected to session management. In addition, mobile devices may provide various login mechanisms, including traditional passwords, gestures, and biometric information such as fingerprints, voice recognition, or other characteristics [40].

5   Evaluation

Due to their recent emergence, cross-platform approaches barely exist for novel mobile device classes (cf. Sect. 2). Therefore, the following evaluation compares PhoneGap to Web apps and native applications with regard to traditional smartphone mobile devices. PhoneGap was chosen due to its perennial popularity as leading cross-platform development tool [12]. The evaluation is by no means a comprehensive survey of the cross-platform framework itself (as provided by [16,32]) but should serve as exemplary comparison in order to discuss our approach of weighted criteria evaluation. Thereby, this evaluation particularly serves as a benchmark for our evaluation framework.

5.1 Weight Profiles

To cater for differences across heterogeneous and evolving mobile device classes, our approach to cross-platform tool evaluation applies a weighting mechanism. Each of the 31 criteria receives between 1 and 7 points with a total of 100 points assigned (not necessarily distributed equally across the categories), constituting the so-called *weight profile*. Each criterion is evaluated on a scale from 0 (criterion unsatisfied) to 5 (optimally fulfilled). The weighting points directly translate to percental values used in calculating the *weighted score*. A weight profile reflects the requirements of a specific device class regarding cross-platform development. It can be individually adapted to the future evolution of the mobile ecosystems, as well as changed to reflect particular needs, e.g. regarding the background of developers. The proposed weight profiles for the device classes presented in Sect. 3 are depicted in Table 2 along with an exemplary evaluation.

In the following, we focus on the *smartphone* device class, which can be backed with empirical and theoretical work. Studies have shown that cross-platform approaches are often developer-oriented [12,52]. From an infrastructure perspective, this means that free and open approaches are considered particularly important. Long-term feasibility benefits from a stabilized smartphone ecosystem with Android and iOS as main players [67]. Distribution channels are mostly limited to platform-specific app stores with a broad set of features.

App developers want to use existing standards and previous knowledge for fast-paced development [12,52]. In contrast, the current practice of smartphone apps apparently does not cover large development teams. As a result, organisational aspects such as scalability, maintainability, and development process integration are not requested by practitioners [52]. UI design seems to be an ongoing challenge for cross-platform frameworks and may even become more important for "standing out from the mass of apps" [1].

On the application side, access to a broad rage of device functionalities is requested, while support for smartphone screens as both input and output device has matured [12]. Apps are still rather developed for social and communication purposes [37], thus business integration and security issues are not prioritized.

With mobile usage soon surpassing desktop usage [37], performance and native look and feel remain important topics for smartphone development. Finally, user management and usage patterns play an inferior role on smartphones as these are mainly designed for single-person usage.

5.2 Web Apps

Web apps are mobile-optimized Web sites built with HTML5 and JavaScript (JS), and executed within the smartphone's browser. They rely on

Table 2. Comparison of approaches and device class weight profiles

Smartphone comparison					Category weights			
Criterion	Weight (%)	Web apps	PhoneGap	Native apps	Tablets	Entertainment	Wearables	Vehicle	Smart home
I1: License	6	5	5	5	5	6	5	3	5
I2: Target platforms	7	5	5	1	5	6	7	4	7
I3: Development platforms	2	5	5	2	2	2	1	1	1
I4: Distribution channels	2	5	3	4	2	3	4	3	3
I5: Monetisation	2	0	3	5	2	1	1	2	2
I6: Global distribution	2	1	3	5	2	2	2	0	1
I7: Long-term feasibility	5	5	5	4	5	3	3	6	5
D1: Dev. environment	7	4	5	5	7	7	5	5	6
D2: Ramp-up time	7	5	4	3	7	7	5	1	5
D3: Scalability	2	3	3	3	2	3	2	3	2
D4: Development process fit	2	3	4	2	2	3	1	4	2
D5: UI design	4	3	3	4	4	5	5	6	3
D6: Test support	3	3	4	5	3	3	4	7	3
D7: Deployment support	3	5	5	3	3	3	4	5	2
D8: Maintainability	2	2	4	2	2	2	1	5	2
D9: Framework extensibility	2	5	5	0	2	2	2	1	2
D10: Native extensibility	2	0	3	5	2	2	1	0	0
D11: Speed of development	4	2	3	0	4	3	3	2	4
A1: Hardware access	5	2	4	5	3	1	6	4	7
A2: Platform functionality	5	2	4	5	5	3	2	3	3
A3: Connected devices	3	0	0	5	2	1	7	4	7
A4: Input heterogeneity	1	4	4	5	3	3	2	2	2
A5: Output heterogeneity	1	4	4	5	1	1	6	3	4
A6: App life cycle	3	0	4	5	3	3	3	3	2
A7: Business integration	2	3	3	5	3	3	1	2	1
A8: Security	3	0	0	1	4	1	3	7	5
A9: Fallback Handling	2	2	4	0	1	4	3	2	1
U1: Look and feel	4	1	3	5	4	2	4	5	3
U2: Performance	4	3	2	5	4	6	3	3	2
U3: Usage patterns	2	0	1	2	4	4	4	3	4
U4: User management	1	0	0	0	2	5	0	1	4
Weighted score		**2.99**	**3.66**	**3.56**					

open standards and are highly cross-platform compatible while using Web development tools (I1–I4). While profiting from an immense community of developers, "app-like" behaviour needs to be implemented manually and distribution cannot be controlled (I5–I6).

Only Web development skills are required; many tutorials and profound tool support is available (D1–D2). The universality of the Web at the same time limits the application to apps, e.g. requiring boilerplate code or providing no guidance on the structure of source code and development (D3–D5). Testability is problematic: desktop browsers emulate the respective mobile counterpart inconsistently and mobile in-browser debugging is hardly supported (D6). Various libraries simplify development, yet native code is unsupported (D9–D10). As a result, Web apps are rather easy to create and modify using established toolchains. However, all aspects regarding app life cycle, integration, security, and fallback have to be built manually without platform-specific abstraction (D7–D8, D11, A6–A9).

Accessing device components is possible only via HTML5 APIs such as Media Capture Stream, which are scarcely supported by mobile browsers (A1–A2) [44]. As the execution happens in the browser, keyboard and gesture support are well established through JS events but limited to Web page behaviour and browser controls (A3, U1). Furthermore, CSS can be used customise the design and target different outputs devices, with the exception of connected devices (A4–A5, A7). Finally, usage patterns and user management are completely up to the developer, whereas the overall performance depends on the smartphone browser and is likely be optimized by the platform provider (U2–U4).

5.3   PhoneGap

PhoneGap was initially developed around 2009 and is still the top-used cross-platform development tool [12, 14]. Freely available under the permissive Apache License, PhoneGap targets all major smartphone platforms in various versions (I1). Technically, apps are developed using HTML5/JS/CSS and executed within a *Web view wrapper* component without browser controls. This allows installing the apps and providing API access to native functionality. Thus, the framework does not adhere to specific platform guidelines but provides a general mobile appearance that can be distributed through any app store but without advanced features such as in-app purchases (I4–I6). Its long existence and stable API has created a large community that in turn supports the long-term perspective (I7).

Similar to Web apps, developers can freely choose their preferred Web development environment and profit from previous knowledge. The framework's structure requires little knowledge and it is well documented (I3, D1–D2). PhoneGap generates a running app skeleton and file structure but does not impose further implications on the development process (D3–D5). All app functionality needs to be implemented manually (A8–A9, U3–U4). Outstanding features are the *cloud deployment* that requires no locally installed SDKs as well as the *remote debugging interface* that connects to real devices (D6–D7). Maintainability is enabled through the extensive and stable API abstracting from platform differences and increasing the speed of development (D8, D11, A1–A2). In addition, numerous plug-ins exist, extending the functionality and covering many of the aforementioned drawbacks, also allowing the execution of native code (D9–D10).

Regarding native behaviour and appearance, the *Event API* provides access to life cycle events and platform settings can be retrieved via the *Device API* to target specific platforms (A6–A7, A9, U1). Support for input and output is similar to Web apps and likewise restricted to the main device (A3–A5). The app performance depends again on the smartphone's browser capabilities with additional framework overhead (U2) [4,50].

5.4   Native Apps

Any cross-platform development approach can be benchmarked against native app development. While it naturally is closest to a platform's capabilities, developing natively not necessarily is the most efficient or elegant option.

Platform SDKs are freely available and fully integrated into the respective app stores. The latter provide a broad set of features for distribution and monetisation (I1, I4–I6). Whereas development might be possible with several technologies, the target platforms are limited to one (I2–I3).

iOS and Android as prevailing platforms and can be treated as reliable on long-term [67]. Platforms typically require specific programming language knowledge, although extensive documentation and community support are available (D2). Moreover, a full ecosystem with tool support for all phases of development is usually provided, with varying degrees of alternatives (D1, D5–D7).

The flexibility of implementation comes at the cost of few guidelines on structuring and subdividing development work (D3–D4). The platforms usually do not provide support for recurring programming tasks (A8–A9, U3–U4). Obviously, the speed of developing multiple native apps is unmatched low (D11).

Native apps can access all possible features of a given platform (A1–A7). Ultimately, a fully native appearance and behaviour as well as performance without runtime overhead can only be reached with native apps (A1–A2).

6   Discussion

The framework presented in the prior sections should provide a step towards a sound theory of cross-platform app development. However, it is by no means static. In fact, we hope it can be the foundation for application and extension by others. Thereby, the framework can stay at eye level with further developments in the field. Specifically, depending on the emergence of novel device classes and the possible proliferation of further kinds of devices, revisions can be applied.

In the following we reflect on our work, starting with a *synthesis of findings*. Our criteria have proven to be useful and applicable in the exemplary use. Categorisation into four perspectives worked well, although it remains to be seen whether an even finer scheme might be advisable to cater for future developments. While the weighting profiles will need further tweaking (see also below), they lead to producible results. In particular, the smartphone profile has proven to be feasible. As could be expected and is widely affirmed by related literature (cf. Sects. 2 and 3), PhoneGap as the leading approach is better suited for cross-platform development that targets smartphones than pure native or Web apps. It should be noted that native development not simply satisfies all criteria *but* cross-platform capabilities; working natively can have its own *overhead*.

The additional weight profiles for now have to be seen as proposals. They should nonetheless be reasonable starting points. In particular, they are well-suited to address idiosyncrasies of specific device classes, e.g. to put weight on security for apps in cars or smart homes.

The tablet profile is rather similar to smartphones, particularly from the infrastructure and the development perspective. Multi-user scenarios and business integration need more attention, and additional means of input play a role. Quite differently, the entertainment profile has less business implications and is less focused on security, sensors and platform-features. Performance requirements might add complexity and support for multiple users is a prerequisite.

For the wearable profile, yet other specialities need to be taken into account. Deploying to and testing on devices is quite hard. User interfaces differ much from platform to platform. Apps typically are very small and must perform with low resource utilisation. At the same time, usage scenarios are simpler and due to high-fluctuation of devices a long-term focus needs to be less emphasized.

Security is of foremost concern in the vehicle profile. Due to the field's fuzziness, it shares similarities with the wearable profile but has more focus on professional software development. Most blurry is the smart home profile, which needs to address the heterogeneity of possible devices along with security concerns.

A number of open questions can be raised. While we deem the evaluation framework to be readily usable, particularly due to its solid literature foundation, the weighting remains open for revisions. Future research will scrutinize whether the device classes have been chosen wisely. There is no easy answer to this since new kinds of devices might be designed with a focus on app-enablement – or not. For example, Tesla announced an own SDK but current work obviously has taken another direction due to security concerns [36]. Moreover, it is hard to predict market development. For example, Android Wear [3] *might* unify development for Wearables or at least consolidate different streams.

It remains to be seen whether the success of Web technology (including frameworks such as PhoneGap) will be repeated for new device classes. On the one hand, devices with hardware that is not powerful enough to run a WebKit-Engine such as some watches might require different approaches. Other devices, such as arguably fitness trackers, do not even pose a platform that would be comparable to Android or iOS. On the other hand, Web technology might be the bridging element for heterogeneity. It is still very hard to image the proper abstraction for devices that fall under the umbrella of smart home technology.

Furthermore, it needs to be questioned whether for all device classes full ecosystems as for smartphones will be established. A Cloud-based middleware, mirroring, or other "remote" approaches could solve issues such as low performance, hardware heterogeneity and security without even relying on devices directly. Moreover, device classes might converge. Modern fitness trackers have smartwatch functionality; a smartwatch was recently hacked to run applications only imaginable on smartphones before [35]. So called *instant apps* can be run without installation [24] and might also contribute to future changes.

Due to the breadth of our work and also due to the novelty of some of the tackled topics, this paper is bound to limitations. While we built upon the literature both for the derivation of criteria and for their exemplary usage, we have not evaluated our work empirically. This is particularly an issue for the weight profiles, which need to be assessed based on the input from practitioners. Moreover, we have made assumptions about the future, most notably considering device classes. It seems unlikely but it might turn out that e.g. app-enabled cars will not gain importance. Even if they do, it is not given that cars (or other device classes) will allow for reasonable cross-platform app development support. Looking towards the future is part of our work but a boundary at the same time.

The limitations do not impede the value of our work, though. In fact, in combination with the above discussed open questions they provide the foundation for our future work. Writing this paper has been *more* than setting out to refresh the view on the topic of mobile computing. It has brought up a host of new ideas for us, particularly revolving around the differences in device classes. We will strive to provide a unified understanding while honouring the particular strengths and possibilities offered by devices. A major source of our future work will be the above mentioned limitations. As a next step, we will work on a broader evaluation of current approaches based on our criteria. Moreover, we will assess possibilities how to get practitioners' feedback on the framework, ideally leading to an empiric validation of our work. This will include a revision of the weights and more concrete advice on approach choice. In particular, we would like to provide recommendations in form of case study-like scenarios for future applications. Finally, we will also seek to make further theory contributions, especially concerning an abstraction from device classes.

7   Conclusion

In this paper, we have presented work on an extended cross-platform app development evaluation framework. It extends existing papers and revised the criteria formerly proposed. In particularly, it takes into account differences in the increasing number of device classes and provides a weighted evaluation. We have not only comprehensively introduced our framework but given an exemplary evaluation. The findings suggest that the framework is well-suited. Nonetheless, much work remains due to the novelty and breadth of the field.

References

1. Amatya, S., Kurti, A.: Cross-platform mobile development: challenges and opportunities. In: Trajkovik, V., Anastas, M. (eds.) ICT Innovations 2013. AISC, vol. 231, pp. 219–229. Springer, Heidelberg (2014). doi:10.1007/978-3-319-01466-1_21
2. Android TV. https://www.android.com/tv/
3. Android Wear 2.0 developer preview. https://developer.android.com/wear/preview/index.html
4. Apache Cordova documentation (2016). https://cordova.apache.org/docs/en/
5. Beal, G.M., Bohlen, J.M.: The Diffusion Process. Agricultural Experiment Station. Iowa State College, Ames (1957)
6. Bouhnick, G.: A list of all operating systems running on smartwatches [wearables] (2015). http://www.mobilespoon.net/2015/03/a-list-of-all-operating-systems-running.html
7. Rahul Raj, C.P., Tolety, S.B.: A study on approaches to build cross-platform mobile applications and criteria to select appropriate approach. In: 2012 Annual IEEE India Conference (INDICON), pp. 625–629 (2012)
8. Carter, J.: Which is the best internet of things platform? (2015). http://www.techradar.com/news/-1302416
9. Chmielewski, J.: Towards an architecture for future internet applications. In: Galis, A., Gavras, A. (eds.) FIA 2013. LNCS, vol. 7858, pp. 214–219. Springer, Heidelberg (2013). doi:10.1007/978-3-642-38082-2_18
10. Ciman, M., Gaggi, O.: Measuring energy consumption of cross-platform frameworks for mobile applications. In: Monfort, V., Krempels, K.-H. (eds.) WEBIST 2014. LNBIP, vol. 226, pp. 331–346. Springer, Heidelberg (2015). doi:10.1007/978-3-319-27030-2_21
11. Ciman, M., Gaggi, O., Gonzo, N.: Cross-platform mobile development: a study on apps with animations. In: Proceedings of the ACM Symposium on Applied Computing (2014)
12. Cross-platform tools 2015 (2015). http://www.visionmobile.com/product/cross-platform-tools-2015/
13. Dalmasso, I., Datta, S.K., Bonnet, C., Nikaein, N.: Survey, comparison and evaluation of cross platform mobile application development tools. In: Proceedings of the 9th IWCMC (2013)
14. Davis, L.: Phonegap: people's choice winner at web 2.0 expo launch pad (2009). http://readwrite.com/2009/04/02/phone_gap
15. Deindl, M., Roscher, M., Birkmeier, M.: An architecture vision for an open service cloud for the smart car. In: Filho, W.L., Kotter, R. (eds.) Mobility in Europe, Green Energy and Technology, vol. 203, pp. 281–295. Springer, Heidelberg (2015)
16. Dhillon, S., Mahmoud, Q.H.: An evaluation framework for cross-platform mobile application development tools. Softw. Prac. Exp. 45(10), 1331–1357 (2015)
17. Dobie, A.: Why you'll never have the latest version of android (2012). http://www.androidcentral.com/why-you-ll-never-have-latest-version-android
18. Dorr, T.: Tesla Model S JSON API (2016). http://docs.timdorr.apiary.io
19. Doud, A.: How important is cross-platform wearable support? (2015). http://pocketnow.com/2015/05/10/cross-platform-wearable-support
20. Durach, S., Higgen, U., Huebler, M.: Smart automotive apps: an approach to context-driven applications. In: SAE-China, FISITA (ed.) Proceedings of the FISITA 2012 World Automotive Congress. LNEE 2012, vol. 200, pp. 187–195. Springer, Heidelberg (2013). doi:10.1007/978-3-642-33838-0_17

21. El-Kassas, W.S., Abdullah, B.A., Yousef, A.H., Wahba, A.: ICPMD: integrated cross-platform mobile development solution. In: Proceedings of the 9th ICCES (2014)
22. Ernsting, J., Rieger, C., Wrede, F., Majchrzak, T.A.: Refining a reference architecture for model-driven business apps. In: Proceedings of the 12th WEBIST, pp. 307–316. SciTePress (2016)
23. Function point languages table: Version 5.0 (2009). http://www.qsm.com/resources/function-point-languages-table
24. Ganapathy, S.: Introducing android instant apps. http://android-developers.blogspot.no/2016/05/android-instant-apps-evolving-apps.html
25. Google Inc.: Android wear 2.0 developer preview. https://developer.android.com/wear/preview/index.html
26. HbbTV overview (2016). https://www.hbbtv.org/overview/
27. Heitkötter, H., Hanschke, S., Majchrzak, T.A.: Comparing cross-platform development approaches for mobile applications. In: Proceedings 8th WEBIST, pp. 299–311. SciTePress (2012)
28. Heitkötter, H., Hanschke, S., Majchrzak, T.A.: Evaluating cross-platform development approaches for mobile applications. In: Cordeiro, J., Krempels, K.-H. (eds.) Web Information Systems and Technologies. LNBIP, vol. 140, pp. 120–138. Springer, Heidelberg (2013). doi:10.1007/978-3-642-36608-6_8
29. Heitkötter, H., Majchrzak, T.A., Kuchen, H.: Cross-platform model-driven development of mobile applications with MD^2. In: Proceedings of the SAC 2013, pp. 526–533. ACM (2013)
30. Heitkötter, H., Majchrzak, T.A., Ruland, B., Weber, T.: Comparison of mobile web frameworks. In: Krempels, K.-H., Stocker, A. (eds.) Web Information Systems and Technologies. LNBIP, vol. 189, pp. 119–137. Springer, Heidelberg (2014)
31. Heitkötter, H., Kuchen, H., Majchrzak, T.A.: Extending a model-driven cross-platform development approach for business apps. Sci. Comput. Program. **97**(Part 1), 31–36 (2015)
32. Hudli, A., Hudli, S., Hudli, R.: An evaluation framework for selection of mobile app development platform. In: Proceedings of the 3rd MobileDeLi (2015)
33. Jie, G., Bo, C., Shuai, Z., Junliang, C.: Cross-platform android/ios-based smart switch control middleware in a digital home. Mobile Inform. Sys. (2015). http://www.hindawi.com/journals/misy/2015/627859/
34. Kim, H., Ahn, M., Hong, S., Lee, S.: Wearable device control platform technology for network application development. Mobile Inform. Syst. (2016). http://www.hindawi.com/journals/misy/2016/3038515/
35. Krawczyk, K.: Hacker installs windows 95 and doom on a samsung gear live smartwatch. http://www.digitaltrends.com/computing/hacker-installs-windows-95-and-doom-on-a-samsung-gear-live-smartwatch/
36. Lambert, F.: Tesla is moving away from an SDK. http://9to5mac.com/2016/01/28/tesla-sdk-iphone-apps-mirror/
37. Lella, A., Lipsman, A., Martin, B.: The 2015 U.S. mobile app report. https://www.comscore.com/ger/Insights/Presentations-and-Whitepapers/2015/The-2015-US-Mobile-App-Report
38. LG Electronics: WebOS for LG smart TVs (2016). http://www.lg.com/uk/smarttv/webos
39. Liu, X., Vega, K., Maes, P., Paradiso, J.A.: Wearability factors for skin interfaces. In: Proceedings of the 7th Augmented Human International Conference, pp. 21:1–21:8. ACM (2016)

40. Luca, A.D., Lindqvist, J.: Is secure and usable smartphone authentication asking too much? Computer **48**(5), 64–68 (2015)
41. Majchrzak, T.A., Ernsting, J.: Reengineering an approach to model-driven development of business apps. In: Wrycza, S. (ed.) SIGSAND/PLAIS 2015. LNBIP, vol. 232, pp. 15–31. Springer, Heidelberg (2015). doi:10.1007/978-3-319-24366-5_2
42. Majchrzak, T.A., Schulte, M.: Context-dependent testing of applications for mobile devices. Open J. Web Technol. (OJWT) **2**(1), 27–39 (2015)
43. Majchrzak, T.A., Wolf, S., Abbassi, P.: Comparing the capabilities of mobile platforms for business app development. In: Wrycza, S. (ed.) SIGSAND/PLAIS 2015. LNBIP, vol. 232, pp. 70–88. Springer, Heidelberg (2015). doi:10.1007/978-3-319-24366-5_6
44. MobileHTML5: Mobile html5 compatibility (2015). http://mobilehtml5.org/
45. Noreikis, M., Butkus, P., Nurminen, J.K.: In-vehicle application for multimodal route planning and analysis. In: Proceedings of the IEEE 3rd CloudNet (2014)
46. Ohrt, J., Turau, V.: Cross-platform development tools for smartphone applications. Computer **45**(9), 72–79 (2012)
47. Palmieri, M., Singh, I., Cicchetti, A.: Comparison of cross-platform mobile development tools. In: Proceedings of the 16th ICIN, pp. 179–186. IEEE (2012)
48. Perakakis, E., Ghinea, G.: HTML5 technologies for effective cross-platform interactive/smart TV advertising. IEEE Trans. HMS **45**(4), 534–539 (2015)
49. Perakakis, E., Ghinea, G.: A proposed model for cross-platform web 3D applications on smart TV systems. In: Proceedings of the 20th Web3D (2015)
50. Phonegap documentation (2015). http://docs.phonegap.com
51. Quaresma, M., Gonçalves, R.: Usability analysis of smartphone applications for drivers. In: Marcus, A. (ed.) DUXU 2014. LNCS, vol. 8517, pp. 352–362. Springer, Heidelberg (2014). doi:10.1007/978-3-319-07668-3_34
52. Research2guidance: cross-platform tool benchmarking (2014). http://research2guidance.com/product/cross-platform-tool-benchmarking-2014/
53. Revest, F.: Asteroidos (2016). http://asteroidos.org/
54. Rodriguez Garzon, S., Poguntke, M.: The personal adaptive in-car HMI: integration of external applications for personalized use. In: Ardissono, L., Kuflik, T. (eds.) UMAP 2011. LNCS, vol. 7138, pp. 35–46. Springer, Heidelberg (2012). doi:10.1007/978-3-642-28509-7_5
55. Ryu, D., Krompiec, P.K., Lee, E., Park, K.: A serious game design for english education on smart TV platform. In: Proceedings of the ISCE (2014)
56. Samsung Electronics Co. Ltd.: Let's toast - samsung smart TV apps developer forum. https://www.samsungdforum.com/Features/TOAST
57. Sansour, R.N., Kafri, N., Sabha, M.N.: A survey on mobile multimedia application development frameworks. In: Proceedings of the ICMCS (2014)
58. Schilit, B., Adams, N., Want, R.: Context-aware computing applications. In: Proceedings of the 1994 1st WMCSA, pp. 85–90. IEEE CS (1994)
59. Schuermans, S., Vakulenko, M.: Apps for connected cars? Your mileage may vary (2014). http://www.visionmobile.com/product/apps-for-cars-mileage-may-vary/
60. Sohn, H.J., Lee, M.G., Seong, B.M., Kim, J.B.: Quality evaluation criteria based on open source mobile HTML5 UI framework for development of cross-platform. IJSEIA **9**(6), 1–12 (2015)
61. Sommer, A., Krusche, S.: Evaluation of cross-platform frameworks for mobile applications. LNI P-215 (2013)
62. Statista. http://www.statista.com/
63. Tizen (2016). https://www.tizen.org/

64. Wasserman, A.I.: Software engineering issues for mobile application development. In: Roman, G.C., Sullivan, K. (eds.) Proceedings of the FoSER 2010, p. 397 (2010)
65. Willocx, M., Vossaert, J., Naessens, V.: A quantitative assessment of performance in mobile app development tools. In: Proceedings of the 3rd International Conference on Mobile Services (2015)
66. Wolf, F.: Will vehicles go the mobile way? Merits and challenges arising by car-apps. In: Proceedings of the 10th ICINCO, vol. 2 (2013)
67. Woods, V., van der Meulen, R.: Gartner says worldwide smartphone sales grew 9.7 percent in fourth quarter of 2015 (2016). http://www.gartner.com/newsroom/id/3215217
68. Xanthopoulos, S., Xinogalos, S.: A comparative analysis of cross-platform development approaches for mobile applications. In: Proceedings of the 6th BCI, pp. 213–220. ACM (2013)
69. XBMC Foundation: Third-party forks and derivatives. http://kodi.wiki/view/Third-party_forks_and_derivatives
70. Zhang, J., Chen, C., Ma, J., He, N., Ren, Y.: Usink: smartphone-based moible sink for wireless sensor networks. In: Proceedings of the CCNC 2011 (2011)

Exploring an Ontological Approach for User Requirements Elicitation in the Design of Online Virtual Agents

Katarzyna Ossowska[✉], Liliana Szewc, Paweł Weichbroth,
Igor Garnik, and Marcin Sikorski

Faculty of Management and Economics, Department of Applied Business Informatics,
Gdansk University of Technology, ul. Narutowicza 11/12, 80-233 Gdansk, Poland
{katarzyna.ossowska,pawel.weichbroth,igor.garnik,
marcin.sikorski}@zie.pg.gda.pl, liliana.szewc@gmail.com

Abstract. Effective user requirements elicitation is a key factor for the success of software development projects. There are many qualitative and quantitative research studies that promulgate particular methods and show the application of user requirements elicitation in particular domains. However, few try to eliminate the burden of ambiguity in gathered data, naturally occurring in different groups of stakeholders. This paper deals with this problem by introducing an ontology-based approach which by design provides a shared and common understanding of a domain. On the other hand, the developed ontology is a feasible communication facility for the stakeholders involved, acknowledged and controlled by a group of experts.

Keywords: Virtual agents · Ontologies · Benefits · Requirements · Elicitation

1 Introduction

Over the two recent decades, we have been able to observe a dynamic growth of e-commerce on a global scale. This has resulted not only in an explosion in the number of online consumers but also in their increased expectations. Customer expectations refer to a wide choice of vendors and attractively priced products, but they equally refer to a mandatory easiness of use and more natural interaction with e-commerce websites.

User-Centered Design [1, 2] is a design approach aimed at increasing the usability of e-commerce websites in terms of improving user task performance, task efficiency and user satisfaction. Subsequently, the User Experience [3, 4] design approach attempts to improve the customers' experience with the website, while the Design Thinking [5] approach aims at increasing the customers' engagement and loyalty to a specific online vendor or brand. In the latter approach, adding novel interactive elements to the website which enhance the customers' relationship with the brand, is the preferred way to distinguish a specific website from others and make it more memorable for the user/customer.

Humanoid virtual agents in particular have become increasingly popular in e-commerce websites. Virtual agents use artificial intelligence modules for the automated answering of typical questions, which customers type into a dialogue box available on the website. While

S. Wrycza (Ed.): SIGSAND/PLAIS 2016, LNBIP 264, pp. 40–55, 2016.
DOI: 10.1007/978-3-319-46642-2_3

some agents display their answers in the textual form in a chat-mode, other agents use a synthesized, modulated voice to express not only the contents but also specific emotions.

Virtual agents have been expected to make interaction with users easier and more natural. However, many users feel reluctant to "talk" with virtual agents because their implementation and behavior are still far from what users expect. As virtual agents are in fact digital robots, to make them a trustworthy conversational partner for the consumer is very difficult, because user expectations of how virtual agents should behave, are usually very vague and imprecise.

This paper deals with the problem of eliciting user requirements when designing virtual agents, and it attempts to use an ontological approach for modelling the expected characteristics of an agent during the analysis phase in an e-commerce website development project.

2 Related Research

2.1 Online Virtual Agents in E-commerce

2.1.1 Application Areas

In the literature, a taxonomy regarding virtual agents is still far from consistent. For instance, the following terms have been in use:

- intelligent agents [6]: software agents which build adaptive, automated dialogue with the user; these agents may not be visible as they work in the background, for instance, text-only chat robots;
- embodied conversational agents [7, 8]: humanoid agents aimed at assisting the user/customer in specific interactive environments like museums, learning, entertainment (can also be off-line, not connected to the internet);
- online virtual agents [9]: humanoid agents built into websites, which interact with the user in textual or conversational mode (or in both).

In this paper, the last definition will be used, as the most relevant to the context of an online e-commerce environment.

Nowadays, virtual agents (VAs) have been used online mostly in the following types of websites [7, 8, 10]:

- websites of utility companies (water, gas, cable TV, telecom, etc. vendors), where VAs answer typical questions from registered online customers; typical questions usually refer to some inconsistencies on recent invoices, frequent questions also concern problems with service quality/availability, VAs may also guide the user in a self-check of the installation before sending a formal complaint, etc.;
- instructional websites, where VAs provide assistance in solving typical users' problems, like configuring the service to individual needs, guidance in conducting repair procedures or helping to self-assemble a product at home;
- promotional or recruitment websites of universities or other organizations, where a VA provides customized, textual or auditory information about perspectives, choices and options suggested for a potential candidate.

In general, apart from providing a new interaction channel with customers, the main motivation for using VAs is to reduce the load (and costs) put on the telephone lines of the service vendor. This is done by redirecting trivial questions (which form most of the calls) to automated processing by a VA and its artificial intelligence dialogue engine, which - in contrary to a human operator - is able to handle multiple dialogues at the same time. Unsurprisingly, due to the significant investment necessary to develop a knowledge base and artificial intelligence engine for VA-based services, a substantial reduction in operational costs is expected mainly in big companies, whose call-centers daily serve thousands of typical, routine, well-specified customer enquiries [8].

2.1.2 User-Perceived Quality of VAs

In designing VAs, it is difficult to define user requirements with a meaning typical for conventional interactive systems [7, 8]. In the case of VAs, users seldom have exact preferences, and they are only able to express vague expectations rather than precise requirements directly useful for the system analyst. Users usually have some requirements as to the quality of the service but not as to the preferred characteristics of the VA itself. It is also difficult to specify usability and UX requirements for VA-based interaction, apart from general guidelines for human-computer dialogue design, which are focused mostly on the ability of the human user to control the dialogue.

Based on the literature survey, the main components of user-perceived VA quality are the following [11, 12]:

- visual appearance, for instance: look, clothing, gender, head/face, hair, dress;
- gestural behavior, for instance: mimics, gesticulation, body movements;
- voice, for instance: timbre, modulation, intonation, vocabulary.

The outcome of all three categories can be described as the agent's credibility, resulting from its overall behavior, including also competent answers, a friendly attitude and good coherence with the company image [11]. Moreover, if a VA is to be perceived as trustworthy, its behavior should be to some degree "intelligent": flexible, adaptable and responsive – simply adequate to whatever the user expects. A VA's general ability to imitate human behavior is sometimes characterized as "social presence" [9], as if the conversation took place with a real person.

2.1.3 VA-Related Design Problems

The acceptability of a VA by users and its attractiveness as a potential conversation partner may depend a lot on how realistic it looks and behaves.

From the system analysis and development side, the implementation of a VA requires the synchronizing of a number of skills [7, 8]:

- graphics, animation, voice engineering,
- text analysis and semiotic understanding of users' queries,
- creating a knowledge base and syntactic engine for generating the VA's answers,
- adaptive mechanisms for providing tolerance to user errors (spelling, syntax, etc.) for adapting the VA's behavior to the user's conversation style.

Implementing a VA for an e-commerce website always involves some risks. Customers will be willing to use the conversation with the VA only if their problems are solved more efficiently (as to time and correctness) than by a human operator on a telephone line. A VA-generated dialogue should be seamless, smooth and error-tolerant, otherwise any deficiency experienced by the user will probably turn him/her back to a conventional call-center phone. Eventually, a poor user experience with a VA is likely to discourage the customer from contacting a VA in the future, and savings expected by the service vendor from using VAs online will never be achieved.

In the literature there is a lack of convincing business and design guidelines, as well as established design methodologies dedicated especially for VAs. Some ready-to-use design frameworks are available only for designing dialogue systems (e.g. [13]) but they do not propose guidelines on how a VA should behave to be trustworthy and attractive as a potential dialogue partner for the user/customer.

What makes the design of a trustworthy VA even more difficult is that users' expectations as to the look or behavior of a VA may vary a lot among various services, like tourism, finance or ticket booking. Failing to meet the customers' expectations may result in the customers' reluctance to interact with a specific VA. This may happen even if a VA seems "technically" correct but appears not to be credible enough or does not fit perfectly to the specific brand or website it is representing.

2.2 Requirements Elicitation Techniques

In an IT project, the appropriate elicitation of user expectations seems to be the most difficult factor for the acceptance of a VA by prospective users/customers.

A number of available requirements elicitation techniques have been so far successfully applied in a variety of software projects. The choice primarily depends on the complexity of the information that needs to be elicited, and the available time and resources assigned to this task [14]. A critical review of the literature was carried out to identify the relevant context-of-use techniques. Among many, the following techniques seem to be potentially useful for designing Vas.

Interview is a conversation in which one or more interviewers ask questions to the interviewee; it is apparently the most traditional and most general requirements elicitation technique [15]; with relatively little effort, it can efficiently and quickly lead to the collection of large amounts of data; in general, there are three types of interviews: structured, unstructured and semi-structured; where in the first a predetermined set of questions is used to gather information, on the contrary, the second does not follow any agenda and thus is conversational and open-minded in nature, and the third is a liberal combination of these two [16].

Questionnaire is a list of open and/or closed questions, printed or electronically presented, submitted to one or more respondents to gain replies, mostly used during the early stages of requirements elicitation; however, to be effective it requires well established terms, concepts and boundaries of the given domain, understood both by respondents and the questionnaire designer [17].

Brainstorming is basically a technique to provoke and encourage creative thinking based on a general idea, during a workshop with a group of participants, including both experts and novices [18].

Storytelling, borrowed from knowledge management, is a well-known technique used to pass along knowledge; in the context of requirements elicitation, storytelling has the potential to elicit unarticulated, but still relevant information, such as context-of-use or usability issues [19].

Prototyping provides a solid foundation for discussion between project stakeholders (designers and users), giving opportunities to learn more about product features and design [20]; a prototype is an initial version of the system, and can take various forms at different fidelity levels: from low paper-based (so-called mock-up) to high extensively-interactive (made with the same methods as the final system), or alternatively "Wizard of Oz" (a human-based simulation of the system's responses to some user inputs) [21].

Ethnography is a study of the "workaday" activities of users within specific contexts; the outcome is detailed descriptions that rely upon real-life task performance in the concerned domain [22].

Role playing is a sort of game or exercise in which participants act as the various stakeholders in a requirements elicitation activity in the context of a predefined task; groups of interests and conflicts might also be revealed, as well as previously neglected users' needs [23].

The process of building an online VA (OVA) brings together experts from various fields, which can possibly lead to ambiguous meanings of concepts represented by the same or synonymous strings. However, none of these techniques can provide semantic foundations nor do they focus on identified relationships between specified and gathered requirements. Moreover, there is no inference engine developed, thus all the necessary tasks are performed alone and manually, although in some cases, and to some extent, supported by dedicated applications. These limitations have induced us to model and represent requirements in the form of an ontology. What is more, the latest advances in the development of ontology implementation environments (e.g. [24]) are promising solutions enabling direct collaboration with other stakeholders. Moreover, our approach supports efficient reuse, maintenance and development, which directly translates into reducing time in modifying an existing OVA or creating a new one, through a clear transfer of requirements from the end-user customer to the developer and graphic designer.

By definition, an ontology is an explicit and formal specification of a shared conceptualization. In practice, this definition can be understood in the following terms:

- we are able to explicitly define the concepts, properties, relationships, functions, axioms and constraints that compose it,
- formal notation provides machine-aided readability and interpretability,
- conceptualization is a simplified view of the requirements model, and
- shared means an uncontested consensus on the gathered information, accepted by a group of experts.

As a consequence, all of these properties, which lay the foundation of the method presented later, might bring significant advantages in requirements elicitation when compared to those techniques presented above. By design, ontologies overcome the limitations of a keyword-based search, reduce the information retrieval problem to a data retrieval task, and the search results are assumed to be always 100 % precise.

3 Method Outline

The aim of the study was to find a way to acquire requirements for online virtual agents used in different types of online services. These requirements would then be used to define the design parameters of VAs. We assume that the source of requirements are internet users who are online service clients. The requirements acquired in such a way should match enough good user/customer expectations, according to a service consultant. However, we do not disregard the situation in which the source of requirements is the owner or management staff of an online service provider.

In order to build the ontology we perform the following steps:

- identify the main concepts,
- build the concepts structure,
- model the relationships as class attributes,
- evaluate the elaborated results,
- implement the ontology,
- maintain and refine.

This is based on the standard procedure in common-use; however, both the laboratory conditions, adding language benefits, and the specifics of the project itself require the work carried out to be extended beyond the accepted standards, and thus present a concept allowing the possibility of using ontologies to gather OVA requirements to be explored.

Our analytic procedure is divided into the ten following steps:

1. Collecting requirements from potential users/customers.
2. Building an ontology of requirements.
3. Collecting the expected benefits from potential users/customers.
4. Classifying the expected benefits among three levels, using UML notation.
5. Ranking the major benefits in terms of their importance.
6. Rejecting unnecessary/redundant benefits.
7. Transferring benefits to the table of benefits to specific levels.
8. Supplementing the benefits table.
9. Entering the agent's features into the benefits table.
10. Identifying links between requirements and benefits.

This method was applied in laboratory settings, in a context not related to a particular IT project.

4   Results

This section presents the results obtained in subsequent steps of the procedure listed in Sect. 3.

4.1   Data Collection (Step 1)

In the first stage of our study we asked 27 respondents (mainly students of two technical universities in Gdansk) to identify the expected characteristics of a VA for the website of a law office. Due to the nature of the service, we expected to acquire a wide range of VA characteristics. In order to obtain the characteristics in a standardized structure we used a specially prepared questionnaire form (Fig. 1) of a tree shape. In this case, the user requirements correspond to the agent's characteristics.

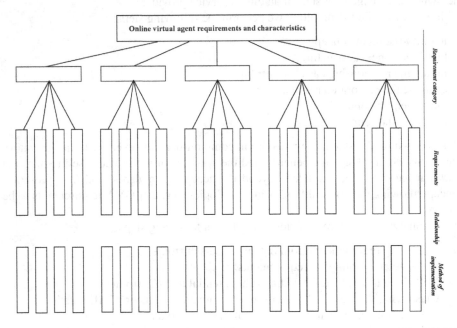

Fig. 1. A template of the questionnaire form used for eliciting the desired characteristics of a VA

The respondents had to define the expected characteristics of the VA, such as visible (appearance, outfit, gestures, etc.) and invisible (e.g. voice) features, behavior, reactions to users' activities, responses to users' questions, and the like. The characteristics had to be grouped in up to five categories. Next, the respondents had to define the method of implementation of each characteristic. The relationship between the characteristics and methods of implementation was not restricted, which means that many methods could be used for implementing one characteristic, as well as many characteristics being implemented by one (or more) method, as shown in Fig. 1.

The respondents, for defining the VA characteristics, were allowed to use natural language. This presents a crucial problem for the requirements elicitation and aggregation process, because users use many different terms for describing the same concept and sometimes it is difficult to precisely translate a characteristic written in natural language into a certain requirement. Therefore, we decided to use an ontological approach to arrange the obtained collection of characteristics into an ordered set of concepts. For further processing, to simplify the structure of the ontology, we abandoned the implementation methods. This also allowed a better focus on the concepts reflecting the users' requirements.

4.2   Requirements Modelling (Step 2)

In order to analyze, synthesize and later infer from the gathered data sheets representing the students' expectations of the attributes of a VA "working" for a law office, we developed a model of the ontology using Ontorion Fluent Editor [24, 25]. It can efficiently support both the requirements engineer and the agent's designer in such a manner which decreases the gap between understanding concepts on the one hand, while on the other hand, delivers a useful tool to "ask" about the present relationships between them.

During the ontology development, we gradually arranged, structured and verified particular bags of words. Next, corrected and coherent concepts were codified on the diagram from top to bottom. On the top, there are unique categories such as: hairstyle, voice, intelligence, competent speech, environment, gender, posture, face, age, appearance, and behavior. They all correspond to the gathered requirements on an analogous level, and occur frequently enough to be taken into account. In some cases, where it was necessary, a few ambiguous concepts were replaced by synonyms that closely reflect the given meaning. In consequence, we resolve the problem of semantic heterogeneity, including confounding and naming conflicts.

Moreover, the defined relationships between the categories and the respondents' requirements are mapped on the ontology for the majority of instances. However, in a few cases, we decided to change a particular category to a subcategory and vice versa. For example, a "face" was pointed out as a requirement (second level) by respondents, and was changed to another category (first level). Such an operation allows an agent to be qualified only when it unconditionally fulfills all input attributes.

The number of gathered sequences in data sheets enabled us to design a semantic network of average complexity. In order to acquire explicit attributes for the agent design we need to use the query and inference tool available in Fluent Editor. The level of the input attribute is irrelevant, because the engine returns both upper and lower attributes. In other words, for a defined and executed query, the list of search results includes both super-sequences and sub-sequences.

Fluent Editor, used in this study (Fig. 2), prompts suggestions in quite a suitable way, based on a dictionary built from the particular ontology, but still limited to the first letters of the sequence being input by a user.

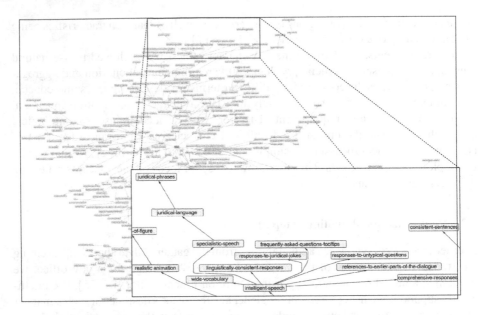

Fig. 2. The ontology elaborated for a VA

In our opinion, there are requirements missing in the gathered data sheets, potentially useful and applicable for the design of the VA. To enrich the developing ontology, during our meetings we organized short brainstorming sessions, where spoken aloud concepts were documented and later analyzed, compared and synthesized.

4.3 Gathering Benefits from Experts (Steps 3–6)

In Step 3 the expected benefits from using the virtual agent were collected from a group of four invited experts – potential users. This invited group was formed from new members, not participating in the questionnaire survey in Step 1, because the questionnaire respondents had problems in distinguishing the expected characteristics of the agent from the expected benefits, where from the latter group a more overall look at the problem was expected. As the method requires identifying and expressing benefits in the same way as requirements are defined and presented, UML (Unified Modeling Language) was a natural choice to use for building a Use Case diagram. The expected benefits have been divided (Fig. 3) into three areas, referred to as levels, due to the fact that they have a hierarchical nature - when satisfying one benefit, another associated one on the upper level can be satisfied, too.

As aforementioned, in general, benefits on the lower levels contribute to satisfying benefits on the upper level and their aggregated outcome is perceived by the user/customer according to individual needs.

Referring to the UML diagram shown in Fig. 3, it can be seen that the benefits of lower levels are included (<<include>>) in the benefits of the upper levels. For

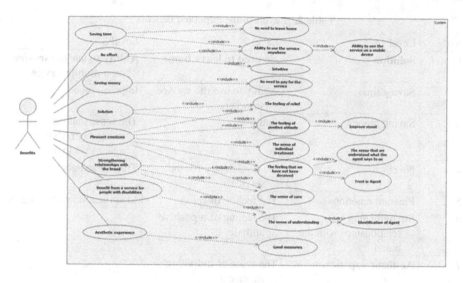

Fig. 3. The UML diagram showing the levels of benefits expected by users

example, the benefits of level 3 are included in the benefits of level 2 and subsequently, the benefits from level 2 contribute in producing the benefits of level 1. The next step was to rank the benefits of level 1 in terms of their importance for the user, according to the following rating scale: the most important, very important, important, less important, unimportant. Moreover, the most important rank may be assigned to only one benefit. Later on, we also rejected the benefits ranked as insignificant (unimportant). Table 1 shows the outcome of these steps.

Table 1. The priorities assigned to benefits

Benefit	Severity
Solution (of the user's problem)	**The most important**
Saving time	Very important
Saving money	Very important
No effort	Important
Pleasant emotions	Important
Strengthening relationships with the brand	Less important
Aesthetic experience	Less important
Benefit from a service for people with disabilities	Not important

Then, according to the levels shown in the Use Case diagram (Fig. 3), all of the expected benefits have been transferred to Table 2 to respective levels.

Table 2. Levels of the expected benefits

No	Level 1	Level 2	Level 3
1	**Solution**	**No need to leave home**	**Ability to use the service on a mobile device**
2	Saving time	Ability to use the service anywhere	Improve mood
3	Saving money	Intuitive	The sense that we understand what the agent says to us
4	No effort	No need to pay for the service	Trust in an agent
5	Pleasant emotions	The feeling of relief	Identification with an agent
6	Strengthening relationships with the brand	The feeling of a positive attitude	
7	Aesthetic experience	The sense of individual treatment	
8	Benefit from a service for people with disabilities	The feeling that we have not been deceived	
		The sense of care	
		The sense of understanding	
		Good memories	

Because the expected benefits have a network-tree hierarchical structure, each expected benefit was given an index corresponding to the column and row in which it is located, according to the template: *number_of_column (level).number_of_line.*

For example, the benefit of "No need to leave home" is in the second column (level 2) and the first line, hence the number assigned to it is 2.1.

In the next step, relating the advantages in a table, each of the main advantages (level 1) is assigned the contained advantages of levels 2 and 3 (Table 3).

Table 3. Relationships among benefits

Level 1	Level 2	Level 3
1.1	2.5, 2.6	3.2
1.2	2.1, 2.2	3.1
1.3	2.4	
1.4	2.2, 2.3	3.1
1.5	2.5, 2.6, 2.7, 2.8, 2.9	3.2, 3.3, 3.4
1.6	2.8, 2.9, 2.10	3.3, 3.4, 3.5
1.7	2.11	
1.8	2.10	3.5

Now we need to find which requirements for the VA meet the specific benefits expected by users. To do this, we complete a table in which the requirements and expected benefits are interrelated (Table 4).

Table 4. Requirements and expected benefits

The direction of filling the table

Requirement	Expected benefits																							
	1.1	1.2	1.3	1.4	1.5	1.6	1.7	1.8	2.1	2.2	2.3	2.4	2.5	2.6	2.7	2.8	2.9	2.10	3.1	3.2	3.3	3.4	3.5	
Legal terminology used correctly																								0
Hints on frequently asked questions		x																						1
Answers to unusual questions																								0
Appropriate sense of humour					x										x									1
Referring to previous parts of the dialogue																								0
Comprehensive responses																								0
	0	1	0	0	1	0	0	0																0
																								0
																								0
																								0
																								0

The number of requirements satisfying a specific benefit from Level 1

The number of benefits from Level 1 related to a specific requirement

It is important for the table to be filled in the correct order, starting from the highest level (in this case, level 3, as shown above), because the benefits gained from the upper level aggregate benefits from the lower levels. In this example, the requirement "Answers to unusual questions" is the fulfillment of the benefit numbered 2.7 "The sense of individual treatment", which in turn is contained within the benefit 1.5 "Pleasant emotions."

In this way, in the final stage of completing level 1 we can see which user requirements (agent characteristics) relate respectively to which benefits expected by users. Moreover, we can also see how many benefits will be met by how many specific requirements (see the comments in the boxes in Table 4). The number of requirements which should be implemented in a virtual agent depends on the importance of the expected specific benefits. Subsequently, in this way the number of requirements which are necessary to provide the expected benefits was proposed as:

- the most important: equal to 100 %,
- very important: min. 80 %,
- important: min. 60 %,
- less important: min. 50 %,
- unimportant min: 30 %.

The number of user requirements (agent characteristics) for each level is related to the fact that there is a possibility of a mutual exclusion of requirements, so we have to make a choice about which of them should be implemented. Such an approach, focusing on the benefits expected by prospective users, allows for a better adjustment of the virtual agent to the needs of the potential user, and it also increases the likelihood of acceptance of such a service by its future customers.

5 Discussion

5.1 Significance of the Obtained Results

Such an approach, focusing on the expected benefits of future users, allows a better adjustment of the virtual agent to the needs of the potential user, and also increases the likelihood of the use of such services by the user in the future.

The requirements elicitation and analysis method presented in this paper has combined two ontologies:

- user requirements (expected characteristics of a virtual agent),
- user-expected benefits from using a virtual agent on a website.

This method promotes a broader use of *benefits* because they are usually easier to articulate by users interviewed by an analyst.

Both requirements and benefits are complex contenders of a hierarchical-networked structure, only a part of which can usually be revealed. Therefore, this method argues that a part of the (least important) information has to be discarded, and the most important elements should be appropriately prioritized.

This method has also coped not only with the problem of assigning priorities to identified elements, but also with identifying relationships among elements scattered across two hierarchies: user requirements and user benefits. An attempt has also been made to estimate how many requirements should be implemented in each group, depending on the priority assigned to a relevant, specific benefit.

All assessments made in the above areas have been made by human experts, using data obtained from human respondents. This is one of the major limitations of this study, which will be discussed in the next section.

The use of ontologies in this study resulted also in the following reflections. During the work on the ontology the main guidelines were the criteria proposed by T. Gruber concerning ontology design. Our model has been built in accordance with the aforementioned objectives, and primarily with the assumption of the possibility of expansion and adaptation to change. However, if the changes are diametric, then we must deal with a new project that will actually require the development of a new ontology. Secondly, an ontology should be designed to anticipate the uses of the shared vocabulary. It should offer a conceptual foundation for a range of anticipated tasks, and the representation should be crafted so that the ontology can be extended and specialized monotonically. In other words, new terms for special uses should be able to be defined based on the vocabulary in a way that does not require a revision of the definitions.

In addition to an experimental use of the ontological approach for requirements elicitation for an OVA, this paper aims at presenting a novelty at least in the following aspects:

- it is an early attempt to formulate and use the "language of benefits" to facilitate communication with users,
- it may open interesting opportunities for a transition from "requirements engineering" to "benefits engineering", which better matches the IT development environment with expectations of users/customers,

- it is an attempt to adapt the language of benefits to the IT domain, used so far in the area of direct sales,
- the "language of benefits" used in the context of OVAs is aimed at a better matching system designed to meet user requirements and reduce the number of project failures due to the poor understanding of customer requirements.

5.2 Limitations of this Study

The following limitations of this study should be pointed out:

1. The subjectivity of raw data obtained from human respondents and the subjectivity of assessments made by human experts. The method in its current state focused on developing a mechanism for "translating" the expected benefits into the required characteristics of an agent, hence no procedures for reducing subjectivity are available at the moment.
2. The human respondents invited to take part in the questionnaire survey (Step 1) often expressed requirements for an agent in terms of reflecting the expected benefits. This may suggest that, instead, an individual interview could be used, allowing the respondents' misconceptions and terminology to be corrected. The quality of the obtained data was also much dependent on how much actual experience a respondent had from interacting with virtual agents (and with how many); this aspect was not included in this study because the sample of available respondents was not large enough. Regarding benefits, both individual and group interviews should be considered as prospective methods for data elicitation from prospective users and existing customers.
3. This method could be much more attractive for the analyst if an interactive tool was available for automating the tabular transformations presented in this paper. The method now is at the stage of a conceptual experiment, aimed at refining its architecture and usefulness and this work is by no means yet complete.
4. The practical validation of this method is under way in two areas:
   - comparing the transformations presented here with other analytic methods from the requirements engineering area;
   - attempting to use the sets of obtained data for the implementation of exemplary virtual agents, but this still remains a laborious and time-consuming task.

5.3 Future Research

There are several areas for further improvements of this method:

- performing data gathering sessions with other groups of users, better informed on understanding the differences between requirements and expected benefits;
- using another rating scale, which would be (to some extent) tolerant to human subjectivity;
- refining the clarity of transformations taking place in this method, as well as a visualization of the outcomes.

Further works are planned to improve both the calculation and notation aspects of the "language of benefits" concept, as well as to promote the "benefits engineering" approach, which surely needs further refinements.

6   Conclusions

Despite these limitations, this study has delivered interesting results, but they should be treated rather as a highlight for the opportunities this method may offer than as a complete and validated solution for analysts.

Because the example of virtual agents was selected as a primary testing field for this method, it is possible that it will work also for systems with other hard-to-specify types of user interfaces, like augmented reality or social media. This method, although early and experimental, after necessary refinements, may offer new opportunities for radical changes in the way analytic work is done in IT projects: instead of intensifying efforts to capture user requirements in the best possible way, a user talking the "language of benefits" and these being subsequently translated into requirements, in the long term, may turn out to be a more prospective approach.

References

1. Dix, A., Finlay, J., Abowd, G., Beale, R.: Human-Computer Interaction. Prentice Hall, Harlow (2004)
2. Lowdermilk, T.: User-Centered Design: A Developer's Guide to Building User-Friendly Applications. O'Reilly, Sebastopol (2013)
3. Garrett, J.J.: The Elements of User Experience. New Riders, Indianapolis (2011)
4. Hartson, R., Pyla, P.: The UX Book: Process and Guidelines for Ensuring a Quality User Experience. Morgan Kaufmann, Burlington (2012)
5. Stickdorn, M., Schneider, J.: This is Service Design Thinking. BIS Publishers, Amsterdam (2010)
6. Abbattista, F., Loops, P., Semerano, G., Andersen, H.: Evaluating virtual agents for e-commerce. In: Falcone, R., Barber, S., Korba, L., Singh, M.P. (eds.) AAMAS 2002. LNCS (LNAI), vol. 2361. Springer, Heidelberg (2003)
7. Cassell, J., Sullivan, J., Prevost, S., Churchill, E.F.: Embodied Conversational Agents. MIT Press, Cambridge (2000)
8. Lester, J., Branting, K., Mott, B.: Conversational agents. In: Singh, M.P. (ed.) The Practical Handbook of Internet Computing. CRC Press (2005)
9. Lunardo, R., Bressoles, G., Durrieu, F.: The interacting effect of virtual agents' gender and dressing style on attractiveness and subsequent consumer online behaviour. J. Retail. Consum. Serv. 30, 59–66 (2016)
10. Cassell, J.: More than just another pretty face: embodied conversational interface agents. Commun. ACM 43(A), 70–78 (2000)
11. Pentina, I., Taylor, D.G.: Exploring source effects for online sales outcomes: the role of avatar-buyer similarity. J. Customer Behav. 9(2), 135–150 (2010)

12. Payne, J., Szymkowiak, A., Robertson, P., Johnson, G.: Gendering the machine: preferred virtual assistant gender and realism in self-service. In: Aylett, R., Krenn, B., Pelachaud, C., Shimodaira, H. (eds.) IVA 2013. LNCS, vol. 8108, pp. 106–115. Springer, Heidelberg (2013). doi:10.1007/978-3-642-40415-3_9

13. Ales, Z., Duplessis, G.D., Serban, O., Pauchet, A.: A methodology to design human-like embodied conversational agents based on dialogue analysis. In: Proceedings of First International Workshop on Human-Agent Interaction Design and Models (HAIDM), AAMAS, pp. 34–50 (2012)

14. Przybyłek, A.: A business-oriented approach to requirements elicitation. In: 9th International Conference on Evaluation of Novel Approaches to Software Engineering, Lisbon (2014)

15. Sommerville, I., Kotonya, G.: Requirements Engineering: Processes and Techniques. Wiley, New York (1998)

16. Scheinholtz, L.A., Wilmont, I.: Interview patterns for requirements elicitation. In: Berry, D. (ed.) REFSQ 2011. LNCS, vol. 6606, pp. 72–77. Springer, Heidelberg (2011). doi: 10.1007/978-3-642-19858-8_9

17. Yu-Cheng, T., Tempero, E.D., Thomborson, C.D.: An experiment on the impact of transparency on the effectiveness of requirements documents. Empirical Softw. Eng. **21**(3), 1035–1066 (2016)

18. Sakhnini, V., Mich, L., Berry, D.M.: The effectiveness of an optimized EPMcreate as a creativity enhancement technique for web site requirements elicitation. Requirements Eng. **17**(3), 171–186 (2012)

19. Gausepohl, K.A., Winchester III, W.W., Smith-Jackson, T.L., Kleiner, B.M., Arthur, J.D.: A conceptual model for the role of storytelling in design: leveraging narrative inquiry in user-centered design (UCD). Health Technol. **6**(2), 1–12 (2016)

20. Sikorski, M.: User-System Interaction Design in IT Projects. Gdansk University of Technology, Gdansk (2012)

21. Weichbroth, P., Sikorski, M.: User interface prototyping. techniques, methods and tools. In: Studia Ekonomiczne. Zeszyty Naukowe Uniwersytetu Ekonomicznego w Katowicach, vol. 234, pp. 184–198, Uniwersytet Ekonomiczny w Katowicach (2015)

22. Prabhala, S., Loi, D., Ganapathy, S.: Ethnography, ethnography or ethnography? what happens when the same word means different things to different people? In: Marcus, A. (ed.) HCII 2011 and DUXU 2011, Part I. LNCS, vol. 6769, pp. 102–110. Springer, Heidelberg (2011). doi:10.1007/978-3-642-21675-6_12

23. Rieu, D., Santorum, M., Movahedian, F.: A participative end-user method for multi-perspective business process elicitation and improvement. Softw. Syst. Model. 1–24, 6 August 2015. doi:10.1007/s10270-015-0489-6

24. Seganti, A., Kaplanski, P., Zarzycki, P.: Collaborative editing of ontologies using fluent editor and ontorion. In: Tamma, V., Dragoni, M., Gonçalves, R., Lawrynowicz, A. (eds.) OWLED 2015. LNCS, vol. 9557, pp. 45–55. Springer, Heidelberg (2016). doi: 10.1007/978-3-319-33245-1_5

25. Kaplanski, P., Weichbroth, P.: Cognitum ontorion: knowledge representation and reasoning system. In: Federated Conference on Computer Science and Information Systems (FedCSIS 2015), pp. 177–184 (2015)

Documenting Agile Architecture: Practices and Recommendations

Mirjana Maric[(✉)], Predrag Matkovic, Pere Tumbas,
and Veselin Pavlicevic

Faculty of Economics in Subotica, University of Novi Sad,
Segedinski put 9-11, 24000 Subotica, Serbia
{mirjana.maric,predrag.matkovic,
pere.tumbas,pavlicevic}@ef.uns.ac.rs

Abstract. Architecture is the foundation of every software product, regardless of the process used for its development. Traditional architecture development based on three architectural phases – architectural analysis, synthesis and evaluation is considered highly ceremonial, due to the great number of artifacts it produces. In agile development, architecture is generated gradually with each iteration, as a result of continuous code refactoring, not some predefined structure. In other words, agile processes do not include any of the traditional phases (analysis, synthesis, and evaluation) of the architecture development process, while self-documenting code is the predominant form agile architecture documentation.

Excessive documentation is considered wasteful in agile development processes. However, complete elimination of documentation results in "evaporation" of architectural information and knowledge, which may compromise the entire development process. Therefore, development of complex software systems requires an architecture documenting strategy positioned between the described extremes.

This paper presents results of theoretical and empirical research on documenting software architecture in agile development processes. Subsequent to the systematic literature review, an empirical research based on the classic Delphi method was carried out on a sample of 20 expert practitioners. In addition to an overview of current architecture documenting practices, the paper proposes structures of two artifacts for documenting agile architecture of complex systems, developed with regard to the results of the empirical research. These artifacts contain short descriptions of architectural decisions and rationale behind them.

Keywords: Agile software development · Software architecture · Architecture documentation

1 Introduction

Documentation is definitely among the most important explicit architectural practices. While overemphasized in traditional development, in agile development it was almost entirely replaced by the practice "source code is the ultimate documentation", in line with the agile principle of "working software over comprehensive documentation".

© Springer International Publishing AG 2016
S. Wrycza (Ed.): SIGSAND/PLAIS 2016, LNBIP 264, pp. 56–71, 2016.
DOI: 10.1007/978-3-319-46642-2_4

Documenting architecture and architectural decisions is among the greatest challenges of complex system development using agile processes. In other words, architecture has a significant role in development of complex business software solutions, and therefore, quality self-documenting code cannot be the only documenting practice; it is necessary to incorporate some of the traditional documenting practices, to an appropriate extent. In agile processes, excessive documentation is considered a waste, which may impair the agility of the development process and compromise early delivery of value to users. On the other hand, complete elimination of this architectural activity results in "evaporation" of architectural information and knowledge, poor comprehension of the architecture, and impaired communication within the development team, which can cause chaos and failure of the development process [9–11].

In line with the arguments made on this issue in the existing literature, we believe that the most important step in overcoming this prevailing problem is to identify explicit architectural activities that could be incorporated into agile development processes, as to ensure that adequate amount of architecture documentation is generated. Hence, the research goal was define the structure of essential architecture documentation in agile processes, based on a set of empirically identified key architectural activities.

The essential purpose of architecture documentation is to help the development team in understanding how the future software solution is organized, how it is supposed to work, and what are the reasons being key architectural decisions made throughout the development process. This provides the development team with a clearly defined architectural strategy, which ensures consistency and reduces the probability of taking wrong turns in the development.

Architectural artifacts must remain visible and transparent throughout the whole development process. This requires explicit statement and inclusion of architectural requirements into the Product Backlog agile artifact. Addition of architecturally significant requirements to the Product Backlog, as an explicit architectural activity, involves compiling a comprehensive list of product requirements – functional, non-functional, and requirements for future system changes, as well as ranking them by significance and required implementation time. Documents shuold not be long and complex, but rather concise and understandable, without burdening details, as to be effortlessly understood, revised, and used for communication purposes.

With regard to the topic and research problem previously described, the following research questions were formulated.

RQ1. What are the most commonly used architecture documenting practices in agile development processes?

The answer to this research question is as result of a state of the art exploration, by means of systematic literature review. Results of the literature review are presented in Sect. 3 – Theoretical Background: Systematic Literature Review.

RQ2. Which explicit architectural activities are significant to documenting architecture in agile development processes?

The answer to this question was obtained thru elaboration on results of qualitative and quantitative components of the conducted empirical research, and served as a basis for the proposed structure of key architecture artifacts for complex systems development using agile processes.

2 Research Methodology

Research design, depicted in Fig. 1, was developed by modifying the framework provided by [1]. Sequence of research activities, along with the techniques used, are presented in Fig. 1. Research problems and research questions described in the introduction represent results of the *research subject identification* phase.

Activity *state of the art exploration* within *theoretical research execution* phase provided the answer to RQ1. The activity was carried out by means of a systematic literature review, in accordance with recommendations by Kitchenham [2]: planning the review, conducting the review, reporting the review. The stages associated with *planning the review* include: (1) identification of the need for a review, (2) development of a review protocol. Stages associated with *conducting the review* are: (1) identification of research, and (2) selection of primary studies, (3) study quality assessment, (4) data extraction & monitoring, and (5) data synthesis. *Reporting the review* is a single stage phase, further described in the Theoretical Background section.

An overview of the total number of hits per each electronic database is given in Table 1. Analysis of search results resulted in 10 relevant papers concerning issues of architecture documentation in agile development processes.

Table 1. Number of hits per each database

Source	Number of hits with the keywords: agile software architecture/agile methods and architecture/agility and architecture/agile documenting	Number of papers selected for further analysis
IEEE Xplore	701	43
ScienceDirect	46	12
ACM Digital library	237	12
Total	984	67

Empirical research realized within the empirical research execution stage involved applying the classic variation of the Delphi method in three iterations [4, 5]. Nature of the research problem necessitated purposive selection of sample units ($n \geq 20$). Hence, the sample was composed of experts experienced in agile development and software architecture design. Results obtained in the empirical research execution phase provided the answers to RQ2.

The first iteration of the empirical research represented its qualitative component. Data collection was carried out by means of a semi-structured interview. The interview consisted of a set of predefined questions, previously evaluated by experts. Interviews were conducted face-to-face and recorded, as to ensure greater accuracy and consistency of collected data. Transcribed interview data was subject to qualitative analysis in NVivo suite (using thematic content analysis technique), in line with recommendations by Miles i Huberman [3]. Results of the first iteration were obtained within the state of the practice exploration activity.

The second and the third iteration of the empirical research constituted its quantitative component. A questionnaire with checklists and Likert-type assessment scales served as the research instrument in both iterations. Gathered data was subject to qualitative analysis in SPSS, using following methods: descriptive statistics, Efron's bootstrapping, Cohen's kappa coefficient, Chaffin-Talley index of individual stability, McNemar's test, and McNemar-Bowker's test.

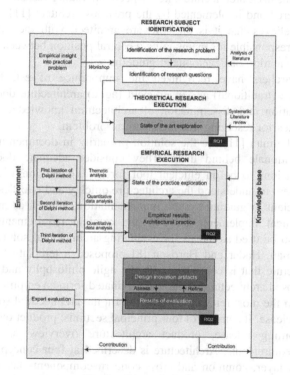

Fig. 1. Research design

3   Theoretical Background: Systematic Literature Review

Results of the literature review indicated that a significant portion of architectural problems originates from an essential conflict between the requirement of minimalism in agile methods and the need for well-documented architecture in complex systems [6]. The need for adequate management of architectural knowledge in agile processes is further amplified by increasingly present global software development [7].

According to the reviewed literature, most cases in the industry belong to one of the extremes: overly extensive documentation or absence of architecture documentation [8].

Poor documentation causes "evaporation" of architectural information and knowledge [9], inadequate architectural understanding, and impaired communication within the development team, which can cause chaos failure of the development process [10]. On the other hand, overly excessive documentation is considered a waste of time, resources, and distancing from the essence [10].

Excessive documentation impairs efficiency of agile processes, since stakeholders, such as programmers, users, and clients lack time and energy to study traditional architectural artifacts in order to understand the architecture. Programmers want clear and decisive design guidelines, while users and clients want to be sure that the architecture supports their business needs. Architects who resume someone else's work want clearly emphasized architecture's key aspects, including reasons for architectural decisions considered and implemented by the previous architect [11].

Faber [12] believes that it is the software architect, with the role of a service provider, who is responsible for maintaining a central position between inadequate and excessive documentation of development guidelines.

Several researchers have recognized the importance of establishing balance between excessive (traditional) and insufficient (agile) architecture documentation, to enhance preservation and dissemination of architectural knowledge, and suggested various approaches for resolving this architectural problem.

Tyree and Akerman [11] see the solution primarily in documenting architectural decisions and rationale behind them. They consider adequate documentation of architectural decisions to be an efficient tool for communication with stakeholders, which enables them to understand the architecture quickly and effortlessly. In addition to that, it is efficient in guiding system implementation, as well as monitoring compliance of technical implementation with the original requirements. Documented decisions can also be used as means for evaluating architectural solutions [11].

Hadar, Sherman, Hadar and Harrison [8] proposed a template for documenting software architecture that is consistent with the agile philosophy and lean documentation. The proposed architectural document originated form an empirical research. It is focused solely on the most relevant information on the architectural solution designed for a particular release. It consists of four principal sections: product overview, product goals for upcoming release, product architecture overview as a whole, and non-functional requirements. Architecture is described at four conceptual levels: system components layer, common and cross concern components layer, external integration components layer, and functional components layer. The approach relies on a tool for automatic documentation generation. The documenting tool is connected with the architecture modeling tool by a common database, so that changes in the model are updated in the documentation [8].

Pareto, Sandberg, Eriksson and Ehnebom [10] proposed a method for prioritizing architectural documentation for projects within large organizations that involve corrective actions over existing architecture. According to them, architecture documentation designates a set of models, viewpoints, and views covering different architectural aspects from various stakeholders' perspectives. The proposed method combines collaborative and analytical techniques involving different stakeholders, aimed at identifying architectural areas that require improvement.

Eloranta and Koskimies [13] see inadequate documentation in agile processes as the obstacle to distribution of architectural knowledge. They point out that, in projects of higher scale and complexity, communication between developers and stakeholders is not sufficient, and propose the concept of Architecture Knowledge Management to be integrated into the Scrum process. The approach involves development of an architectural knowledge base and utilization of a method for evaluating architectural decisions. The proposed method (DCAR) analyses each architectural decision the moment it is made, from bottom to top. Due to its incremental nature, which enables piecewise evaluation of architecture, DCAR method is suitable for agile processes. After analysis, architectural decisions and their justifications are recorded in the architectural knowledge base, which is a sort of an information system. Architectural database can automatically generate (on-line or printed) architectural reports or documents for specific purposes, using stored information [13].

In his research on documentation issues in agile processes, Babar [14] highlighted the use of a modified traditional documentation practice in the form of a Software Architectural Overall Plan, however, limited only to conceptual description of architecture. Remaining design decisions are described in Wikis. Responsibility for analysis and selection of an architectural solution is shifted to the client. Architectural evaluation carried out by the Architecture Review Board, where programmers evaluate proposed solutions, is rather informal [14].

However, Falessi et al. [15] have shown that agile programmers have positive attitudes towards software architecture, and that they perceive architectural artifacts as beneficial to communication between developers, later design decisions, documentation and product evaluation [15].

4 Results of the Empirical Research

Quantitative results suggest that agile teams recognize the importance of architectural documenting, since the proportion of respondents who rated this explicit architectural practice as significant was 0.85.

Analysis of qualitative data related to one of the identified categories – architectural documenting – lead to a conclusion that, in practice, agile teams develop a set of informal software architecture documents, covering some basic development guidelines, such as code standards, error handling, etc.

As opposed to traditional documenting, which involves making formal artifact with views describing different perspectives of the architecture (e.g. RUP 4 + 1 view), agile teams tend to use Wikis, without a predefined form.

Architectural decisions are most commonly made and clarified to team members in front of the whiteboard. Hence, the most common manner of documenting architectural decisions and rationale behind them are informal diagrams drawn on a whiteboard, which are later photographed and stored in a Wiki, or distributed to system stakeholders via email. Documents in the form of images are also used for communication and collaboration with stakeholders.

Most of the respondents emphasized use of tools that ease documenting activities. Most frequently used tools include Jira, GitHub, Word and Excel, which are also used for collaboration with stakeholders.

Development of formal models and use of specialized tools, such as Rational Rose or Enterprise Architect are typical to traditional development. Unlike in the traditional development, where implementation is preceded by comprehensive diagramming, agile teams dismissed this as a waste of time and resources, stating that development and maintenance of such diagrams is not possible in a dynamic, volatile environment.

Basic UML diagrams are made only for communication within the development team, when there is no better way to present a particular solution. However, UML is avoided in communication with external stakeholders, since software development practitioners feel that business people have difficulties understanding it.

Architectural documentation contains a description of the problem being solved, descriptions of architecturally significant functional and non-functional requirements, as well as the decision on the technology stack. Some of the non-functional requirements are extracted from descriptive elements, i.e., what clients expect from the system throughout its use; they are subsequently specified as non-functional requirements and their validity is checked with the client in the verification process.

The documentation also contains the initial architectural solution, up to an intermediate level of abstraction. Defining classes, their attributes and methods is not a common practice, unless the system is exceptionally complex, and team members lack skills and experience in design. Respondents also noted that architecture documentation is very helpful when new team members join the development team.

Architectural documents most commonly contain some initial deployment model and an initial database model. Information obtained thru analysis of the user story being implemented is also recorded during development. Most commonly, this involves examples of positive and negative tests for that user story, impact on security aspects of the architecture, and similar.

In several cases, the documenting process begins with the development of acceptance tests in a Word document, and ends with integration tests, which represent the final specification of the product.

Several respondents highlighted that it is useful, even desirable when architectural documentation is formally revised and verified by a team of experts, and that the implementation of the solution should begin only after the architecture had been approved. However, this is rarely the case in practice, as is remarked by one of the respondents: "… Once software architect completes that document, it is not good practice to upload it to an internal site and be done with it; it is desirable to send it to other software architects, head of QA and head of security for their verification. If they say that 'this is it', it is finally sent to chief architect for approval. Once they read the whole document and approve it, than it is set for implementation. Implementation of user stories should not begin prior to the approval; however, this is not the case, since the chief architect lacks time to read the document, so every document ended up pending approval."

Qualitative analysis of respondents' answers revealed that explicit architectural activity of documenting detailed design should not be incorporated into agile development processes. The proportion of respondents who classified this practice as significant was 0.1. In other words, 90 % of surveyed experts classified documenting detailed design as insignificant. Such high level of agreement among experts indicates that practitioners find documenting this activity unnecessary in agile processes. They stated several reasons, including that it requires additional time and effort, as well as that programmers already possess skills necessary to independently, or with technical guidance from a software architect, develop the detailed design.

Results indicate that there nearly all agile practitioners agree on the importance of the explicit architectural practice of Product Backlog prioritization. Numerous respondents noted that the architecture owner's participation in Product Backlog prioritization is just as important as the product owner's. Product owner, as a representative of the user, sets priorities from the point of value delivered to the user, while architecture owners need to prioritize technical features and the order of their implementation over iterations, based on previous technical dependency analyses and risk assessments. Architecture owner's technical suggestion depends on availability of team members, tools, and so on. The architecture owner should rank architectural requirements in accordance with the following factors.

- Value delivered to stakeholders with the implementation of a particular architectural requirement: critical/important/useful.
- Requirement's impact on architecture: none/extends/alters. Some functional requirements can be classified as critical (high priority from the point of value to stakeholders), and yet have no impact on architecture, and vice versa.
- Risks to be mitigated (performance, availability, component suitability)
- Other tactical goals and limitations.

The Product Backlog must be updated throughout the development process, after each iteration and after each release.

Creation and maintenance of a Product Backlog can be done efficiently using agile project management tools, which usually come bundled with templates. For that reason, this artifact was not particularized in this paper, that is, its structure is not proposed in the following section. We only point out that this agile artifact needs to encompass all kinds of requirements: functional, non-functional and requirements for future system changes.

All architectural activities, identified as a result of the empirical research, that were classified as significant to the development of software architecture in agile development processes are given in Table 2. This comprehensive list of significant practices served as a basis for developing structures of two key architectural artifacts – the Vision Document and the Software Architecture Document, which will be presented in the following chapter.

Table 2. Empirically identified explicit architectural practices significant to development of complex software solutions using agile processes

Empirically identified explicit architectural practices	Proportion of respondents who classified the practice as significant
Functionality interdependence analysis	1
Forming a suitable team and choosing a software architect with regard to the problem being solved	0.95
Understanding of the business problem	0.95
Code review	0.95
Development of coding rules and other guidelines for system design	0.95
Reviewing present architectural solutions	0.95
Active discussions with stakeholders aimed at analyzing and understanding the business	0.9
Identification of architecturally significant requirements	0.9
Risk analysis aimed at identifying and isolating complex areas	0.9
Examining technology suitable for implementation	0.9
Identification and definition of basic structures (modules) for the system core, as well as their relations	0.9
Testing system performance and other critical non-functional requirements	0.9
Identifying common components and common infrastructure of the functionality set of the future release	0.9
Use of Use Case technique	0.9
Managing dependencies with external systems that the system interacts with throughout a release	0.9
Static code analysis	0.9
Test Driven Development with focus on non-functional requirements	0.9
Explicit identification of non-functional requirements	0.9
Prioritizing Product Backlog, with regard to business value, architectural risk, and architectural impact	0.9
Project scoping	0.85
Analysis of dependencies between functional requirements and architectural elements during release planning	0.85
Configuration management	0.85
Tracking architectural task in the Backlog or a Kanban board throughout the whole development process	0.85

(*Continued*)

Table 2. (*Continued*)

Empirically identified explicit architectural practices	Proportion of respondents who classified the practice as significant
Generating top level documentation	0.85
Architecturally significant requirements are identified as a result of consultations with stakeholders, analysis of functional and non-functional requirements, and anticipation of future business goals	0.85
Creation of a Product Backlog, with all functional, non-functional, and requirements for future system change	0.85
Architectural planning beyond one release	0.85
Evaluation of present architecture before a new release	0.85
Continuous review of architecture	0.85
Prioritization of the Product Backlog	0.8
Defining the basic data architecture	0.8
Development of a deployment model	0.8
Validation of critical architectural requirements and design concepts using prototypes	0.8
Specification of integration tests	0.8
Estimation of technical user stories and time required for their development	0.8
Selection of a suitable implementation framework	0.8
Assessment of the existing infrastructure in the target organization	0.8
Identification of architectural elements that need to be more flexible	0.8
Architectural spikes	0.8
Prototyping	0.8
Evaluation of architecture by the architectural board	0.85
Scenario analysis of stakeholders' interaction with the system, with focus on non-functional requirements	0.85
Identification of key stakeholders	0.75
Formal architecture review	0.75
Regression testing	0.75
Load testing future architecture	0.75
Specification of test cases	0.75
Examining third-party libraries	0.75
Identification of future goals and business development	0.75

(*Continued*)

Table 2. (*Continued*)

Empirically identified explicit architectural practices	Proportion of respondents who classified the practice as significant
Release planning that includes a strategy for examining legacy systems, dependencies with partner or other third-party products, and backward compatibility of data	0.7
Specification of acceptance tests	0.7
Development of QA tests	0.7
Time boxed proof of concept	0.7
Market research and domain analysis aimed at better identification of architectural requirements	0.7
Analysis of dependencies between functional and non-functional requirements	0.7
Identification of necessary changes to the architecture, prior to the next release	0.7
Explicit identification of requirements related to geographic dispersion of the future system	0.7

4.1   Structure of Artifacts for Documenting Software Architecture of Complex Business Systems in Agile Processes

The Vision Document, states the business problem that the future system should solve, as well as the set of business requirements essential for identifying architecturally significant requirements. In addition to that, it includes an overview of the target organization's existing infrastructure, and other restrictions that also influence the choice of an architectural solution. The document consists of 11 main sections: Problem Being Solved, System Stakeholders, Target Organization's Business and Information Architecture, Organization's Goals and Development Paths, Features of the Future System, Target Organization's Software and Technical Infrastructure, List of Architectural Risks, Team, Architecturally Significant Requirements, Technological Issues, Choice of the Architectural Solution.

The Software Architecture Document contains information on the design of the architectural solution. The intention was that it should contain only the most relevant architectural decisions and be as comprehensible as possible. Such straightforward overview should simplify communication between the software architect and all stakeholders, particularly the development team, which can use it to effectively guide the implementation of the system. The Document is comprised of 8 main sections: Modules of the Main Part of the System and Their Dependencies, Defining Subsystems and Layers for the Identified Modules, Defining Key Elements, Interactions and Design Mechanisms, Architectural Decisions on the Data Model, Identification of Architectural Elements That Need to Be More Flexible, Architectural Decisions on Deployment Model, and Architectural Decisions on the Implementation Model. The listed sections contain rationale of architectural decisions and graphical representation based on informal models, drawn on paper or a whiteboard, and captured as photographs. With such a concise document, reviewers can be more effective, that is, quickly provide precise comments and recommendations. The section "Decisions on Changes in the Architecture and Rationale behind Them" allows for effortless tracking of changes made in the architecture in different releases.

The structure of the documents is given below.

A. Vision Document
Problem Being Solved

Problem statement	
Key benefits of a successful solution to the problem	

System Stakeholders

Stakeholder title	Key responsibilities	Present expectations/expectations from the future system

Target Organization's Business and Information Architecture
Organizations workflow presented with an informal flowchart.
Organization's Goals and Development Paths
A short description that will serve as a basis for compiling a list of requirements for future system changes.

Features of the Future System

Business need	System feature (general level)	Reason for implementation of the feature (value for customer)

Target Organization's Software and Technical Infrastructure

- Software application currently in use within by the organization (brief description);
- How the present software applications are used (brief description);
- Interdependence of present software applications;
- Existing relevant hardware infrastructure;

After the analysis and documenting of software and technical infrastructure, it is necessary to answer the following questions:

- Is the technology already implemented within the target organizations suitable for the new system?
- Would the implementation of new technology increase risk?
- Does development success depend on novel technologies that have not yet been fully tested?
- Is reuse of software components that exist in the target organization justified?
- Are existing software components developed or purchased?
- Do dependencies on other systems include ones outside the organization?
- Do interfaces for their communication already exist, or should they be developed with the new system?

List of Architectural Risks

Risk	Architecture's exposure to risk	Risk scope	Mitigation strategy

Systems scoping involves updating the list of risks in the table, by answering the following set of questions:

- Is the amount of transactions the system is expected to support reasonable?
- Is the amount of data the system should operate with reasonable?
- Are there any unusually technically challenging requirements that the development team has not encountered so far?
- Are the identified requirements relatively stable and clear?
- Are there any extremely inflexible non-functional requirements (e.g. that the system must never fail), are requirements complex?
- Are domain experts available?
- Does the team have enough people, with adequate skills and experience?

Risks identified during verification and implementation of the architecture
Team

Name	Experience, skills, expertise	Assigned position/responsibilities

Architecturally Significant Requirements:

- Key non-functional requirements
- Non-functional requirements
- Requirements for future changes
- Requirements associated with geographic distribution
- Real-world limitations

Technological Issues

- Decision on the technology stack
- Results of option trend analysis
- Selected implementation framework
- Selected programming language
- Decision on use of existing class libraries
- Decision on reuse of existing software components

Choice of the Architectural Solution

- Defined criteria for selecting an architectural solution
- Selection of a technique for evaluating potential architectural solutions
- Results of analysis and evaluation of potential architectural solutions (strengths/weaknesses)
- Justification of the choice of architectural solution

B. Software Architecture Document

Modules of the main part of the system and their dependencies

Graphic representation based on an informal model, drawn on paper or a whiteboard and captured as a photograph. General overview of the architecture illustrates the essence of the proposed architectural solution and main building blocks (elements, modules) that will constitute the architecture of the system.

Defining subsystems and layers for the identified modules

Graphic representation based on an informal model, drawn on paper or a whiteboard and captured as a photograph. Organization of subsystems for each identified module should represent the system design at the highest level of abstraction.

Defining key elements, interactions and design mechanisms

- Graphic representation based on an informal model, drawn on paper or a whiteboard and captured as a photograph. The representation contains initial design elements that will be modified and detailed during implementation, as well as interactions between key abstractions, which specifies a method of communication between design elements.
- This section should also include a list of identified design mechanisms.
- Decision on the method of their implementation is documented in the implementation phase.

Architectural decisions on the data model

- Decision on the type of database to be developed.
- Problems and solutions related to data compatibility.
- Initial setup of a data model, which will be extended and detailed during implementation

Identification of architectural elements that need to be more flexible

Decision on architectural elements that need to be more flexible, due to the nature of identified requirements for future system changes.

Architectural decisions on the deployment model

– Decision on deployment model solution
– Initial conception of the deployment model

Key decisions on the implementation model

Key decisions on the implementation model, without many details.

Decisions on changes in the architecture and rationale behind them

Includes decisions that resulted from verification and review of the system architecture throughout the implementation.

5   Conclusion

Results presented in this paper are a part of the research conducted for the development of the doctoral dissertation "Methodological Framework for Developing the Software Architecture of Business Software in Agile Processes". The results indicate that agile practitioners do not renounce architecture documenting activities, but rather consider them significant in the development of complex systems.

Based on the results of this research, the authors recommend that the structure of key artefacts for documenting architecture be formally defined. For this reason, this paper proposes the structure of two key artefacts, which can be tailored to specifics of the projects. The basic idea is that documents should not be too extensive, and should only cover the most important architectural decisions and rationale behind them. Architectural decisions would still be made in an agile manner, using informal models and means for representation both the team and the stakeholders are already accustomed to.

The proposed artifacts facilitate preservation of architectural knowledge, improve team collaboration, and assist in understanding the business problem and solutions to it, which altogether should reduce the possibility of taking wrong turns in the development. In addition, the proposed artifacts do not obstruct the agility of the development process, since they do not rely on traditional documenting practices, which involve use of formal languages for modeling software architecture.

References

1. Hevner, S., March, S.T., Park, J., Ram, S.: Design science in information systems research. MIS Q. **28**(1), 75–105 (2004)
2. Kitchenham, B.: Procedures for performing systematic reviews (2004)
3. Miles, M.B., Huberman, A.: Qualitative Data Analysis: An Expanded Sourcebook, 2nd edn. Sage, Thousand Oaks (1994)
4. Helmer, O., Rescher, N.: On the epistemology of the inexact sciences. Manage. Sci. **6**(1), 25–52 (1959)
5. Keeney, S., Hasson, F., McKenna, H.: The Delphi Technique in Nursing and Health Research, 1st edn. Wiley, London (2011)

6. Hadar, I., Sherman, S.: Agile vs. plan-driven perceptions of software architecture. In: 2012 5th International Workshop on Co-operative and Human Aspects of Software Engineering (CHASE), pp. 50–55 (2012)
7. Clerc, H., Lago, V., Vliet, P.: Architectural knowledge management practices in agile global software development. In: Sixth IEEE International Conference On Global Software Engineering Workshops, pp. 1–8 (2011)
8. Hadar, J.J., Sherman, I., Hadar, S., Harrison, E.: Less is more: architecture documentation for agile development. In: 2013 6th International Workshop Cooperative and Human Aspects of Software Engineering (CHASE), pp. 121–124 (2013)
9. Hadar, G.M., Silberman, E.: Agile architecture methodology: long term strategy interleaved with short term tactics. In: Companion to the 23rd ACM SIGPLAN Conference on Object-oriented Programming Systems Languages and Applications, OOPSLA Companion 2008, pp. 641–651 (2008)
10. Pareto, S., Sandberg, L., Eriksson, A., Ehnebom, P.: Prioritizing architectural concerns. In: 2011 Ninth Working IEEE/IFIP Conference on Software Architecture (WICSA), pp. 22–31 (2011)
11. Tyree, A., Akerman, J.: Architecture decisions: demystifying architecture. IEEE Softw. **22** (2), 19–27 (2005)
12. Faber, R.: Architects as service providers. IEEE Softw. **27**(1), 33–40 (2010)
13. Eloranta, K., Koskimies, V.P.: Aligning architecture knowledge management with scrum. In: Proceedings of the WICSA/ECSA 2012, pp. 112–115 (2012)
14. Babar, M.A.: An exploratory study of architectural practices and challenges in using agile software development approaches. In: 2009 European Conference on Software Architecture. Joint Working IEEE/IFIP Conference, pp. 81–90 (2009)
15. Falessi, D., Cantone, G., Sarcia', S.A., Calavaro, G., Subiaco, P., D'Amore, C.: Peaceful coexistence: agile developer perspectives on software architecture. IEEE Softw. **27**, 23 (2010)

Architectural Element Points: Estimating Software Development Effort by Analysis of Logical Architectures

Luís M. Alves[1(✉)], Pedro Ribeiro[2], and Ricardo J. Machado[2]

[1] Polytechnic Institute of Bragança, School of Technology and Management Department of Informatics and Communications, Bragança, Portugal
lalves@ipb.pt
[2] Centro ALGORITMI, Engineering School of University of Minho, Guimarães, Portugal
{pmgar,rmac}@dsi.uminho.pt

Abstract. Empirical studies are important in software engineering to evaluate new tools, techniques, methods and technologies. In object-oriented analysis, use case models describe the functional requirements of a software system, so they can be the basis for software measurement and sizing. The purpose of this study is to develop a new metric called *Architectural Element Points* (AEPoint) that enables to calculate the effort required to develop a software solution, using the *4-Step Rule Set* (4SRS) method. This paper describes a case study with 60 undergraduate students grouped in four teams that developed a software system (Web application) for a real customer. In this study, we used the AEPoint metric to estimate the resources needed to develop a software system. The results of the AEPoint and *Use Case Points* (UCP) metrics and the real software development effort are compared, conclusions drawn and recommendations are proposed.

Keywords: Empirical studies · Software engineering management · Software quality · Software requirements · Software metrics

1 Introduction

In last decades, the software engineering community researchers have developed several empirical studies to evaluate tools, techniques, methods and technologies. The main goal is to provide to the practitioners the research results found in laboratories in order to improve their software products and processes. Thus, the practitioners can have evidence about innovative products and processes in order to assess their value and the risks that must be managed during their institutionalization.

In 1992, Basili *et al.* introduced the concept of *experience factory* [1]. Basically, the *experience factory* is an organizational schema that shows how to institutionalize the collective learning of an organization [2]. This schema presents two entities, the *project organization* that plan and execute the project and the *experience factory* that collect

This work has been supported by COMPETE: POCI-01-0145-FEDER-007043 and FCT – Fundação para a Ciência e Tecnologia within the Project Scope: UID/CEC/00319/2013.

© Springer International Publishing AG 2016
S. Wrycza (Ed.): SIGSAND/PLAIS 2016, LNBIP 264, pp. 72–84, 2016.
DOI: 10.1007/978-3-319-46642-2_5

and package experiences and reuse the empirical results in order to diffuse, generalize, analyze the knowledge contained.

That Basili *et al.* schema was designed based on many years of the *Software Engineering Laboratory* (SEL) work. Empirical studies developed within the SEL involved students from different USA (United States of America) universities and industry partners.

In our case, to perform empirical studies we created an environment similar to an industrial set involved graduated and undergraduate students. All this students attend computer science and information systems program degrees of University of Minho (Portugal). We collected knowledge from the literature to build an environment where each student knows very well her/his role in the project. In a previous work we presented in detail our research environment [3].

As a factor of success it is important to estimate the total amount of resources early in developing process in order to ensure compliance, in terms of cost, schedule and quality of an IT (*Information and Technology*) project. In the development of a software system, the most complex activity is probably the transformation of a requirements specification into an architectural design. The process of designing software architectures is less formalized and often is greatly an intuitive ad-hoc activity, poorly based on engineering principles [4]. Since the architecture of a software system constrains the solution space, the design decisions made during the architectural design should be done very carefully, whereas they typically have a large impact on the quality of the final system. The *4-Step Rule Set* (4SRS) method employs successive model transformations in order to obtain a logical architecture that satisfies the previously elicited user requirements. It is based on the mapping of UML (*Unified Modeling Language*) use case diagrams into object diagrams. The iterative nature of the method and the usage of diagrammatic models help to ensure that the obtained logical architecture reflects the user requirements [4].

The *Use Case Points* (UCP) can predict the total amount of resources at the beginning of a software development process. It is easier to plan and predict the remaining project if there is a metric that allows to know the expected effort during the development phase of the project. With these metrics we can make a better analysis of the costs and the time it will take to complete a project [5].

The existence of a metric on the 4SRS process gives an estimate of the software development effort more precise than the UCP. With 4SRS implementation there is already an architecture aligned with the solution and not just an alignment with the problem. For this purpose we developed a metric to apply on 4SRS that allows to estimate the effort required in the software process development. This metric will be called *Architectural Element Points* (AEPoint).

After the development of the metric, the next step was to test it. In this sense, we considered to perform an empirical study in educational context. We intend to answer the following research question: the AEPoint metric gives a rough estimate of the resources that we should allocate to projects with this complexity level? Mainly, we hope that this metric gives an approximate number of hours to perform all steps of the software development.

In our empirical study we used graduate and undergraduate students of our university. The students were distributed in random groups in four teams. Each team developed a software system of medium/high complexity. We applied the original UCP method for estimate the effort needed to develop each one of that software systems.

In this paper, a description of 4SRS is presented in Sect. 2. Section 3 describes related work with *Use Case Points* methods. In Sect. 4, we present in detail the AEPoint metric that we use in the next section. In Sect. 5 we briefly describe the empirical study we have developed to initially assess the effectiveness of using AEPoint metric in educational context. Finally, in Sect. 6 we present the conclusions and future work.

2   Purpose of the 4-Step Rule Set Method

The 4SRS purpose is to make the bridge between user requirements and the design elements of a complex system. The most complex activity during development of software systems is probably the transformation of a requirement specification into an architectural design [4]. These diagrams represent the logical architecture of the system, integrating the system-level entities, their responsibilities and the relationships between them. The logical architecture captures the functional and nonfunctional requirements of the system.

The 4SRS method for identifying the system components for such architecture (the conceptual model) requires the software engineer to start the development by defining the functional model (use case diagram) that reflects the system functionalities offered to its users from their perspectives. The method is based on a sequence of steps that are inscribed in a tabular representation that is used to derive the software architecture for a focused part of the global system. The method's iterative nature and the use of graphical models ensure that architectures reflect user requirements [4].

The 4SRS method is based on use cases and transformation rules that create other elements (objects). The elements are created and their names are prefixed with a code in brackets, which is used to ensure the uniqueness and easy visual identification. It uses an approach whereby a use case is realized by a collaboration of three types of components: *control*, *data* and *interface*. After this initial transformation, a series of steps with rules is proposed to transform the initial component model in a consistent component model, which is compatible with the requirements. Basically, at each step a set of refactoring rules are applied by modifying the initial model components across groups, divisions or removal of components. Some of these rules can be automated, but others depend on human intervention [4].

As advantages for 4SRS approach, we can point out that the identified classes properly represent the system requirements as they are identified through a recursive process embedded in the 4SRS method that ensures the elimination of redundancy and the identification of missing requirements. Additionally, the recursive nature of the 4SRS method permits that several components of a system can be treated one at a time (each one with its own 4SRS execution) [4].

This approach reduces the complexity of the overall system design, avoiding the construction of a global and massively complex class diagram for the whole system. Instead, we obtain a single class diagram for each system component, when the 4SRS executions adopt the recursive approach. When compared to the existing approaches, the current version of the 4SRS method adopts a complementary approach by using both object-driven artefacts and use cases to support the complex process of identifying class diagrams from user requirements. A complete description of the 4SRS method can be found in [4].

3 Effort Estimation Methods

We can find in the literature great efforts and contributions to measure the size of a software system and estimate the effort needed to develop it. Measuring the size of a software system is different to estimate the effort needed to develop it, although the two concepts are connected. The first is an activity that consists to assign a measurement unit to represents the size of a software system while the second estimates the effort required to developing it. The relationship between the size of a software system and effort required to develop it is given by the productivity of the software development team.

Metrics are measurement methodologies whose main objective is to estimate the size of software system and assist, as an indicator, the project management of software system development. The estimated size is one of the most commonly used metrics for software size, since has direct impact on development effort and project management. It is an indicator of the amount of work to be performed and this kind of knowledge can be used to help us to estimate the cost and the lead time for the project [6]. According to Pressman, measurement enables managers to plan, monitor, improve and enhance the software process development [7].

The size of the software system means the amount of work to be performed in a project development. Each project can be estimated according to the physical size (which is measured through the requirements specification, analysis, construction and testing), based on the functions that the user gets, in the complexity of the problem that the software system will solve and in the reusability of the project, which measures how much the product will be copied or modified from another existing product [8, 9].

3.1 Use Case Points

The UCP metric was defined to estimate *Object Oriented* (OO) projects based on the same philosophy of *Function Points* and in the process "*Objectory*", where the use case concept was developed. Later, Ivar Jacobson developed "*Object-Oriented Software Engineering (OOSE)*", methodology based in use cases, a technique widely used in industry to describe and collect the functional requirements of the software. Considering that the use cases model was developed to collect the requirements based on use and users vision, it makes sense to base the estimation of size and resources of software projects in use cases [10].

The UCP metric was developed to predict the resources needed for a specific project in early developing process e.g. after the requirements analysis. With such an early estimation, one could more easily plan and predict for the rest of the project [6]. The first description of the method was published by Gustav Karner [6] with the aim of creating a model that would allow estimating the resources required to develop a software system under *Objectory AB* (later acquired by Rational Software).

The UCP method consists in calculating a metric called *Use Case Points* that give us an estimation of the size and complexity of a software project. If we know the development team productivity (to be obtained based on previous projects), we can derive an estimate of the effort required to develop the software project. The UCPs are related to functional, technical and environmental complexity of the software project.

When applying the method, we must first calculate the complexity of actors and use cases in the system to quantify the variables *Unadjusted Actor Weight* (UAW) and *Unadjusted Use Case Weight* (UUCW), respectively. When combined with their weight, we obtain an inadequate measure of the size and complexity of the system called *Unadjusted Use Case Points* (UUCP). The next step is to adjust this measure with a number of technical factors and environmental factors given by *Technical Complexity factor* (TCF) and *Environmental Factor* (EF) variables, respectively. These factors combined with the UUCP variable will produce the effective number of UCPs that reflect the size and complexity of the software project. In the following subsections we detail the steps needed to calculate the UCPs. For space reasons we do not present in detail the UCP method, however, it can be found in [6, 11, 12].

4   The Architectural Element Point (AEPoint)

In software projects there is a significant conceptual difference between the problem domain and solution domain. When there are such differences between the specified requirements and design decisions, the architecture can become unsynchronized with the specific requirements of the system. Thus, the 4SRS method support the transition of the system requirements to software architectures and elements of design. In this sense, it is useful that there is a method that allows to predict the total amount of resources at the beginning of the development process. Although there is already the UCP method, in this paper we propose a new metric, called *Architectural Element Points* (AEPoint). This metric will provide some advantages: it provides an estimate of the total amount of resources closer to reality because the metric runs on 4SRS method and there was already an alignment between the problem domain and solution; it provides data that allow allocate and reallocate resources, since we already take into account the software architecture and its elements of design.

The AEPoint metric will run on 4SRS method and is based on the UCP method. This metric is based on three key factors, namely: *Unadjusted Architectural Element Point* (UAEP), *Technical Complexity Factor* (TCF) and *Environmental Factor* (EF). The AEPoint are then calculated by the product of these three factors.

$$AEPoint = UAEP \times TCF \times EF \qquad (1)$$

After calculating the AEPoint, we obtain a result about the architectural elements, lacking a factor to convert estimation points to effort in person hours. After application of the UCP method in three real projects, Karner found that it takes 20 man hours to complete one UCP [6]. This factor has been accepted as an historically collected figure representing productivity [10, 13]. In a previous work, also in an educational context, we find that in average it takes 9 man hours to complete one UCP [11]. This discrepancy between Karner value and our value to the productivity can be explained by several factors. In our view, the main factors are the environment context, using students instead of professionals and the partial implementation of the uses cases. Since we are evaluating metrics applied early in software development process and that there is no more literature about this subject we consider that an AEPoint also corresponds to 9 man hours of work.

4.1 Unadjusted Architectural Element Point (UAEP)

This factor must be calculated based on two components, namely, the *Architectural Element Impact* (AEI) and the *Architectural Element Complexity* (AEC). As Eq. (2) shows the calculation of UAEP is obtained by adding the two components that comprise it.

$$UAEP = AEI + AEC \qquad (2)$$

The AEI indicates the impact that a given element has to architecture. The impact is related to the links of this elements. We created a scale to quantify the impact. This scale is then applied to the effect that Software Architects, Analysts and Developers attribute to a particular architectural element. Note that the impacts attributed by the work team's members consider a scale from 0 to 1 at intervals of 0.1. Table 1 shows the levels of impact considered, as well as a correlation with impact attributed by the work team members and their respective weights. The assignment of the impact by the team members will be obtained by averaging the impact that members assign to a particular architectural element.

Table 1. Architectural Element Impact (AEI)

Impact	Impact assigned by team members	Weight
Low	0 to 0.3	1
Average	0.4 to 0.7	2
High	0.8 to 1	3

The AEI variable is calculated by the sum of the products of the weight impacts by the number of architectural elements in each category impact.

Another component that allows us to infer the size and effort of a software architecture is the complexity of an architectural element. The complexity is related to the internal structure of this elements. As greater the complexity of an architectural element, greater the effort required to develop it and consequently its weight in the architecture.

We created a scale to quantify the impact. This scale is then applied to the effect that Software Architects, Analysts and Developers attribute to a particular architectural element. Note that the impacts attributed by the work team's members consider a scale from 0 to 1 at intervals of 0.1. Table 2 shows the levels of impact considered, as well as a correlation with impact attributed by the work team members and their respective weights. The assignment of the impact by the team members will be obtained by averaging the impact that members assign to a particular architectural element.

Table 2. Architectural Element Complexity (AEC)

Impact	Impact assigned by team members	Weight
Very low	0 to 0.2	1
Low	0.3 to 0.4	2
Average	0.5 to 0.6	3
High	0.7 to 0.8	4
Very high	0.9 to 1	5

The AEC variable is calculated by the sum of the products of the weight impacts by the number of architectural elements in each category impact.

4.2 Technical Complexity Factor (TCF)

The size of the software system depends also, on the quality characteristics of the system. Therefore, there are a number of technical or non-functional factors that must be considered to measure the size of the system based on what was agreed between the customer and the supplier. A list describing all technical factors proposed by Karner is shown in Table 3 [6].

Table 3. *Technical Factors* contributing to complexity

Factor	Description	Weight
T1	Distributed systems	2
T2	Performance	2
T3	Efficiency	1
T4	Complex internal processing	1
T5	Code reusability	1
T6	Installation ease	0.5
T7	Usability	0.5
T8	Portability	2
T9	Changeability	1
T10	Concurrency	1
T11	Security	1
T12	Accessibility of others	1
T13	Training	1

The impact of each factor within the project is rated on a scale 0, 1, 2, 3, 4 and 5, where 0 means that it is irrelevant and 5 means it is essential. If the factor is neither important nor irrelevant it must be rated with the value of 3 [5, 12, 14, 15]. The rate of the factor must be multiplied by the associated weight as shown in Table 3. The sum of all the products calculates the *TFactor* value, which is used to calculate the *Technical Complexity Factor* (TCF):

$$TCF = 0.6 + (0.01 \times TFactor) \tag{3}$$

Karner based the constants 0.6 and 0.01 on the adjustment factors of *Function Points* created by Albrecht [16].

4.3 *Environmental Factor* (EF)

The characterization of the software development teams is also important to obtain a measure of the size and complexity of the software project; thus there is a set of aspects related to the development environment that must be weighed. A list describing all environmental factors proposed by Karner is shown in Table 4 [6]. We believe that as on the UCP method the environment factors also influence the software architecture development, then we decide to consider these factors in our AEPoint metric.

Table 4. *Environmental Factors* contributing to efficiency

Factor	Description	Weight
E1	Experience with a software development process	1.5
E2	Development experience with similar projects	0.5
E3	Experience with OOP	1
E4	Maturity in OO analysis	0.5
E5	Motivation	1
E6	Stability of requirements	2
E7	Part time workers	-1
E8	Experience with technologies adopted	-1

The impact of each factor within the project is rated on a scale 0, 1, 2, 3, 4 and 5, where 0 means that it is irrelevant and 5 means it is essential. If the factor is neither important nor irrelevant it must be rated with the value of 3. The rate of the factor must be multiplied by the associated weight as shown in Table 4. The sum of all the products calculates the *EFactor* value, which is used to calculate the *Environmental Factor* (EF):

$$EF = 1.4 + (-0.03 \times EFactor) \tag{4}$$

The constants 1.4 and −0.03 were obtained by Karner from interviews performed to the resources projects analyzed. The evaluation of UAEP and technological factors occurred by contact with development teams. The environmental assessment factors occurred by online questionnaires realized in milestones defined by teacher's staff.

5   Case Study

Based on the previously described approach for calculating the AEPoint, a case study was developed to determine the productivity of some student software development teams.

The teams were constituted by second year students of the course 8604N5 Software System Development (SSD) from the Integrated Master's in Engineering and Management of Information System in University of Minho (the first University to offer in Portugal, DEng, MSc and PhD degrees in Computing). The teams had 60 people (1 team with 16, 2 teams with 15 and 1 team with 14). Each team receives a sequential identification number (Team 1, Team 2, Team 3 and Team 4) and the description of the customer problem.

The teams developed a software project of medium complexity, using the *Unified Modeling Language* (UML) notation encompassed in an iterative and incremental software development process, in this case, the *Rational Unified Process* (RUP). The teams followed the guidelines established by the RUP reduced model, executing the phases of inception, elaboration and construction according to the best practices suggested by CMMI-DEV v1.3 ML2. The project lasted 4 months. This software project was to develop a Web solution using object-oriented technologies (Java or C#) and relational databases (SQL Server or MySQL), to support the information system of one local professional handball team that provided all the information about the organization and interacted directly with the teams. The logical architecture of the software project was built through the 4SRS method presented in section two.

The main goal of case study was to apply the AEPoint metric in a real software development project although in an educational context. The impact and complexity analysis of 4SRS elements in order to calculate the AEI and AEC components was made based on documentation provided by the teams. Table 5 shows the results of AEPoint and UCP metrics obtained from the software development projects.

Table 5. Results of the software development teams

Description	Team1	Team2	Team3	Team4
Number of elements	15	16	15	14
Total effort [hours]	3321	3542	3321	3099
Architectural Element Impact (AEI)	144	58	209	51
Architectural Element Complexity (AEC)	132	79	325	57
Unadjusted Architectural Element Point (UAEP)	276	137	534	108
TFactor	47.5	52.5	48.0	45.0
Technical Complexity Factor (TCF)	1.075	1.125	1.08	1.05
EFactor	10	10	10	10
Environmental Factor (EF)	1.1	1.1	1.1	1.1
***Architectural Element Point* (AEPoint)**	326	170	634	125
Use Case Points (UCP)	477	225	513	281

In order to validate the results obtained with the AEPoint metric we decided also to calculate the UCP of the four project teams. Table 6 shows the comparison of the AEPoint and UCP metrics results. In this table, we also present the average of the real effort recorded by the teams.

Table 6. Comparison of the AEPoint and UCP metrics results

AEPoint		Effort (Hours)	UCP	Effort (Hours)	Real effort
Team1	326	2934	477	4293	3321
Team2	170	1530	225	2027	3542
Team3	634	5706	513	4619	3321
Team4	125	1125	281	2526	3099

As referred previously, based on our previous work, we consider that it takes 9 man hours to complete one UCP [11]. We used that reference value to estimate the software development effort by the teams, thus, we assume that the time to apply one UCP is the same as the time to apply one AEPoint.

From the analysis of Table 6 we can draw some interesting conclusions. It is in Team2 that is a greater closeness between the values obtained from the two metrics, approximately 500 h of difference. In the case of Team1 and Team4 the difference is greater, approximately 1400 h of difference. Regarding Team3 we can see that there is a difference of about 1000 h, but the effort is almost 6000 h so the difference is not as significant. We can also verify from Table 6 analysis that the efforts obtained by the metrics presents some difference from the real effort declared by the teams. AEPoint metric gives a close value to the real effort for the Team1 and UCP metric gives a close value to the real effort for the Team4 and also for the Team1. For both metrics and for the other teams the difference is above of 1000 h. In Fig. 1 we can check this analysis throughput with a graph.

AEPoint metric gives a considerable different value to the real effort for the Team3. In our opinion, this happen because it is the team that has a more robust software architecture, but, in its final application, its implement only part of that architecture.

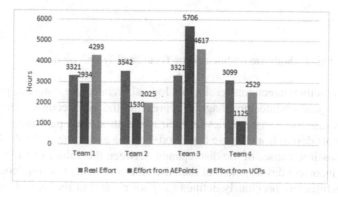

Fig. 1. Comparison of the real effort and effort got from AEPoint and UCP metrics

Analyzing the traceability matrix we can check that the final solution only implements part of the architecture designed. In this matrix we can analyze what were modeled, what were designed and what were implemented in the final solution.

Table 7 shows the number of architectural elements of the teams software applications and their final grade in the SSD course. This table shows that team3 has the highest number of architectural elements, but they has not the highest grade. This reinforce the previous analysis, in the sense that this team presented a very optimistic architecture, but in their final application we can find implemented just some parts of the global architecture. In other and, Team1 has the most realistic architecture, in terms of what they intended to implement and what they implemented. This team got the best grade because, among other factors, they built the most complete application. Team2 and Team4 have the lowest number of architectural elements. As the Team3, Team4 just implemented some part of the architecture, thus, your grade was the lowest.

Table 7. Number of architectural elements versus student assessment

Architectural elements		Grade (0–20)
Team1	59	17
Team2	21	15
Team3	84	14
Team4	22	13

Figure 2 shows the software architecture of the Team2 and Team3 applications. This figure is intentionally not zoomed (and thus not readable), just to show the complexity of each one of the architectures.

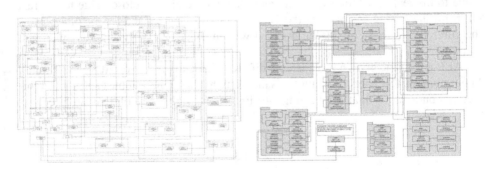

Fig. 2. Software Architecture of Team2 and Team3 applications

The 4SRS method execution results in a logical architecture diagram, presented in Fig. 2. This logical architecture diagram represents the architectural elements, from which the constructors can be retrieved, their associations and packaging. The architectural elements derive from the use case model by the execution of the 4SRS method.

We find possible causes of the discrepancy between the values of the metrics (see Table 6): (1) incorrect development of the AEPoint metric; (2) non-implementation of the overall architecture previously defined (3) poor control of the real effort record by the project manager and team members; (4) poor quality of inputs, including use cases and 4SRS models. The quality of artifacts, mainly the use case models, are limited by the reduced experience of the teams in requirements specification. We could observe in all teams, use cases with poor quality, leading to a subjective interpretation to identify transactions in the main and alternative courses. Additionally, the majority of the use cases were classified as *simple* according the UCP method because it had few transactions. It was not easy to analyze the use cases diagrams to identify transactions. Sometimes we had to analyze activity and sequence diagrams as a way to validate the existence of transactions.

Throughout the semester, we observed a difference between use cases and architectural elements between projects of different teams, although the purpose of the project was the same. Furthermore, we observed some discomfort in the technological factors evaluation by team members due to lack of knowledge. These facts might have led to a poor quality of inputs.

Since the quality of inputs was one of the factors that most influenced the results, the use of methods that achieve better quality in defining architectures would be an asset. In our research, we propose the *Active Review for Intermediate Designs* (ARID), *Architecture Tradeoff Analysis Method* (ATAM) and *Software Architecture Analysis Method* (SAAM). As a future work, we can use one or a combination of that methods to improve the inputs collected from uses case and 4SRS models.

6   Conclusions

The software development effort in man hours obtained from UCP and AEPoint metrics are relatively close. For some teams, the estimate effort obtained by the metrics is so close to the real effort declared by the teams, but, for other teams there is a considerable difference. It should be needed further research to find the reason of this discrepancy. With some tune in the metric parameters we believe that we can use AEPoint metric to estimate the resources that we should allocate to projects with the medium/high complexity. Furthermore, we also believe, that empirical studies involving students on these subjects are important for the scientific community and the industry.

As future work, we suggest the following actions: (1) partial implementation of ARID, SAAM and ATAM methods early in development process to improve the quality of inputs and solution architecture; (2) application of the AEPoint metric on projects that have teams with more experienced and mature elements; (3) Reviewing the AEPoint metric trying to tune the weights and variables needed to calculate it; test AEPoints metric in different approaches, away from the UCP method. We suggest for future editions of the SSD courses that all teams use a development tool, for example *Teamwork Project Manager* [17] in order to accurately determine the effective involved effort. We intent to assess the influence of this tool in the teams performance.

As a strong validation of the AEPoint metric, we will test it in real design of information systems and we will carry out action research in order to allow practitioners to develop metric as well.

Acknowledgments. The authors would like to thank the referees for their valuable comments.

References

1. Basili, V., Caldiera, G., McGarry, F., Pajerski, R., Page, G., Waligora, S.: The software engineering laboratory-an operational software experience factory. In: 14th ICSE, pp. 370–381. ACM (1992)
2. Visaggio, G.: Empirical experimentation in software engineering. In: Lucia, A.D., Ferrucci, F., Tortora, G., Tucci, M. (eds.) Emerging Methods, Technologies and Process Management in Software Engineering, p. 227. Wiley, Hoboken (2008)
3. Alves, L.M., Ribeiro, P., Machado, R.J.: Project-Based Learning: An Environment to Prepare IT Students for an Industry Career. Overcoming Challenges in Software Engineering Education: Delivering Non-Technical Knowledge and Skills, pp. 230–249. IGI Global (2014)
4. Machado, R.J., Fernandes, J.M., Monteiro, P., Rodrigues, H.: Transformation of UML models for service-oriented software architectures. In: 12th IEEE International Conference and Workshops on the Engineering of Computer-Based Systems (ECBS 2005), pp. 173–182 (2005)
5. Karner, G.: Resource Estimation for Objectory Projects. Objectory Systems SF AB (1993)
6. Karner, G.: Use Case Points: Resource Estimation for Objectory Projects. In: Objective Systems SF AB. (1993)
7. Pressman, R.S.: Software Engineering: A Practitioner's Approach. McGraw-Hill, New York (2005)
8. Fenton, N.E., Neil, M.: Software metrics: roadmap. In: CFSE 2000, pp. 357–370. ACM, 336588 (2000)
9. Fenton, N.E., Pfleeger, S.L.: Software Metrics: A Rigorous and Practical Approach. PWS Publishing Company, Boston (1997)
10. University of Houston-Victoria. http://bfpug.com.br/Artigos/UCP/Damodaran-Estimation_Using_Use_Case_Points.pdf
11. Alves, L.M., Sousa, A., Ribeiro, P., Machado, R.J.: An empirical study on the estimation of software development effort with use case points. In: 2013 Frontiers in Education Conference, pp. 101–107. IEEE (2013)
12. Ochodek, M., Nawrocki, J., Kwarciak, K.: Simplifying effort estimation based on use case points. Inf. Softw. Technol. **53**, 200–213 (2011)
13. Anda, B., Dreiem, H., Jørgensen, M.: Estimating software development effort based on use cases-experiences from industry. In: Gogolla, M., Kobryn, C. (eds.) UML 2001. LNCS, vol. 2185, pp. 487–502. Springer, Heidelberg (2001)
14. Anda, B., Benestad, H.C., Hove, S.E.: A multiple-case study of software effort estimation based on use case points. In: International Symposium on Empirical Software Engineering, pp. 407–416 (2005)
15. Yavari, Y., Afsharchi, M., Karami, M.: Software complexity level determination using software effort estimation use case points metrics. In: 5th Malaysian Conference Software Engineering (MySEC 2011), pp. 257–262 (2011)
16. Albrecht, A.J.: Measuring application development productivity. In: IBM Application Development Symposium, pp. 83–92. IBM Press (1979)
17. http://www.teamworkpm.net/

Business Models of Internet of Things

Dariusz Kralewski[✉]

Faculty of Management, Department of Business Informatics,
University of Gdańsk, Gdańsk, Poland
dariusz.kralewski@ug.edu.pl

Abstract. *Background.* This article focuses on one of the most important topic for future life and economy – Internet of Things.

Research aims. Indicate business models that apply to the Internet Things.

Method. Theoretical analysis of the phenomenon of Internet of Things. Analysis of fifty-five business models. Indication of thirty-three models of the Internet of Things.

Key findings. Analyzing a broad variety of companies (up to 400 cases) Gassmann, Frankenberger and Csik identify fifty-five business model patterns that either individually or together build the fundament of the majority of currently existing business models. These models can be the basis of creating business models Internet of Things. The author of this article from fifty-five models selected thirty-three models and pointed their application in the field of Internet of Things. These thirty-three models can be successfully used in the Internet of Things on four specified layers and in eleven areas. These models may also be the starting point for creating new business models or inspiration for the creation of a completely new, innovative models. Specification of these new models will be the target for further studies.

Keywords: Business models · Internet of Things

1 Introduction

There are many papers and articles on business model innovation and the Internet of Things (IoT). They share a common consensus that the IoT will enable companies to create new business models. Suitable business models will play an important role when it comes to leveraging the opportunities of the Internet of Things. But what is the basis for these new business models? How will the IoT provide us with these many business opportunities?

This article analyzes the innovative aspects Internet of Things. Article begins with defining the Internet of Things. Analysis of applications associated with detailing the layers of the Internet of Things is the basis to indicate the places where they can be used or created models of the Internet of Things. Then focused on the theme of business models and business model canvas described by the nine elements.

Analyzing a broad variety of companies (up to 400 cases) Gassmann, Frankenberger and Csik identified fifty five business model patterns that either individually or together build the fundament of the majority of currently existing business models [1]. These

© Springer International Publishing AG 2016
S. Wrycza (Ed.): SIGSAND/PLAIS 2016, LNBIP 264, pp. 85–103, 2016.
DOI: 10.1007/978-3-319-46642-2_6

models were the base of this study. Instead of reinventing the wheel, when identifying a new business model it is often sufficient to (re-) combine (i.e., transfer, combine, or repeat) these existing patterns [2]. Of course, these patterns are helpful for creating Internet of Things business models as they cover diverse industries and sectors and layers of Internet of Things. Internet of Things has of course the potential to create completely new business model patterns. This article is the beginning of research on the exploration of such models.

2   Review of Background

2.1   Internet of Things

Internet of Things is the networking of almost all types of devices. Behind this concept lies the vision of a future world in which digital and physical device or everyday objects are connected through appropriate infrastructure, in order to provide a whole range of new applications and services [3]. Internet of things is a combination of two worlds known to us (digital and physical), and in the coming years, we will have the opportunity to observe how fundamentally changing the way we use and interact both with the outside world of digital devices and the physical world [4].

The Internet of Things is an extension of networking and computing capabilities on objects, devices and sensors that are not normally considered to be computers. These intelligent objects require minimum human intervention to create, exchange and retrieval of data. The concept of Internet of Things is based on three concepts: anytime, anyplace, anything [5] (Fig. 1).

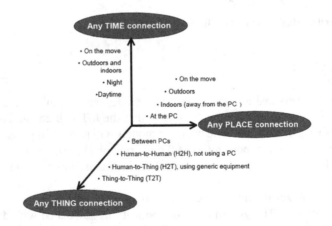

Fig. 1. Communication on the Internet of Things, the source: ITU-T

The definition of Internet of things is based on three pillars relating to the characteristics of smart objects: allow for the identification of himself (everything is able to introduce), provide communication (everything can communicate) and interact (everything can interact).

Implementing the concept of Internet of Things we can observe every day. Systems for remote meter reading, monitoring resource consumption or environmental conditions, health monitoring, are just some of them [6]. What we see today is just the beginning, and the range of potential applications seems to be endless [7]. At the moment, the Internet is used by over two billion people around the world: web browsing, sending and receiving e-mail, browsing the various types of multimedia content, playing, using social networks and many other. In addition, the number of people having access to a global network will increase. Soon we will see a big technological leap, when the Internet will be not only a global platform for users, but also for machines, sensors, smart objects that will be able to communicate with each other, exchange information, count and initiate a number of different kinds of activities. It is said that the fastest growing group of "users" of the Internet are just objects [8].

Many companies and research organizations are trying to predict the potential impact of the Internet of Things on the Internet and the economy in the next five to ten years. Cisco, for example, predicts more than 24 billion objects with Internet access until 2019 [9], Morgan Stanley 75 billion networked devices by 2020 [10] and Huawei expects 100 billion connected devices by 2025 [11]. Although these predictions are inconsistent and difficult to indicate precise calculation, however, they present a picture of a significant increase of Internet of Things [12].

2.2 Applications of the Internet of Things

In order to fully imagine the scale of the phenomenon and the number of devices that can be found within the Internet of Things, here we are potential areas [13].

Smart Environment includes automated systems used to monitor the current status and estimate the probability of natural disasters (e.g. the risk of fire, earthquake), control of air pollution (CO_2 emissions), life protection of wild animals (e.g. tracking them with GPS/GSM) or tourism.

Smart Water Management includes, for example the impact of water resources on the environment, their use and protection, deficits, regulation of rivers and protection against floods, waterways, hydropower or security. With solutions Internet of Things is possible live management of the process water supply, starting from the control of its suitability for consumption and storage, through supply and water supply tightness, after monitoring the consumption of end users. Use of the Internet of Things can have of great importance for the protection of the environment (e.g. monitoring the state of the soil), industry and agriculture (including issues such as the degree of fertilization and pollution, fields irrigation and greenhouses) or in solutions for water management in smart cities (e.g. monitoring of fertility and irrigation green areas).

Smart Industry is an area of the Internet of Things entering into solutions for various sectors of the national economy. Possible areas of application include monitoring the state of resources (e.g. the state of cisterns - water, fuel, gas), silo solutions (filling level of storage and weight of stored goods), diagnostics (e.g. self-diagnostics of machines, system failure detection), working conditions (e.g. monitoring inflammatory and dangerous gases, temperature) or processing of products (e.g. detection level of ozone, which is particularly important in plant foods).

Smart Manufacturing, like smart industry, includes solutions that fall within specific sectors of the economy. These include issues related to agriculture (e.g. temperature control and irrigation in order to avoid drying out or becoming moldy), breeding (monitoring living conditions and grazing livestock), and control production lines (readers, sensors, video surveillance - useful in the management and inspections) or control the rotation of products on store shelves and in warehouses.

Smart Transport is next to the above mentioned, the key segments of supporting the economy. This category includes such issues as: the location of transported goods (e.g. control of routes of hazardous materials, delicate or precious), control of transport conditions (e.g. hit, shock) or storage conditions (e.g. flammable materials). The Internet of Things comes also in issues related to the organization of transport, which is, for example reservation of seats at charging stations for electric vehicles, automatic tolls in congested places and self-diagnostics. This way of using the Internet of Things can be critical for fleets, car rental, and even defense systems.

Smart Energy covers a range of solutions that enable you to manage the media. These include the monitoring of electricity consumption of households, businesses, factories and processes for its production and use (e.g. in solar systems, windmills and water management).

Smart City is another area in which the Internet Things can play an increasingly important role, starting with the organization of the movement of pedestrians and traffic (such as monitoring traffic congestion, parking spaces, intelligent road, informing about the state of the road surface, traffic alerts, weather or accidents on the road) diagnosis safety (e.g. vibration and strength of materials in buildings, bridges, historic buildings), noise, lighting (e.g. adaptive to the level of cloud cover) and waste management (e.g. filling level of containers). This area is particularly important in areas such as security (video monitoring, alerting fire), the city's image and comfort of residents and tourists (e.g. tourist information).

Smart Building is a whole range of facilities, such as monitoring the property (fences, windows, doors), motion sensors, smart irrigation, thermostats with automatic learning. Possible solutions include surveillance of external conditions and internal (e.g. to detect the presence of water in buildings and threats installation, supervision, level of temperature, lighting). Monitoring can also include information about location-specific risks (e.g. smoke, CO2).

Smart House is a category of equipment, which are typically individual use, such as refrigerators (informing about content, shelf life, the need to replenish inventories), remote washing machines (enabling the use of lower energy tariffs), cookers (for remote setting of the oven). With solutions in this category, it is possible to control media consumption (by controlling light bulbs, thermostats, air conditioning) and security (surveillance of child, camcorders, alarm).

Smart Health covers a wide range of applications used in the monitoring of the health and physical activity (e.g. the elderly), vitality (e.g. people active in sport), patient safety (both in hospital and at home). Thanks to the Internet of Things it is possible to e.g. control of sleep (thanks to intelligent mattresses) and teeth (using the smart brushes). For applications at industrial level is the monitoring of hygiene (e.g. informing about the need to wash hands in factories), the state of the goods (e.g. refrigerators medical monitoring) and security (e.g. the level of UV or radiation in nuclear power plants).

Smart Life is a whole range of consumer solutions for comfort and safety. These include e.g. support purchases (compliance with the preferences of purchasing, monitoring the presence of the allergic components, expiration date), remote control equipment to avoid accidents, monitoring weather conditions (temperature, humidity, atmospheric pressure, wind strength and rain) and protection of personal rights (wallets, jewelry).

2.3 Architecture for Internet of Things

Chen Min [14] presents a four-layer architecture for Internet of Things (Fig. 2):

- Object sensing and information gathering: The first step of enabling smart services is to collect contextual information about environment, "things" and objects of interest.
- Information delivering: Various wireless technologies such as wireless sensor networks (WSNs), body area networks (BANs), WiFi, Bluetooth, Zigbee, GPRS, GSM, cellular and 3G, etc. can be used for delivering the information.
- Information processing: Pervasive and autonomic services are provided through ubiquitous machines in both "autonomic" and "smart" way.
- Application and smart services: Heterogeneous network performance in terms of bandwidth utilization, computing capability and energy efficiency are improved according to different users' requirements, and application-specific design.

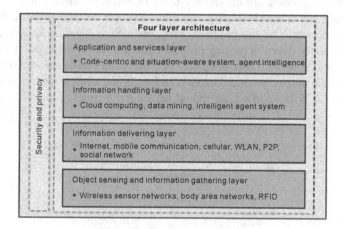

Fig. 2. Layers of Internet of Things

Each company can participate into more than one layer, and create its own business model [15]. The combination of the Internet of Things applications with layers indicates the location of a potential business models (Fig. 3).

Layers	Smart											
	Environment	Water	Management	Industry	Manufacturing	Transport	Energy	City	Building	House	Health	Life
Object sensing and information gathering	x		x		x		x	x	x	x	x	x
Information delivering	x		x		x		x	x	x	x	x	x
Information processing	x		x		x		x	x	x	x	x	x
Application and smart services	x		x		x		x	x	x	x	x	x

Fig. 3. The use of business models on different layers

2.4 Business Model

Business models is a way to describe activities of the company permanently operate in the landscape business. Also in Poland, this concept is constantly present in the discussions between the beginner start-ups and investors. One of the most popular concepts in defining the business model is a business model canvas by Alexander Oterwalder. This model accurately describes how organizations create and deliver value to its customers. The concept has been lined in the book "Business Model Generation", released in 2010, which Osterwalder wrote with Yves Pigneure, Alan Smiths and 470 business practitioners from 45 countries [16].

Before starting explaining the operation of the concept of business model canvas must first understand exactly what is the business model. As already mentioned, we can say that it describes the behavior of the company. At a more general level of understanding it is a system of assumptions, concepts and relationships between them allowing to describe (to model) in the approximate way some aspect of reality. In this case, the business reality. This can be both theoretical and physical object, whose analysis or observation allows learning characteristics different examined (modeled) phenomenon, process or object. Models are commonly used in business. Model at the same time simplifying and clarifying the reality and allows people to take right decisions thus allowing management. The aim of creating models include leveling knowledge so that all participants in the decision making process started from the same point and said the same thing. Looking at the business model "X", everyone should see clearly where the company takes the money, what sells, to whom it sells and when it recognizes that it has achieved success. What in that case should be a good business model? Ideally, to be

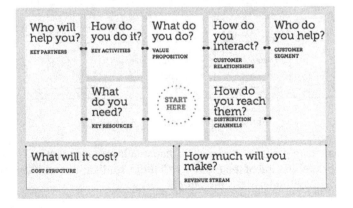

Fig. 4. Business model canvas

simple, adequate to reality and understand. It can not simplify and falsify the complex reality in which the enterprise operates. As adopted by Alex Osterwalder approach, called business model canvas the reality in which the company operates is described by the nine elements that illustrate the following graphics (Fig. 4).

The nine blocks are the elements that represent different aspects of the enterprise. Filled with the content, connected elements describe the product or service that the company provides to its customers.

2.5 Elements of the Business Model Canvas

The business model proposed by Alex Osterwalder was built as the sum of resources and activities, which the company organizes and implements in order to provide a specific value for a particular client. The template is divided into nine interdependent components: Key Partners, Key Activites, Key Resources, Value Proposition, Channels, Cost Structure, Revenue Streams, Customer Segment and Customer Relationships. Description of individual components should start from the most important of them, customer segmentation.

Customer Segmentation (Customer Segment). This is the basic element of the model. It defines the different groups of customers, which provides the added value produced by the company. Customers are the heart of every business model. Without them and without their finances no company can exist. To better understand and more effectively meet the needs of customers, businesses divided them into groups differing from each other needs, behavior or other properties. In the business model, you can define one or more customer segments. The basis for distinguishing customer segments may be such features as:

- Satisfying the needs of the customer segments requires a reasonable business and a distinctive offer.
- Customers in this segment be reached through the use of specific distribution channels (Channels).
- Characterized segment generates specific patterns of behavior and build relationships with customers (Customer Relationship).
- Each customer segments has a separate profitability.
- Customers from different segments are unable to pay differently for different services of the company.

Considering the above criteria clients can be divided for example:

Mass customer. The business model focused on client mass does not make explicit target groups. Value Proposition, Distribution Channels and Customer Relationship focuses on a large group of customers with similar problems and needs. An example of such a business can be a client in the field of consumer electronics, as well as most of the fast moving products (FMCG).

Niche market. Companies operating in niche markets supplying specific, specialized customer segment. In this case, the added value (Value Proposition), distribution

channels (Channels) and Customer Relationships are adapted to the needs and requirements of specific market niche. An example can be specialized thematic channels (STAR
Cricket - TV sports for lovers of cricket).

The market segmented. Some business models exude segments differ slightly from
each other's needs and problems. Most banks segments of its customers for large groups
with less assets and fewer of the larger portfolio. For example, Polish bank PKO BP for
nearly half a million customers, with a monthly income of 3 to 20 thousand PLN offers
service under personal banking. In contrast, private banking covers only 60 thousand
customers. Both of these segments have similar, but differentiating their needs and
problems. This has an impact on other elements of the business model, such as the Value
Proposition, distribution Channels and Customer Relationships or the Revenue Streams.

Diversified. A company with a diversified segment provides product several target
groups with different needs and problems. A good example is the company Amazon,
known as the largest online bookstore in the world. Using its experience in the field of
conducting a powerful website, Amazon began selling cloud computing services. In this
way, he began to share virtual servers and data storage to companies in Internet industry.

Value Proposition. Services or products that the company provides to customer
segments make up the so-called value proposition. That value proposition is the reason
why customers choose one company over another. The value for the customer is to
satisfy their specific needs or solving his problems. In other words, the value proposition
is a set of benefits that the company offers to its customers. Sometimes the value proposition can be innovative and offer benefits previously unheard of in the market. Another
added value is to offer products or services already existing in the market fortified by a
certain characteristic or attribute. Value proposition can be expressed quantitatively
(price, delivery time of service) or quality (design, customer experience in dealing with
the product/service, full service). When determining the value added for a given segment
we must ask the question: what problems or what needs meets a particular product or
service that helps solve the problems of potential customers. In the case of innovative
value may be the freshness of the product (e.g. new features in mobile phones). Qualitative value can emphasize its uniqueness by associating with the desired feature of (e.g.
a manufacturer of electronic equipment Apple combines its products with feature of
creativity) or a shift towards socially desirable values (e.g. the ethical investment funds).
Quantitatively added value can be expressed by the speed of execution of services
(FedEx), or the promise of high income (Forex).

Value proposition can promise perform the work for the buyer. A good example is
the rental company of car fleets. In this situation, customers do not have to think about
the technical condition of the car or other similar matters. Another added value is the
appropriate design, an important example in the fashion industry or consumer electronics. The element that adds value is also a brand. All well associated brands, such as
Rolex and Harley Davidson products companies have long been symbols of personal
success. In turn, offer similar value-added at a lower price is a typical way of satisfying
the customer's needs, which draws attention to the price. An example is Ryanair, which
designed their business model to be able to provide service flights at competitive prices.
He homesteaded customer segment, which was far excluded from the market of

passenger air transport. In the B2B segment firms often offer their clients added value in the form of cost reduction, such as companies providing software CRM (Client Relationship Management - systems that enable the company in an orderly manner to develop a relationship with the client which translates to greater satisfaction with customer service, and hence reduction of costs associated with the loss of a client, customer acquisition, etc.). In creating value by reducing the risk of helping all kinds of warranties on products purchased. Another element is the availability of value-added services, as in the case of urban bicycle loan scheme.

Channels. Channels is the way the company communicates and tries to segment customers (Customer Segment) to provide added value (Value Proposition). Communication, distribution, sale are the places where the company is in contact with the client, and therefore play an important role in making the consumer experience. Channels fulfill several functions:

– They provide customer knowledge of products and services
– Help customers evaluate the Value Proposition of company
– Allowing users to purchase products or services
– They provide after-sales support

   According to convention, business model canvas channels have five phases. The channel may contain some or all of them. The key is finding the right channel configurations in order to provide added value to the market (Value Proposition). In the first phase channel provides the client information about the products or services so as to be aware of their existence. In the second phase it should allow the customer to verify the added value (Value proposition). The next step is the purchase and delivery of the product. The last stage is the after-sales support. Good business model covers all five phases.

Customer Relationships. Customer relationships describe the type of interaction that the company establishes with separate customer segments. The relationship can range from personal, direct contact to the fully automated contact. It all depends on the expectations of customers segment. Personal relationship is based on direct customer interaction. The client can communicate with the consultant - supervisor, who will advise when selling a product or service. Dedicated personal contact is far more common in the B2B industry where customer relationships are built for a long time and decision about buying by the customer requires a lot of support from the dealer. A completely different type of relationship is self-service. We can meet it in the car wash or bike rentals. Another type of contact: co-creation goes beyond the traditional types of relationships. In this type, the customer co-creates value of the company. Examples are reviews of books in bookstores or online consumer reviews such Opineo.pl. Choosing the type of relationship also depends on cost, and integration with other elements of the business model.

Revenue Streams. This element describes the way in which the company generates revenue from various segments (Customer Segments). The company must ask the question: at what Value Proposition the Customer Segment really want to pay? The mechanisms may be different, based on a single purchase of the customer or multiple purchase.

Probably the most popular model is the sale of rights to ownership of physical goods. Another way to generate a revenue stream could be the fee charged for using the service or product. The more or frequently you use of the service, the more you pay. The simplest example are the hotels, movie rentals, courier companies and mobile operators. Another type is a subscription fee - in this case the company charge a fee for access to the service. In this way operate fitness clubs or online games where you pay for access to the server and the ability to play. Licensing is a stream of income, which is widely used in the media industry. Applications created by corporations like Adobe or Microsoft are available on the license terms. Copyright is retained by the manufacturer and the user can use the product according to the agreement. Another revenue stream is to generate funds from advertising, for example, in the software industry. Internet services: Google or Facebook generates its revenue primarily from advertising. Revenue streams can be combined. For example, car rental may charge a fee for signing up and for the use of the car. Computer game can be purchased physically in the box and pay extra for the opportunity to play on the network in the other levels.

Key Resources. This element describes the key resources needed to generate Value Proposition and to reach Customer Segments through distribution Channels. Key resources can be divided into the existing physical, that are machines, car, sales, servers. They are usually very capital intensive. Tesco has a huge network of warehouses and logistics infrastructure. Facebook must have a large and very expensive server farms. Another important source are the intellectual resources. Brand, patent, copyright or customer data are a very important part of any business model. These resources are difficult to manufacture, but owned able to build a very strong value. Microsoft and SAP base their strength on intellectual property developed over the years. Resource of very great importance are also people: especially in innovative companies or based on knowledge distribution. The last resource is money. Certain business models require a large amount of money in order to deliver a new product to market or gain new distribution Channels.

Key Activites. It's the most important steps that a company must perform in order to provide added value (Value Proposition), establish a relationship with the customer (Customers Relationship) and generate revenue structure (Revenue Streams). Key activities can be divided into production, troubleshooting and operating the platform/network. Production is nothing like the design, manufacture and supply of products in specified amounts. Troubleshooting is an activity consisting in the support of the client in understanding the ambiguity or help with unexpected situations. In this way, operate consulting companies, hospitals, third sector institutions. Business models of these organizations require activity such as knowledge management or regular staff training. The business model of Allegro.pl or eBay needs to constantly modernize. Platforms for e-learning (LMS) also constantly developing its solutions to fit the new requirements of technology and customers.

Key Partners. The concept of key partners describes the network of suppliers and contractors, who make the company operates. This could be the most important supplier, joint venture established to provide a new product or service, the strategic partnership between competitors or strategic alliance with a company from another industry. The motivations for creating partnerships can be different. Sometimes it's about optimization and economies of scale. The company that makes cars does not produce all the parts on their own, because often it is simply profitable. It includes strategic partnerships with manufacturers of necessary parts, which are delivered just-in-time. Another reason for the creation of partnership agreements is the need to acquire specific resource needed to improve business efficiency. Affiliation in order to reduce the risk and uncertainty when introducing a new product or service is more frequent. This was the case for optical media Blu-ray. Companies producing Blu-Ray joined forces to promote the new technology, so that it displaced the DVD. All the while they competing with each other in the sale of its own products Blu-ray.

Cost Structure. The cost structure describes all the costs, which generates business model. Creating and delivering additional value (Value Proposition), maintaining relationships with customers (Customer Relationships) and generating revenue (Revenue Streams) generate costs. It can easily be calculated by defining Key Resources, Key Activities and Key Partnerships. Business models are focused on minimizing costs wherever this is possible. Typical examples are bus lines Polski Bus or airline Ryanair. On the other hand, companies whose business model is based more on providing value could care less about its cost. This category includes luxury hotels and Rolex watches type.

Described in this way, the business model is intuitive and easy to present. Presented in the article approach it is also characterized by high flexibility, which allows you to describe business models operating in different industries. Another advantage is its location in the center of the value proposition. In this perspective, the organizations' efforts are focused on providing the customer what you really want or need.

3   Method

A necessary condition for accurate and reliable research, next to correctly formulated problems and hypotheses is the choice of appropriate methods, techniques and research tools. Methods and research tools are determined by the research problem. In this study, literature analysis, analysis of business models and inference was used.

Analyzing a broad variety of companies (up to 400 cases) Gassmann, Frankenberger & Csik identify 55 business model patterns that either individually or together build the fundament of the majority of currently existing business models. These models are: Add-on, Affiliation, Aikido, Auction, Barter, Cash Machine, Cross-selling, Crowdfunding, Crowdsourcing, Customer Loyalty, Digitisation, Direct Selling, E-commerce, Experience Selling, Flat Rate, Fractional Ownership, Franchising, Freemium, From Push to Pull, Guaranteed Availability, Hidden Revenue, Ingredient Branding, Integrator, Layer Player, Leverage Customer Data, Licensing, Lock-in, Long Tail, Make More of It, Mass Customisation, No Frills, Open Business, Open Source, Orchestrator, Pay Per Use, Pay What You Want, Peer to Peer, Performance-based Contracting, Razor and Blade, Rent Instead of Buy, Revenue Sharing, Reverse Engineering, Reverse Innovation, Robin Hood, Self-service, Shop in Shop, Solution Provider, Subscription, Supermarket, Target the Poor, Trash to Cash, Two-sided Market, Ultimate Luxury, User Design, White Label [17]. A description of all these 55 models would be too extensive for this article.

These models were the base of this study. Instead of reinventing the wheel, when identifying a new business model it is often sufficient to (re-) combine (i.e., transfer, combine, or repeat) these existing patterns. Of course, these patterns are helpful for creating Internet of Things business models as they cover diverse industries and sectors and layers of Internet of Things. Internet of Things has of course the potential to create completely new business model patterns. This article is the beginning of research on the exploration of such models.

The conceptualization of the business model consists of four central questions (Fig. 5): (1) Who is the customer? In other words, What are the distinctive customer segments; (2) What is being offered? In other words, What is the value proposition?; (3) How is the value proposition to be fulfilled? In other words, What are the organization's activities, processes, resources and capabilities for delivering what it promises?; (4) How is (financial) value created? In other words, What are the cost structure and the income flows: the earning model?

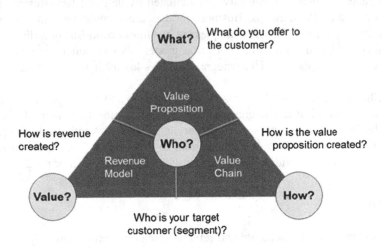

Fig. 5. Business model definition – the magic triangle.

A concrete pattern example is "add-on" – performed, e.g. by Ryanair – where customers are offered a very price competitive basic offering (What?) with additional, variable, and (generally) expensive options to book on top (Revenue?). This business model attracts price sensitive customers, who intend to only pay for what they consume (Who?) and is based on very cost conscious processes (How?).

4   Results

Based on the analysis and reasoning, the following are the business models that are applicable to the Internet Things. Next to their names find a short description. From the 55 business models, 33 models can be applied to the Internet Things.

Add-On - The core offering is priced competitively, but there are numerous extras that drive the final price up. In the end, the costumer pays more than he or she initially assumed. Customers benefit from a variable offer, which they can adapt to their specific needs. Internet of Things devices can activate their activities with expressed needs of the user. For an additional fee, they can be activated e.g. elements of artificial intelligence, or delivered to the customer additional data.

Affiliation - The focus lies in supporting others to successfully sell products and directly benefit from successful transactions. Affiliates usually profit from some kind of pay-per-sale or pay-per-display compensation. The company, on the other hand, is able to gain access to a more diverse potential customer base without additional active sales or marketing efforts. The company also can get access to the data, the ownership of which can significantly increase the value of its own data and thus offer a more complete service.

Cross Selling - In this model services or products from a formerly excluded industry are added to the offerings, thus leveraging existing key skills and resources. In retail especially, companies can easily provide additional products and offerings that are not linked to the main industry on which they were previously focused. Thus, additional revenue can be generated with relatively few changes to the existing infrastructure and assets, since more potential customer needs are met. Companies can addition to their own devices, sensors and data sources to offer an external device and the data expanding its offer and making it more comprehensive.

Digitization - This pattern relies on the ability to turn existing products or services into digital variants, and thus offer advantages over tangible products, e.g., easier and faster distribution. Ideally, the digitization of a product or service is realized without harnessing the value proposition which is offered to the customer. In other words: efficiency and multiplication by means of digitization does not reduce the perceived customer value. Many things that are currently performed manually sensors, devices and data from Internet of Things can realize for us.

Direct Selling - Direct selling refers to a scenario whereby a company's products are not sold through intermediary channels, but are available directly from the manufacturer or service provider. In this way, the company skips the retail margin or any additional costs associated with the intermediates. These savings can be forwarded to the customer and a standardized sales experience established. Additionally, such close contact can improve customer relationships. Internet of things devices themselves can order supplies and replenish stocks when they are below the minimum directly from the manufacturer. The devices can themselves be ordered at the time of injury.

Experience Selling - The value of a product or service is increased with the customer experience offered with it. This opens the door for higher customer demand and commensurate increase in prices charged. This means that the customer experience must be adapted accordingly, e.g., by attuning promotion or shop fittings. More information drawn from the Internet of Things devices and in-depth analysis by the company are direct increase in the customer experience.

Flat Rate - In this model, a single fixed fee for a product or service is charged, regardless of actual usage or time restrictions on it. The user benefits from a simple cost structure while the company benefits from a constant revenue stream. The customer can pay a fixed fee for the use of the Internet of Things devices and aggregates.

Fractional Ownership - Fractional ownership describes the sharing of a certain asset class amongst a group of owners. Typically, the asset is capital intensive but only required on an occasional basis. While the customer benefits from the rights as an owner, the entire capital does not have to be provided alone. In this model, e.g. city districts, companies can co-create the network of the Internet of Things for the achievement of the common good.

Freemium - The basic version of an offering is given away for free in the hope of eventually persuading the customers to pay for the premium version. The free offering is able to attract the highest volume of customers possible for the company. The generally smaller volume of paying 'premium customers' generate the revenue, which also cross-finances the free offering. For example, the company can provide the client basic information obtained from the Internet of things devices, while accurate, aggregated, combined with artificial intelligence may offer a fee.

From Push-To-Pull - This pattern describes the strategy of a company to decentralize and thus add flexibility to the company's processes in order to be more customer focused. To quickly and flexibly respond to new customer needs, any part of the value chain - including production or even research and development - can be affected.

Guaranteed Availability - Within this model, the availability of a product or service is guaranteed, resulting in almost zero downtime. The customer can use the offering as required, which minimizes losses resulting from downtime. The company uses expertise and economies of scale to lower operation costs and achieve these availability levels. In this model, the company may charge a fee for the guarantee of continuous operation of devices Internet of Things.

Hidden Revenue - The logic that the user is responsible for the income of the business is abandoned. Instead, the main source of revenue comes from a third party, which cross-finances whatever free or low-priced offering attracts the users. A very common case of this model is financing through advertisement, where attracted customers are of value to the advertisers who fund the offering. This concept facilitates the idea of 'separation between revenue and customer'. The value for the company will be the same data obtained from the Internet of Things devices. The company having the data can monetize.

Ingredient Branding - Ingredient branding describes the specific selection of an ingredient, component, and brand originating from a specific supplier, which will be included in another product. This product is then additionally branded and advertised with the ingredient product, collectively adding value for the customer. This projects the positive brand associations and properties on the product, and can increase the attractiveness of the end product. The attractiveness of the product can be enhanced through embedding the device the Internet of Things, which will be supported by a well-known brand.

Integrator - An integrator is in command of the bulk of the steps in a value-adding process. The control of all resources and capabilities in terms of value creation lies with the company. Efficiency gains, economies of scope, and lower dependencies from suppliers result in a decrease in costs and can increase the stability of value creation. Integration of devices, data from different devices Internet of Things is its core.

LAYER PLAYER - A layer player is a specialized company limited to the provision of one value-adding step for different value chains. This step is typically offered within a variety of independent markets and industries. The company benefits from economies of scale and often produces more efficiently. Further, the established special expertise can result in a higher quality process. The company, through its pioneering approach to the Internet of Things can use this model. Other companies that wish to enter the market will use its ideas and products.

Leverage Customer Data - New value is created by collecting customer data and preparing it in beneficial ways for internal usage or interested third-parties. Revenues are generated by either selling this data directly to others or leveraging it for own purposes, i.e., to increase the effectiveness of advertising. This model is the core of the Internet of Things.

License - Efforts are focused on developing intellectual property that can be licensed to other manufacturers. This model, therefore, relies not on the realization and utilization of knowledge in the form of products, but attempts to trans-form these intangible goods into money. This allows a company to focus on research and development. It also allows the provision of knowledge, which would otherwise be left unused and potentially be valuable to third parties. Ideas, licenses, property rights can be the basis for the functioning of some of the companies involved in Internet of Things. This field is new and innovative, and appear and will appear new solutions and patents.

Lock-In - Customers are locked into a vendor's world of products and services. Using another vendor is impossible without incur-ring substantial switching costs, and thus protecting the company from losing customers. This lock-in is either generated by technological mechanisms or substantial interdependencies of products or services. The lack of standards and the lack of interoperability may cause lock-in devices Internet of Things.

Long Tail - Instead of concentrating on blockbusters, the main bulk of revenues is generated through a 'long tail' of niche products. Individually, these neither demand high volumes, nor allow for a high margin. If a vast variety of these products are offered in sufficient amounts, the profits from resultant small sales can add up to a significant amount. Such a large range of applications the Internet of Things will generate a lot of market niches.

Make More of it - Know-how and other available assets existing in the company are not only used to build own products, but also offered to other companies. Slack resources, therefore, can be used to create additional revenue besides those generated directly from the core value proposition of the company. Cooperation and sharing knowledge certainly will take place on a new, innovative market, the Internet of Things.

Mass Customization - Customizing products through mass production once seemed to be an impossible endeavor. The approach of modular products and production systems has enabled the efficient individualization of products. As a consequence, individual customer needs can be met within mass production circumstances and at competitive prices. This is the basic premise of Industry 4.0 and industrial Internet of Things.

Open Business Model - In open business models, collaboration with partners in the ecosystem becomes a central source of value creation. Companies pursuing an open business model actively search for novel ways of working together with suppliers, customers, or complementors to open and extend their business. Create Internet of Things ecosystem is the foundation of its development.

Open Source - In software engineering, the source code of a software product is not kept proprietary, but is freely accessible for anyone. Generally, this could be applied to any technology details of any product. Others can contribute to the product, but also use it free as a sole user. Money is typically earned with services that are complimentary to the product, such as consulting and support. Interoperability and related open standards are the basis for the dynamic growth of the Internet of Things. McKinsey Global Institute report states that interoperability can generate 40 percent of the Internet of Things and generate income of over 4 billion USD per year in 2025, with total revenue of 11.1 trillion [18]

Pay Per Use - In this model, the actual usage of a service or product is metered. The customer pays on the basis of what he or she effectively consumes. The company is able to attract customers who wish to benefit from the additional flexibility, which might be priced higher.

Pay What You Want - The buyer pays any desired amount for a given commodity, sometimes even zero. In some cases, a minimum floor price may be set, and/or a suggested price may be indicated as guidance for the buyer. The customer is allowed to influence the price, while the seller benefits from higher numbers of attracted customers, since individuals' willingness to pay is met. Based on the existence of social norms and morals, this is only rarely exploited, which makes it suitable to attract new customers.

Peer-To-Peer - This model is based on a cooperation that specializes in mediating between individuals belonging to an homogeneous group. It is often abbreviated as P2P. The company offers a meeting point, i.e., an online database and communication service that connects these individuals (these could include offering personal objects for rent, providing certain products or services, or the sharing of information and experiences). Companies can exchange with each other data gathered from the Internet of Things.

Razor and Blade - The basic product is cheap or given away for free. The consumables that are needed to use or operate it, on the other hand, are expensive and sold at high margins. The initial product's price lowers customers' barriers to purchase, while the subsequent recurring sales cross-finance it. Usually, these products are technologically bound to each other to further enhance this effect. The basic version of the Internet of Things can be very cheap, but its any reconfiguration may require large expenditures.

Reverse Engineering - This pattern refers to obtaining a competitor's product, taking it apart, and using this information to produce a similar or compatible product. Because no huge investment in research or development is necessary, these products can be offered at a lower price than the original product. The dynamic growth of the Internet of Things can lead to the popularization of this model.

Reverse Innovation - Simple and inexpensive products, that were developed within and for emerging markets, are also sold in industrial countries. The term 'reverse' refers to the process by which new products are typically developed in industrial countries and then adapted to fit emerging market needs. Internet of Things devices can be produced in a variety of markets. May differ craftsmanship, sensitivity of sensors and collected data.

Self-Service - A part of the value creation is transferred to the customer in exchange for a lower price of the service or product. This is particularly suited for process steps that add relatively little perceived value for the customer, but incur high costs. Customers benefit from efficiency and time savings, while putting in their own effort. This can also increase efficiency, since in some cases, the customer can execute a value-adding step more quickly and in a more target-oriented manner than the company. Future model Build Your own The Internet of Things (BYIoT) is slowly becoming the present. Are becoming increasingly popular. For example projects Arduino and Raspberry Pi n some dimension are BYIoT.

Solution Provider - A full service provider offers total coverage of products and services in a particular domain, consolidated via a single point of contact. Special know-how is given to the customer in order to increase his or her efficiency and performance. By becoming a full service provider, a company can prevent revenue losses by extending their service and adding it to the product. Additionally, close contact with the customer allows great insight into customer habits and needs which can be used to improve the products and services.

Subscription - The customer pays a regular fee, typically on a monthly or an annual basis, in order to gain access to a product or service. While customers mostly benefit from lower usage costs and general service availability, the company generates a more steady income stream.

User Designed - Within user manufacturing, a customer is both the manufacturer and the consumer. As an example, an online platform provides the customer with the necessary support in order to design and merchandise the product, e.g., product design software, manufacturing services, or an online shop to sell the product. Thus, the company only supports the customers in their undertakings and benefits from their creativity. The customer benefits from the potential to realize entrepreneurial ideas without having to provide the required infrastructure. Revenue is then generated as part of the actual sales. This is the basic premise of Industry 4.0 and industrial Internet of Things.

5   Limitations on the Research Design and Material

Quite a few limitations have been identified with this research.

- Article is the beginning of in-depth research on models of the Internet of Things,
- Research method is based on inference and deduction of the author. Another part of the study will also include the appropriate use cases.
- The article includes only the business models of the Internet of Things based on already known business models. No new business models of Internet of Things. Their occurrence will be part of further research.

6 Conclusion

The business model is adopted by the company the long-term method to increase and use of resources in order to provide customers the offer exceeding the offer of competition, while ensuring the profitability of the organization. Good business model is to obtain and maintain at a later stage, a competitive advantage. Business models are constantly transformed. What constituted a good solution several years ago, can not check the current reality, which is why it is so important to keep track of changes and trends in your market. Keep in mind that each newly formed model is burdened with more or less defects, which is soon captured by his opponents. Analyzing a broad variety of companies (up to 400 cases) Gassmann, Frankenberger & Csik identify 55 business model patterns that either individually or together build the fundament of the majority of currently existing business models. These models can be the basis of creating business models Internet of Things. The author of this article from 55 models selected 33 models and pointed their application in the field of Internet of Things. These 33 models can be successfully used in the Internet of Things on four specified layers and in 11 areas. These models may also be the starting point for creating new business models or inspiration for the creation of a completely new, innovative models. Specification of these new models will be the target for further studies.

References

1. Gassmann, O., Frankenberger, K., Csik, M.: The St. Gallen Business Model Navigator, University of St. Gallen. www.bmi-lab.ch
2. Rudny, W.: Business models and the process of value creation in the digital economy. J. Manage. Finan. **13**(3), 1 (2015)
3. Bucherer, E.: Business models for the internet of things. In: Uckelmann, D., Harrison, M., Michahelles, F. (eds.) Architecting the Internet of Things. Springer, Heidelberg (2011)
4. Waher, P.: Learning Internet of Things. Packt Publishing, Birmingham (2015)
5. Vermesan, O., Friess, P.: Internet of Things: Converging Technologies for Smart Environments and Integrated Ecosystems. River Publishers, Aalborg (2013)
6. Jamoussi, B.: IoT Prospects of Worldwide Development and Current Global Circumstances, Comunication Standardization Bureau (2010). www.itu.int/ITU-T/go/IoT
7. Greengard, S.: The Internet of Things. The MIT Press, Cambridge (2015)
8. Thierer, A., Castillo, A.: Projecting the Growth and Economic Impact of The Internet of Things, George Mason University, Mercatus Center (2015). http://mercatus.org/sites/default/files/IoT-EP-v3.pdf
9. Cisco: Cloud and Mobile Network Traffic Forecast Visual Networking Index (VNI) (2015). http://cisco.com/c/en/us/solutions/serviceprovider/visual-networking-index-vni/index.html
10. Danova, T., Morgan, S.: 75 Billion Devices Will Be Connected To The Internet Of Things By 2020, Business Insider (2013). http://www.businessinsider.com/75-billion-devices-will-be-connected-to-the-internet-by-2020-2013-10
11. Huawei Technologies Co. Ltd., Global Connectivity Index (2015). http://www.huawei.com/minisite/gci/en/index.html
12. Fleisch, E., Weinberger M., Wortmann, F.: Business Models and the Internet of Things (2014). www.iot-lab.ch

13. Vermesan, O., Friess, P.: Internet of Things – From Research and Innovation to Market Deployment. River publishers, Aalborg (2014)
14. Chen, M.: Towards smart city: M2M communications with software agent intelligence. Multimed. Tools Appl. **67**(1), 167–178 (2013)
15. Chan, H.C.Y.: Internet of things business models. J. Serv. Sci. Manage. **8**, 552–568 (2015)
16. Osterwalder, A., Pigneur, Y.: Business Model Generation: A Handbook for Visionaries, Game Changers, and Challengers. Wiley, New York (2010)
17. Gassmann, O., Frankenberger, K., Csik, M.: The Business Model Navigator 55 Models That Will Revolutionise Your Business. Pearson, New York (2015)
18. Manyika, J., Chui M., Bisson P., Woetzel J., Dobbs R., Bughin J., Aharon D.: The Internet of Things: Mapping the Value Beyond the Hype, McKinsey Global Institute (2015). http://www.mckinsey.com/insights/business_technology/the_internet_of_things_the_value_of_digitizing_the_physical_world

Towards De-duplication Framework in Big Data Analysis. A Case Study

Jacek Maślankowski[✉]

Department of Business Informatics, University of Gdańsk, Gdańsk, Poland
jacek@ug.edu.pl

Abstract. Big Data analysis gives access to wider perspectives of information. Especially it allows processing unstructured and structured data together. However lots of data sources do not mean that the quality of data is enough to provide reliable results. There are several different quality indicators related to Big Data analysis. In this paper we will focus on two of them that are the most critical in the first phase of data processing: ambiguousness and duplicates. The goal of this paper is to present the proposal of the framework used to eliminate duplicates in large datasets acquired with Big Data analysis.

Keywords: Business informatics · Big Data · Unstructured data · Data analysis · Data quality

1 Introduction

Big Data gives lots of opportunities for researchers who want to make analysis based on several data sources available on the Internet. One of the most common examples is to make analysis based on the content gathered from webpages. Usually such data sources are unstructured. However in many cases webpages used for a specific analysis can be semi-structured. Examples of such webpages are related to the following analysis: real-estate market, job offers, twitter content, etc. For instance, if there is a need to make analysis of real-estate market, several different webpages present offers in a similar way, which means that some data can be extracted using specific structure enhanced with tags. This allows preparing a good quality dataset for further analysis. However if more than one data source are used, the same information can be collected two or more times. This is the reason of creating the proposal the framework that will eliminate duplicates in large datasets.

The purpose of this paper is to propose a framework that can be used to eliminate duplicates for Big Data analysis. Although the popularity of Big Data analysis is increasing, there is still no framework that can be used to eliminate duplicates from large unstructured datasets. In this paper we will not focus on preliminary tasks related to data analysis, such as selecting keywords or attributes. We will concentrate only on the framework of eliminating duplicates which is a contribution of this paper.

Reliability of the data analysis depends on the number of duplicates in the source dataset. The hypothesis used in this paper is as follows: eliminating duplicates in the data source by comparing selected attributes extracted from unstructured dataset will

© Springer International Publishing AG 2016
S. Wrycza (Ed.): SIGSAND/PLAIS 2016, LNBIP 264, pp. 104–113, 2016.
DOI: 10.1007/978-3-319-46642-2_7

give more reliable results than typical de-duplication that matches all attributes related to observation.

The paper consists of six parts. After introduction, in the second part of the paper there are theoretical fundamentals of Big Data Quality. In the third part there is a discussion on de-duplication issues with suggested approach to eliminate duplicates. In the fourth part a case study is briefly presented. The fifth part shows a proposal of suggested framework for eliminating duplicates. The conclusions are presented in the sixth part of this paper.

2 Big Data and the Quality

The importance of Big Data quality may be perceived in almost every type of the data, including structured and unstructured [1]. Three different facets for which data quality can be checked are input, process and output [10]. In this paper we will focus on the quality related to data processing to eliminate duplicates. As mentioned above, de-duplication is one of the key issues regarding receiving high quality data. It concerns both data and metadata. When trying to identify a specific keyword used to describe an object, usually we can use an automated form. In some cases semi-automated detection can be used to give better results [9]. In the article [11] published in Communications of the ACM it was demonstrated that common set of attributes allows re-identifying a specific object and link two different datasets as shown in Fig. 1.

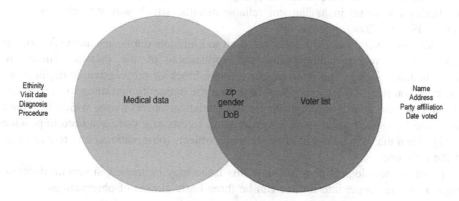

Fig. 1. Re-identification in combined two datasets Source: Own elaboration based on [11].

To de-identify the dataset the first step is to determine the method of anonimization requirements used for the specific set. In Fig. 1 the common set of attributes for both datasets (medical data and voter list) are zip code, gender and date of birth. Other attributes and values are collected based on two different datasets. Therefore the main goal is to find syntactic and semantic levels of data integration [16]. Although lots of new knowledge is produced, we should be concerned that combining several different data sources can face some ethical aspects of the possibilities of tracking people [15].

Surveys conducted by academic researchers showed the existence of several problems especially with identifying popular elements. For instance, in [2] we can find that Dublin Core study identified that DC.title and the DC.subject elements did not add any value for retrieval purposes, while the DC.creator, DC.publisher and DC.contributor elements presented inconsistent name formats. This means that not all of the attributes in any dataset are relevant for data comparing.

The importance of Big Data quality is not only an issue in unstructured datasets. It can also be a relevant aspect of Supply Chain Management process [4]. There are new proposals of using multidimensional date cubes from heterogeneous data sources like Big Data [12]. The same topic was discussed in Business Intelligence Journal in the article by [13], in which data warehouses are evolving to fulfil Big Data requirements. It is especially important in terms of decision making by using real-time data [14]. Thus Big Data ecosystem can also be regarded as a high quality service tools [3].

Because webpages are one of the most common data source nowadays, there are different approaches to assess its quality [8]. In that case the data quality is based on content semantics analysis.

3   De-duplication of Datasets

Typical use of de-duplication is to reduce amount of data stored in datasets [5]. The purpose of this method is usually to increase performance in data processing [6]. De-duplication is a technique that is used by MapReduce algorithms to enable parallel execution of data-intensive tasks but it cannot find duplicates in adjacent block [7]. Duplicates can result in having not reliable results, which was strongly visible in Google Flu and Ebola outbreaks [17].

There are several techniques that are used to eliminate duplicates however most of them are referred to compression and replication of the dataset. These are single-instance storage and fixed-block, variable-block or progressive de-duplication. The common rule of these methods is to reduce the dataset to minimum to save space. In our case, the goal is to eliminate similar statistical observations, which in a case study can be a specific real-estate advertisement. In this case there is a need to provide an algorithm that will be used to find the same objects (observations) and reduce them to the only one.

From methodological point of view this issue may be treated in several different ways. Looking deeper into it there can be three basic classes of observations:

Case 1: observation is the same including business metadata and data;
Case 2: observation is the same in business metadata but differs in values;
Case 3: observation is different in business metadata but it refers to the same object.

These cases were illustrated in Table 1 based on the data on real-estates. The case number indicates the way the algorithm can be used to eliminate duplicates in the dataset. In our case study only 1 and 2 case were used to identify the observations that occur at least twice.

Table 1. Classification of duplicates based on real-estate example

Case number	Comparison		
	Metadata	Data	Action
1	City, Street, Size, Number of rooms, Equipment, Additional Data	*Same:* Price	Eliminate
2	City, Street, Size, Number of rooms, Equipment, Additional Data	*Different:* Price	Eliminate
3	City, Street, Size, Number of rooms, *Different:* Equipment, Additional Data	*Same or Different:* Price	Eliminate or Add

As shown in Table 1, the decision of eliminating or not may depend on the metadata and data completion. If there is the same business information on the specific object, this observation definitely will be eliminated. For some reasons if a particular metadata is different but the others are the same including the price, the object in most cases will not be included in the analysis.

4   Case Study

In this paper we don't concentrate on basics of using Big Data tools to retrieve the data from unstructured data source. We will focus only on testing the environment to fulfill user expectations on eliminating duplicates in a source dataset.

The case study used in this paper is to provide data on real-estate market based on the data from various different websites. To accomplish this task several different data sources were used. The goal was to see how the suggested framework works with duplicates. For this case study Apache Hadoop ecosystem was used with Apache Spark as the front gateway. Algorithms for the framework were implemented and tested using Python programming language.

The first step of the case study was to identify business metadata and match them with the metadata from different sources. In this step the main goal was to identify all of the keywords used in specific data sources to describe a specific offer and match them with the keywords used in other data sets.

In Table 2 there is an example of the data reduction by using de-duplication framework proposed in the part 5 of this paper.

Table 2. Reduction of observations by eliminating duplicates

Number of data sources	Comparison		
	Number of observations	Reduction ratio	De-duplication class
2	2000	31 %	1, 2
3	3000	52 %	1, 2
4	4000	61 %	1, 2

As it was shown in the Table 2, the reduction of observations was significant. It means that data derived by suggested framework for eliminating duplicates is more reliable comparing to traditional data processing. Observations used in this case study were limited to one region and selected by date – newest 1000 observations. The reason for doing such analysis was that mostly it should be presented in time series. Therefore the case study was limited to the newest advertisements.

To avoid any ambiguousness and prepare reliable weights, the best way is to find the number of discrepancies in various expressions used to find duplicates in the data source. An example written in Python below show how to do this without applying MapReduce. This algorithm was also included in the phase of finding discrepancies in the input dataset. The following part of the script written in Python compiled in Apache Spark can be used to show what is the rate of dataset ambiguousness.

Listing 1. Part of the script for discrepancy identification
```
from pyspark import SparkContext
file="realestates"
sc=SparkContext("local","Aplikacja AiB")
data=sc.textFile(file).cache()
k1= data.filter(lambda s: 'London, Ealing' in s).count()
k2= data.filter(lambda s: 'London, Eal.' in s).count()
print("Number of observations: %i,  : %i" % (k1, k2))
```

The reduction of the dataset is very promising as it was shown below. Listing 2 is the output of Apache Spark processing with the RDD job finished with success.

Listing 2. Output of Apache Spark
```
16/05/21 18:39:25 INFO MemoryStore: Block rdd_1_0 stored as
bytes in memory (estimated size 51.1 KB, free 295.0 KB)
16/05/21 18:39:25 INFO BlockManagerInfo: Added rdd_1_0 in memory
on localhost:42842 (size: 51.1 KB, free: 511.2 MB)
16/05/21 18:39:25 INFO PythonRunner: Times: total = 259, boot =
214, init = 19, finish = 26
16/05/21 18:39:25 INFO Executor: Finished task 0.0 in stage 0.0
(TID 0). 2704 bytes result sent to driver
```

As it was written above, the reduction is more than 30 % for just two datasets. Larger datasets with well-defined weights and attributes can reduce more than 50 % of the data observations.

5   Suggested Framework for Eliminating Duplicates

Firstly, we need to define the rate of data reliability. For this purpose a specific function was proposed. This function is fitted to Big Data Apache Hadoop ecosystem, especially when defining MapReduce algorithms. Therefore observations that are duplicated should be eliminated. MapReduce paradigm is designed to map and reduce data but not to delete them. Thus a specific algorithm must be implemented in the second stage of data reduction. It is presented below.

The suggested framework for eliminating duplicates consists of two steps. The first step is to design the function to eliminate duplicates. The second step is to use machine learning tool to extend the function to other cases and data sources. As it was shown in a case study, the results of using this approach are very promising. It can be said that the more observations are eliminated, the more reliable results are. The proposed function for eliminating duplicated observations is as follows:

$$f(x) = w1 * k1 + w2 * k2 + \ldots + wn * kn$$

where:

- 1, 2, n is the number of attribute tested for matching;
- wn is the weight used to give priority of attributes;
- kn has the value of 1 when attribute match and value of 0 when don't match.

In the function above the total sum of weights should not exceed 1. That means that for each attribute the value of weight will be decimal. For k1-kn the value can be only matching (1) or not matching (0). No other values are possible.

An example of weights calculations for real-estate market analysis was presented in Table 3.

Table 3. Weights and attributes used for calculations

Case number	Calculation		
	Attribute	Weight	Notes
1	City	0.30	
2	Street	0.30	
3	Size	0.09	May differ depending on web portal
4	Number of rooms	0.12	May differ depending on web portal
5	Equipment	0.05	
6	Property	0.06	
7	Others	0.08	

As shown in Table 3 the decision of eliminating or not may depend on various different attributes. For example, in many different web portals the same flats or houses had a different value of number of rooms or size.

In the case study the threshold value was amounted to 0.7. It means that at least city and street must be matched. Other values are not necessary as it was written before. The threshold value with 0.7 may also provide to eliminate observations that are quite similar but refers to different real estates.

The way the function is used has been presented in Fig. 2.

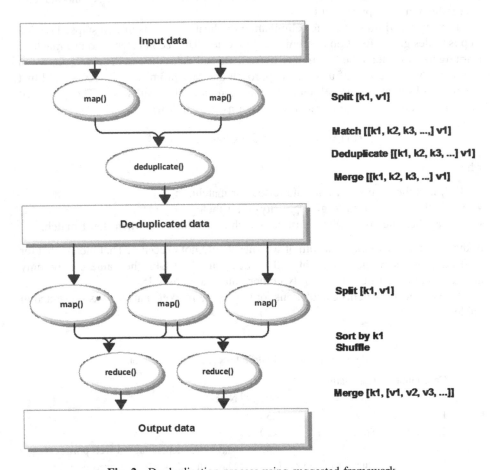

Fig. 2. De-duplication process using suggested framework

In Fig. 2 the main difference is to add new functionality to MapReduce framework to reduce duplicates in the dataset. Otherwise similar observations will be counted as many times as they are included in datasets. Input data are the representation of several different datasets. The suggested framework gives access to functions that allows data cleansing in the following order:

- split(),
- match(),
- deduplicate(),
- merge().

The aim of the first function is to split the data set into different observations. As it is usually not an issue when making analysis of semi-structured datasets, the data scientist should select what type of attributes will be analysed. Other attributes should be omitted. Then the dataset will be ready to match all observations to find the similarities between different observations.

The next step is to match observations and find any relations between them. To do this, data scientist should decide about weights of each attribute used for data comparison. The weights should count to 1 as it was shown in Table 3. Because of the fact that preparing good weights is not trivial, the data scientist should make the preliminary analysis of differences and discrepancies in values used to describe the same characteristics of observation. Having prepared good weights the function of de-duplication process can be used.

Deduplicate() function use all weights and attributes characteristics to find any matches based on the algorithm presented above. The goal is to save all observations that fulfil the threshold criteria defined by data scientist in the second step of the first step. All observations that don't fulfil this criteria should be excluded from the dataset.

The last step works in the similar way as in MapReduce framework. It is used to merge all the observation in one dataset and provide cleansed output data for further analysis by MapReduce algorithms.

After that the dataset is ready and can be processed in any language using MapReduce paradigm. In the case study we used Python to provide a final output. The de-duplication framework proposed in this paper does not affect any of the step of MapReduce. Therefore the dataset can be used to give a reliable result.

The MapReduce paradigm use a typical data processing steps which are: split, sort, shuffle and merge. Please not that suggested de-duplication framework is using a different way of mapping than in typical MapReduce paradigm. In a proposed framework we have classified all the attributes (observation characteristics) as one key. Therefore comparing to typical MapReduce job, our key is complex and consists of several separated attributes. In MapReduce the key can be also complex but it is usually presented by one value that is used to combine all keys into one key.

6 Conclusions

In this paper a case study showed that processing large datasets can provide a significant number of duplicated records that should be eliminating to provide better results. This leads to the need of creating several different rules for data filtering that will be processed by MapReduce algorithms. In the proposed concept, data filtering to eliminate duplicates is the first step and should be done before MapReduce paradigm is used.

The goal of the paper was to show that eliminating duplicates is a crucial step in Big Data analysis. The proposed framework of de-duplication is relevant in almost every type of Big Data analysis, not only on unstructured data but also structured data that comes from several different data sources. Because of the fact that the unstructured data are much more difficult to process, the solution based on percentage values (counted to 1) was used. Although there is a risk that more observations can be eliminated than it should be, it is still much more reliable solution than a typical Big Data processing. We have to be concerned that Big Data sources have so many values (data and metadata) that the sample in the survey is usually significant larger than in a typical survey. This leads to the conclusion that the data source will never be fully clear and cleanse.

The risk of having not reliable Big Data source is almost the same like in a typical survey where standard error measure is used. However the case study used in this paper has the total number of observations that covers at least 80 % of total population. This means that statistical testing will not be performed as the population is not the random sample.

The hypothesis of the better results when using selected attributes to find duplicates can be reconfirmed. The number of duplicates covered by suggested de-duplication framework is much higher than eliminating them in traditional way by matching all characteristics of the observation.

References

1. Maślankowski, J.: Data quality issues concerning statistical data gathering supported by Big Data technology. In: Kozielski, S., Mrozek, D., Kasprowski, P., Małysiak-Mrozek, B. (eds.) BDAS 2014. CCIS, vol. 424, pp. 92–101. Springer, Heidelberg (2014)
2. Rousidis, D., Garoufallou, E., Balatsoukas, P., Sicilia, M.: Metadata for Big Data: a preliminary investigation of metadata quality issues in research data repositories. Inf. Serv. Use 34(3/4), 279–286 (2014)
3. Hucheng, Z., Jian-Guang, L., Hongyu, Z., Haibo, L., Haoxiang, L., Tingting, Q.: An empirical study on quality issues of production Big Data platform. In: ICSE: International Conference on Software Engineering, pp. 17–26 (2015)
4. Hazen, B., Boone, C., Ezell, J., Jones-Farmer, L.: Data quality for data science, predictive analytics, and Big Data in supply chain management: an introduction to the problem and suggestions for research and applications. Int. J. Prod. Econ. 154, 72–80 (2015)
5. Di Pietro, R., Sorniotti, A.: Proof of ownership for deduplication systems: a secure, scalable, and efficient solution. Comput. Commun. 82, 71–82 (2016)
6. Mao, B., Jiang, H., Wu, S., Tian, L.: Leveraging data deduplication to improve the performance of primary storage systems in the cloud. IEEE Trans. Comput. 65(6), 1775–1788 (2016)
7. Kun, M., Fusen, D., Bo, Y.: Large-scale schema-free data deduplication approach with adaptive sliding window using MapReduce. Comput. J. 58(11), 3187–3201 (2015)
8. Han, J., Chen, K., Wang, J.: Web article quality ranking based on web community knowledge. Computing 97(5), 509–537 (2015)
9. Polidoro, F., Giannini, R., Lo Conte, R., Mosca, S., Rossetti, F.: Web scraping techniques to collect data on consumer electronics and airfares for Italian HICP compilation. Stat. J. IAOS 31(2), 165–176 (2015)
10. Agafiţei, M., Gras, F., Kloek, W., Reis, F., Vâju, S.: Measuring output quality for multisource statistics in official statistics: some directions. Stat. J. IAOS 31(2), 203–211 (2015)
11. Angiuli, O., Blitzstein, J., Waldo, J.: How to de-identify your data. Commun. ACM 58(12), 48–55 (2015)

12. Maté, A., Llorens, H., de Gregorio, E., Tardío, R., Gil, D., Muñoz-Terol, R., Trujillo, J.: A novel multidimensional approach to integrate big data in business intelligence. J. Database Manage. **26**(2), 14–31 (2015)
13. Clegg, D.: Evolving data warehouse and BI architectures: the Big Data challenge. Bus. Intell. J. **20**(1), 19–24 (2015)
14. Akbay, S.: How Big Data applications are revolutionizing decision making. Bus. Intell. J. **20**(1), 25–29 (2015)
15. Martin, K.E.: Ethical issues in the Big Data industry. MIS Q. Executive **14**(2), 67–85 (2015)
16. Goes, P.B.: Big Data and IS research. MIS Q. **38**(3), iii–viii (2014)
17. Kugler, L.: What happens when Big Data blunders? Commun. ACM **59**(6), 15–16 (2016)

Information Systems Management

Mapping Between Artefacts and Portfolio Processes from the PMI Standard for Portfolio Management

Ana Lima[1,2(✉)], Paula Monteiro[1,2], Gabriela Fernandes[2], and Ricardo J. Machado[1,2]

[1] CCG/ZGDV Institute, Guimarães, Portugal
ana.lima@ccg.pt
[2] ALGORITMI Research Centre, Universidade do Minho, Guimarães, Portugal

Abstract. Among the decisions that software development organizations need to take is to define which projects should developed, as these are, ultimately, the reason for their existence. This decision is part of a broader decision-making process than the strictly project management efforts of every day, involving aspects that go beyond the limits of a project itself, such as: strategic alignment, economic viability, risks that an organization is willing to assume, the capacity of available resources and the returns that will be achieved. These concerns are within the scope of project portfolio management. The Project Management Institute (PMI) has developed the 'Standard for Portfolio Management', whose objective is to propose a strategy for project portfolio management throughout processes. This paper presents the dependencies between all portfolio management process and artefact's from that PMI standard with Software Process Engineering Metamodel (SPEM).

Keywords: Project portfolio management · Processes · Artefacts · SPEM analysis

1 Introduction

The Software Engineering discipline had emerged in the 1960s and, like many other areas of knowledge, also requires the use of decision support techniques throughout the development and evolution of software-based systems. In this context, one can highlight that methodologies for supporting decision-making are crucial for any organization that seeks continuous learning because [1]: (i) it facilitates the structuring of problems under investigation; (ii) it helps the understanding of information necessary for making efficient decisions; (iii) it drives the generation and evaluation of alternative solutions by using explicit models to prioritize the alternatives.

Given the current complexity of the software-based systems, the pace of technological progress, the constant change of requirements, along with the competitive market and resource constraints, bad decisions and subsequent need of additional work become increasingly harmful for organizations. Hence, it is paramount to explicitly and

© Springer International Publishing AG 2016
S. Wrycza (Ed.): SIGSAND/PLAIS 2016, LNBIP 264, pp. 117–130, 2016.
DOI: 10.1007/978-3-319-46642-2_8

consciously support decision-making throughout the development and evolution of software-based systems.

The adoption of methods, techniques and tools which support implementation of the organization's strategy, promote necessary changes and help achieve strategic objectives is extremely important. One example of such method is project portfolio Management [2, 3]. This decision is part of a broader decision-making process than the project management (PM), involving aspects that go beyond the limits of an individual project, such as: strategic alignment, economic viability, risks that an organization is willing to assume, the capacity of available resources and the returns that will be achieved. These concerns are within the scope of project portfolio management.

Traditionally, PM has been concerned with the management of an 'individual project' [4]. Project is defined as *"an organisation unit dedicated to the attainment of a goal – generally the successful completion of a development product on time, within budget, and in conformance with predetermined performance specifications"* [5]. PM offers a structure which ensures achieving the project goals [6], through the planning and control of variables including resources, cost, productivity, schedule, risk and quality [7]. Practitioners and academics have been showing an increasing interest in the use of PM for strategic purposes [8]. This new approach to PM requires the use of the program and portfolio approaches. A program can be defined as *"a framework for grouping existing projects or defining new projects, and for focusing all the activities required to achieve a set of major benefits"* [9]. Projects in a program have common outputs while projects in a portfolio share inputs.

Project portfolio is defined as a group of projects that are carried out under the sponsorship and/or management of a particular organization. Since there are usually not enough resources to carry out every proposed project which meets the organization's minimum requirements on certain criteria (such as potential profitability, etc.), the projects must compete for scarce resources (people, finances, time, etc.) made available from the sponsor [10]. This paper focuses on portfolio management.

Organizations initiate and sponsor projects to improve their innovative capacity, to carry out system-wide change efforts, and to enhance their adaptive capability [11]. These projects focus on the future vision for the organization and may include technology, product or process development, product/service launch, business process reengineering or new capacity development [12, 13], further referred as internal projects. On the other hand, organizations initiate projects to accommodate complex business activities [14], such as, the development of software to support organizational processes (Enterprise Resource Planning Systems (ERP), Manufacturing Execution Systems (MES), etc.), further referred as external projects. Such activities have been common in the construction industry for several decades, and have also become significant on a range of other industries and sectors, as technology-based and service providing organizations, that increasingly organize their operational activities in different kinds of projects and customer delivery projects [15]. Since the projects are of high importance for organizations, top management must approve and maintain constant vigilance on these projects and determine which of them can provide a real contribution to the organization to achieve its strategic objectives [16]. Thus, the portfolio management has become a significant factor in the "successful long-term" organization's oriented projects [17].

The main goals of portfolio management (PfM) are the maximization of the financial value of the portfolio, linking the portfolio to the organization's strategy, and balancing the projects within the portfolio, taking into account the organization's capacities [18].

PfM is defined as a dynamic decision process, whereby a business's list of active new product (and R&D) projects is constantly updated and revised. In this process, new projects are evaluated, selected, and prioritized. Also, existing projects may be accelerated, "killed" or de-prioritized. Additionally, resources can be allocated and re-allocated to the active projects. The portfolio decision process is characterized by uncertain and changing information, dynamic opportunities, multiple goals and strategic considerations, interdependence among projects, and multiple decision-makers and locations [19].

The Project Management Institute (PMI) [20] defines PfM as the centralized management of one or more portfolios, which includes identifying, prioritizing, authorizing, managing, and controlling projects, programs, and other related work, to achieve specific strategic business objectives.

Several inputs can be used to guide an organization in improving PfM, by selecting the most appropriate tools and techniques in a given context, including various Bodies of Knowledge. The PfM body of knowledge is the sum of knowledge within the profession of portfolio management. The complete PfM body of knowledge includes proven traditional practices that are widely applied, as well as innovative practices that are emerging in the profession [4].

This paper presents the mapping between artefacts and all PfM processes, which have been established by performing a systematic analysis of the process groups and artefact's categories of the PfM standard from PMI. The identified dependencies between artefacts and processes have been modelled by using the Software Process Engineering Metamodel (SPEM) notation. The authors expect that clarifying the dependencies between PfM processes and its artefacts, particularly the practitioners interested in increasing their performance in the management of portfolios have a more complete understanding of which involves project portfolio management.

This paper is organized as follows. Section 2 presents a brief description of the processes and artefacts for PfM. Section 3 describes the dependencies between artefacts and portfolio processes for PfM. Section 4 specifies the dependency between PfM artefacts and processes with SPEM. Finally, conclusions are presented, as well as some highlights for further research.

2 Synopsis of the PfM Standards from PMI

The fundamental PfM concepts were introduced for investment, in 1981. The main idea was to promote the balance between higher risk and lower risk investments so that the resources would be invested in lower risk projects, and part would be invested in higher risk projects. In [21], McFarlan says that the governance of organizations must also make use of a risk-based approach, for the portfolio selection and management of IT projects. McFarlan developed the foundations for the PfM concepts in Information Technology (IT) projects. The author observed that unbalanced portfolios can take the organization undergoing disruptions or leave "gaps" for competitors.

Table 1. Internal alignment between process groups, knowledge areas, and portfolio processes of PMI PfM standard

Portfolio Management Process Groups (PMPG)	Portfolio Management Knowledge Areas (PMKA)	Portfolio Processes (PP)	Acronym
PG-1 Defining Process Group	Portfolio Strategic Management (PSM)	Develop Portfolio Strategic Plan	{PP 1} DPSP
	Portfolio Strategic Management (PSM)	Develop Portfolio Charter	{PP 2} DPC
	Portfolio Strategic Management (PSM)	Define Portfolio Roadmap	{PP 3} DPR
	Portfolio Governance Management (PGM)	Develop Portfolio Management Plan	{PP 4} DPMP
	Portfolio Governance Management (PGM)	Define Portfolio	{PP 5} DP
	Portfolio Performance Management (PPM)	Develop Portfolio Performance Management Plan	{PP 6} DPPMP
	Portfolio Communication Management (PCM)	Develop Portfolio Communication Management Plan	{PP 7} DPCMP
	Portfolio Risk Management (PRM)	Develop Portfolio Risk Management Plan	{PP 8} DPRMP
Aligning Process Group	Portfolio Strategic Management (PSM)	Manage Strategic Change	{PP 9} MSC
	Portfolio Governance Management (PGM)	Optimize Portfolio	{PP 10} OP
	Portfolio Performance Management (PPM)	Manage Supply and Demand	{PP 11} MSD
	Portfolio Performance Management (PPM)	Manage Portfolio Value	{PP 12} MPV
	Portfolio Communication Management (PCM)	Manage Portfolio Information	{PP 13} MPI
	Portfolio Risk Management (PRM)	Manage Portfolio Risks	{PP 14} MPR
PG-3 Authorizing and Controlling Process Group	Portfolio Governance Management (PGM)	Authorize Portfolio	{PP 15} AP
	Portfolio Governance Management (PGM)	Provide Portfolio Oversight	{PP 16} PPO

In [21], Reyck et al. identify some good practices for the development of PfM within organizations: centralization of information, analysis restrictions, risk analysis and financial, and existence of a systemic process for prioritization, alignment and selection.

The process defined by PMI [20] for PfM assumes that the organization has a strategic plan, knows its mission and has established its vision and goals.

The use of PfM may help evaluate how well the portfolio components and the portfolio as a whole as to how well they are performing in relation to the key indicators and the strategic plan [22].

The Standard for Portfolio Management from PMI describes the steps defined to deploy PfM processes in a set of 16 portfolio processes, divided into five knowledge areas: (1) strategic management; (2) governance management; (3) performance management; (4) communication management and; (5) risk management and three process groups: (1) the *defining* process group to establish the strategy and the organization's objectives that will be implemented in a portfolio; (2) the *alignment* process group to manage and optimize the portfolio; (3) the *authorizing and controlling* process group to determine who authorizes the portfolio, as well as the ongoing oversight of the portfolio.

In order to implement a concrete PfM approach in organizations, the following steps are, typically, used: (1) identify the government strategic objectives; (2) identify and categorize components; (3) evaluate and select components; (4) identify and

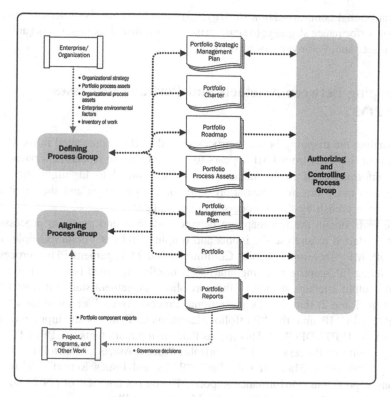

Fig. 1. PMI PfM process group interactions by artefacts [20]

analyse the portfolio risks; (5) prioritize components; (6) balance portfolio; (7) monitoring and controlling process group and; (8) closure [22].

Table 1 depicts the internal alignment of the PMI PfM standard in terms of process groups, knowledge areas and portfolio processes [20]. To help the discussion in Sect. 3, Table 1 includes a column to define an acronym for each portfolio process {PPn}, where PP stands for portfolio process, and n corresponds to the number of the process.

PfM processes occur as a series of interrelated processes or bridges between the organizational strategy and the implemented programs/projects. These are part of the tactical work of the organization to meet the goals, objectives and strategies of the organization [20].

The generic data flow diagram about the process depicted in Fig. 1 shows the basic flow and interactions between the three process groups by identifying the artefacts that are created or necessary for the implementation of PfM processes.

The PMI standard categorizes all the artefacts in the following content types: enterprise documents, portfolio documents, and portfolio reports [20]. For example, the enterprise documents artefacts are: (1) organizational strategy and objectives;

(2) organizational communication strategy; (3) organizational risk tolerance; (4) organizational performance strategy; (5) enterprise environmental factors; (6) organizational process assets and; (7) inventory of work.

3   Mapping Between Artefacts and Portfolio Processes for PfM

Understanding the mapping between processes and artefacts presented in the Portfolio Management Standard from PMI appears to be limited. The researchers based on the detailed information of input and output artefacts aimed to highlight the existing mapping and made the implementation order of the processes and the input output interrelation establish by these processes more explicitly.

In order to obtain the full mapping between artefacts and portfolio processes, the researchers started to analyse the inputs and outputs artefacts. As an example, for the {PP7} DPCMP "Develop Portfolio Communication Management Plan" process, the corresponding PP7-centric mapping analysis is briefly explained below. Analyzing the input and output artefacts section of the portfolio management standard from PMI we can read (in Table 2) that the "Organizational Process Assets" are an input artefact of the {PP7} DPCMP and the "Portfolio Management Plan" is an input and output artefact of the {PP7} DPCMP. This means that the input artefacts of {PP7} DPMP are the "Organizational Process Assets", "Portfolio Process Assets", "Portfolio", "Portfolio Roadmap", "Portfolio Management Plan", "Risks and Issues Report", "Governance Decisions Report" and "Performance Report". The output artefacts of {PP7} DPMP are "Portfolio Process Assets" and "Portfolio Management Plan".

Table 2. {PP7} DPCMP matrix line

	Enterprise Documents Artefacts							Portfolio Documents Artefacts							Portfolio Reports Artefacts					Number of Artefacts	INPUT Number of Artefacts - Internal Process	INPUT Number of Artefacts - External Process	OUTPUT Number of Artefacts - Internal Process	OUTPUT Number of Artefacts - External Process
	Organizational Strategy and Objectives	Organizational Communication Strategy	Organizational Risk tolerance	Organizational Performance Strategy	Enterprise Environmental Factors	Organizational Process Assets	Inventory of Work	Portfolio Process Assets	Portfolio Strategic Plan	Portfolio	Portfolio Roadmap	Portfolio charter	Portfolio Risk Management Plan	Portfolio Management Plan	Resources	Risks and Issues	Value and Benefits	Governance Decisions	Performance	Financial					
PCM {PP 7} DPCMP M,C,I						IN-E-A		I/O-A		IN-A	I/O-A			I/O-A		IN-A		IN-A	IN-A		10	7	1	2	0

All these relations are represented in Table 2 matrix, where an "IN" stands for input artefact (variant, "IN-A" corresponds to internal artefacts of the portfolio processes and "IN-E-A", corresponds to external artefacts of portfolio processes), "OUT-A" for output artefact, and "I/O-A" for input and output artefact (variant, "I/O-A" corresponds internal artefact of the portfolio processes and "I/O-E-A", corresponds external artefact of the portfolio processes). Each matrix row represents the portfolio process source under analysis and the columns represent the mapped artefact, both in the input and output perspectives.

The elementary dependency analysis was performed for all the PfM processes, in order to create the complete matrix between artefacts and PfM processes (see Table 3). For a better understanding of the effective impact of the dependencies between all artefacts and all the portfolio processes, the matrix is sorted by process groups (note the red gradient) and artefacts categories ("Enterprise Documents", "Portfolio Documents" and "Portfolio Reports").

Table 3. Mapping between all the portfolio processes and all artefacts

4 Specification of the Dependency Analysis with SPEM

4.1 Elementary Dependency Analysis

In this Section, we describe how we characterize the elementary dependency between artefacts of a particular portfolio process; what we call the PPn-centric dependency analysis (n is the number of the process portfolio; see Table 1).

As an example, we will analyse the {PP4} DPMP "Develop Portfolio Management Plan" through their interaction with artefacts depicted in Fig. 2.

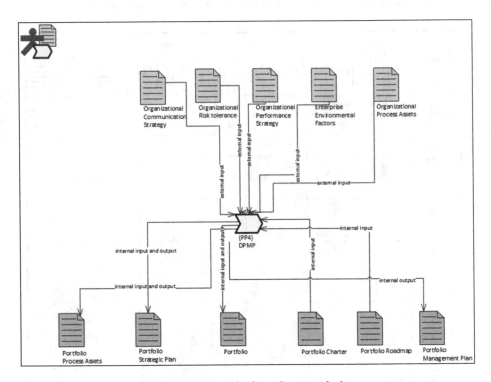

Fig. 2. PP4-centric dependency analysis

The {PP4} DPMP process receives information through the artefacts organizational communication strategy, organizational risk tolerance, organizational performance strategy, enterprise environmental factors, organizational process assets, portfolio charter, portfolio roadmap, and sends information to the portfolio management plan. The following artefacts are input and output of {PP4} DPMP: portfolio process assets and portfolio strategic plan, as during this process ({PP4} DPMP) sometimes is necessary to conduct updates in these particular artefacts. All processes in the depicted graph are positioned in the respective process group lane (as an example, the PP4 {DPMP} is located in the lane of the *Defining* process group).

Elementary dependencies between artefacts are perfectly identified in the portfolio management standard from PMI. However, the overview of all PfM artefacts organized by process groups is not easily perceived. A Process Group includes the constituent PfM processes that are linked to the respective inputs and outputs (artefacts and processes), where the result or outcome of one process becomes the input to another. The Process Groups should not be thought of as PfM phases [20]. This is why our systematic analysis is applied to highlight all the detailed overall dependencies between the complete set of portfolio artefacts.

For the mapping of dependencies between PfM processes and artefacts was used SPEM version 2.0, which is an Object Management Group Standard and is based on a metamodel containing three main elements: activity, work product and process role [23]. SPEM2.0 is the standard dedicated to software process modelling. It aims at providing organizations with means to define a conceptual framework offering the necessary concepts for modelling, interchanging, documenting, managing and presenting their development methods and processes [23].

4.2   Process Group Centric Dependency Analysis

The objective of centric dependency analysis is to focus on the dependencies between artefacts and portfolio processes related to a specific process group. For this purpose, three additional models have been created. They are called *PG-n Centric Dependency Analysis Model* (where *n* corresponds to the process group under study, 1 – *defining*, 2 – *aligning* and 3- *authorizing and controlling*).

Figures 3, 4 and 5 present, respectively, the PG-1, PG-2 and PG-3 Centric Dependency Analysis Model. As an example, the construction of the PG-1 Centric Dependency Analysis Model uses the information of the first 8 rows of the global matrix (Table 3) that correspond to the *defining* process group.

To better understand the creation of the PG-1 model, the {PP1} Develop Portfolio Strategic Plan, {PP2} Develop Portfolio Charter and {PP7} Develop Portfolio Communication Management Plan are analysed as an example. To represent in the model the dependencies faced by the {PP1} DPSP process with the artefacts we must parse the matrix row that corresponds to {PP1} DPSP as shown in Table 1. This process presents a considerable number of dependencies from organizational: organizational strategy and objectives, organizational communication strategy, organizational risk tolerance, organizational performance strategy, enterprise environmental factors, organizational process assets, inventory of work, portfolio process assets, portfolio strategic plan and portfolio. The artefacts in red tone are "Enterprise Documents" category, in light grey tone is "Portfolio Documents" category and in dark grey tone are "Portfolio Reports" category.

The {PP1} DPSP has a high dependency in external artefacts ("Enterprise Documents" category), artefacts which are developed out of the PfM process. The dependency on external artefacts ("Enterprise Documents" category) for the execution of {PP1} DPSP may create risks for the performance of this process.

The {PP2} DPC is only dependent on the external artefact "Enterprise Environmental Factors," and receives information already created by {PP1} DPSP, the

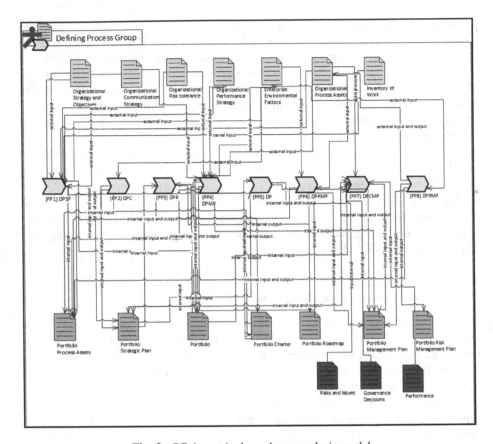

Fig. 3. PG-1 centric dependency analysis model

"Portfolio strategic plan" and "Process Portfolio Assets" artefacts. The artefact generated for {PP2} DPC is "Portfolio charter".

The {PP7} DPCMP is the only process, for *defining* process group, which has as input artefact, "portfolio reports" category, namely, "risks and issues", "governance decisions" and "performance" reports.

Within the context of the "aligning" process group, PG-2 Centric Dependency Analysis Model is presented in Fig. 4. The model emphasizes the fact that the aligning process group receives more information from the "Portfolio Documents" category and produces more outputs for the "portfolio reports" category, it is concluded that the *"aligning"* process group is the process group that is already implemented in monitoring the portfolio, with few dependencies there are organizational artefacts, more focused on PfM, with develop of PfM documents and control reports for the organization.

From the {PP 10} OP process until the {P13} MPI process there are many inputs from artefacts of the "Portfolio Report" category and also outputs to the "Portfolio Documents" and "Portfolio Report" categories.

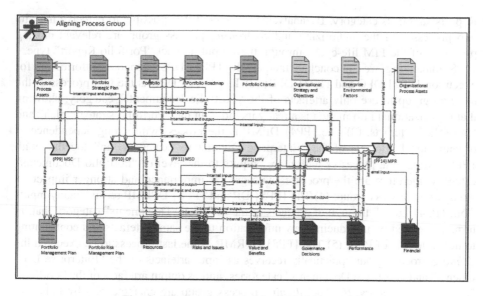

Fig. 4. PG-2 centric dependency analysis model

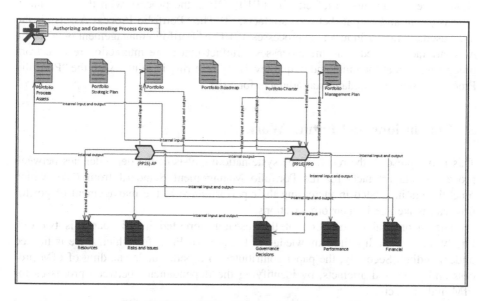

Fig. 5. PG-3 centric dependency analysis model

Figure 5 shows the PG-3 centric dependency analysis model that supports the dependency analysis of the only two existing processes within the *authorizing and controlling* process group: the {PP15} AP and the {PP16} PPO. These two processes are mainly recipients of information of the "Portfolio Documents" and "Portfolio

Reports" artefacts category. By analysing the model it is possible to perceive that the two processes of the authorizing and controlling process group are relevant closing processes of the PfM life-cycle, through the output artefact "Portfolio Report" type.

Summarizing, we can conclude that: (1) the {PP1} DPSP generates information for execution {PP2} DPC and {PP3} DPR; (2) The {PP3} DPR is the first process of the *defining* group to use only artefacts of the "Portfolio Documents" category, showing that organizational information is already included in the "Portfolio strategic plan" and "portfolio" artefacts; (3) The {PP4} DPMP is the process with strong dependence of organizational artefacts of the "Enterprise Documents" category, and together with {PP5} DP are the processes with more outputs to the level of "Portfolio Documents" category, therefore are the processes with greater importance and stronger impact on the *defining* process group; (4) The {PP5} DP and {PP6} DPPMP receive many inputs from {PP4} DPMP through of artefacts of the "Portfolio Documents" category that, in turn, are refined by introducing new information to the same artefacts and contributing to new artefacts of PfM; (5) The {PP8} DPRMP as the last process to be executed the *defining* process group, practically receives as input artefacts of the "Enterprise Documents" and "Portfolio Documents" categories, and as output artefacts of the "Portfolio Documents" category; (6) The *aligning* process group are characterized by failure to use of "Enterprise Documents" artefacts, except the {PP14} MPR, which as well as receiving as input artefact an "Enterprise Documents" artefact, also contributes to an "Enterprise Documents" artefact; (7) {PP10} OP is the process with the most interactions (input and output) between artefacts; (8) The "Portfolio Process Assets" is the most used artefact as input in the processes; (9) The "Portfolio management plan" is the most artefact updated from the processes (artefact that more interaction receive from processes, both at the input and output level), by referring in jointly with the "Portfolio Process Assets" as fundamental artefacts for PfM.

5 Conclusions and Future Work

This paper presents the result of the systematic analysis of the dependencies between processes and artefacts for the Portfolio Management Standard from PMI, which practitioners interested in increasing their performance in the management of portfolios, can make use in their organizations.

The theoretical contribution of the research reported in this paper is twofold. Firstly, this research builds knowledge in the area of PfM, for which there is limited understanding. Secondly, the paper contributes to a better understanding of PfM process and generated artefacts, by identifying the dependencies between processes for PfM and artefacts.

In software development companies, the {PP4} DPMP process, with a strong dependency in organizational artefacts, is particularly important in order to establish the project requirements boundaries. Requirements definition in software projects is often very complex, namely, because of the high number of stakeholders involved and the complexity of the scope definition. The implementation of the {PP16} PPO process, which receives inputs mainly through internal artefacts, needs to take into account the different approaches to managing software projects. In software development companies it is common to coexist more traditional approaches and more agile approaches for managing different types of software projects, which brings many implications on how to monitor the portfolio to ensure alignment with the organization's strategy and objectives.

Moreover, through of the "Process Portfolio Assets", "Portfolio Management Plan" and "Portfolio" artefacts, it is verified the need for inputs of the artefacts generated from the management of software development projects, because of the particularity of the development process (agile or waterfall) and outputs generated by the software project, whose goal is to enrich the "Portfolio" artefact with characteristics and criteria of software projects.

After thorough knowledge of the dependencies between PfM process and artefacts, future work will be to compare this study of PfM process and artefacts from PMI with a framework created specifically for the software area from the Office of Government Commerce [24] to understand the processes or artefacts that are might missing, and which processes that might be adapted to ensure that the PfM is suitable to the context of software development organizations. In order, to propose a PfM model for software development projects with customized processes and artefacts for software area, based on these two authoritative references in literature. The proposed PfM model will be later implemented in a case study of a portfolio management of IT projects in the context of an R&D organization.

Acknowledgements. This work has been supported by COMPETE: POCI-01-0145-FEDE R-007043 and FCT – Fundação para a Ciência e Tecnologia within the Project Scope: UID/CEC/00319/2013, and project: AICEP-PIN- iFACTORY-P1013.

References

1. Ruhe, G.: Software engineering decision support – a new paradigm for learning software organizations. In: Henninger, S., Maurer, F. (eds.) LSO 2003. LNCS, vol. 2640, pp. 104–113. Springer, Heidelberg (2003)
2. Cobbold, I., Lawrie, G.: Why do only one third of UK companies realise significant strategic success? 2GC Working Paper: Realising Significant Strategic Success (2001)
3. Moore, S.: Strategic Project Portfolio Management: Enabling a Productive Organization. Wiley.com (2010)
4. Andersen, E.S., Jessen, S.A.: Project maturity in organisations. Int. J. Proj. Manag. **21**, 457–461 (2003)
5. Gaddis, P.O.: The Project Manager. Harvard University, Boston (1959)
6. Morris, P.W.G.: The Management of Projects. Thomas Telford, London (1997)
7. Hodgson, D.: Disciplining the professional: the case of project management. J. Manag. Stud. **39**, 803–821 (2002)
8. Shenhar, A.J.: One size does not fit all projects: exploring classical contingency domains. Manag. Sci. **47**, 394–414 (2001)
9. Pellegrinelli, S.: Programme management: organising project-based change. Int. J. Proj. Manag. **15**, 141–149 (1997)
10. Archer, N.P., Ghasemzadeh, F.: An integrated framework for project portfolio selection. Int. J. Proj. Manag. **17**, 207–216 (1999)

11. Wikström, K., Artto, K., Kujala, J., Söderlund, J.: Business models in project business. Int. J. Proj. Manag. **28**, 832–841 (2010)
12. Chin, G.: Agile Project Management: How to Succeed in the Face of Changing Project Requirements. AMACOM Division of American Management Association, New York (2004)
13. Shenhar, A.J., Dvir, D.: Project management research-the challenge and opportunity. Proj. Manag. J. **38**, 93 (2007)
14. Hobday, M.: Product complexity, innovation and industrial organisation. Res. Policy **26**, 689–710 (1998)
15. Hobday, M.: The project-based organisation: an ideal form for managing complex products and systems? Res. Policy **29**, 871–893 (2000)
16. Cleland, D.I.: The strategic context of projects. In: Project Portfolio Management: Selecting and Prioritizing Projects for Competitive Advantage. Center for Business Practices, West Chester, PA (1999)
17. Dye, L.D., Pennypacker, J.S.: Project Portfolio Management: Selecting and Prioritizing Projects for Competitive Advantage. Center for Business Practices, West Chester (1999)
18. Meskendahl, S.: The influence of business strategy on project portfolio management and its success a conceptual framework. Int. J. Proj. Manag. **28**, 807–817 (2010)
19. Cooper, R., Edgett, S., Kleinschmidt, E.: Portfolio management for new product development: results of an industry practices study. R&D Manag. **31**, 361–380 (2001)
20. Project Management Institute (PMI): The Standard for Portfolio Management. Project Management Institute, Newtown Square (2013)
21. Reyck, B.De, Grushka-Cockayne, Y., Lockett, M., Calderini, S.R., Moura, M., Sloper, A.: The impact of project portfolio management on information technology projects. Int. J. Proj. Manag. **23**, 524–537 (2005)
22. Yu, S., Wang, J., Guo, N.: The application of project portfolio management in the government investment projects. In: International Seminar on Business and Information Management, 2008, ISBIM 2008, pp. 513–516 (2008)
23. Object Management Group (OMG), Inc.: Software Process Engineering Metamodel (SPEM) 2.0
24. OGC of G.C.: MoP™ Management of Portfolios, London (2011)

Solving Problems During an Enterprise System Adoption: Does Employees' Age Matter?

Ewa Soja[1(✉)], Piotr Soja[2], and Grażyna Paliwoda-Pękosz[2]

[1] Department of Demography, Cracow University of Economics, Kraków, Poland
Ewa.Soja@uek.krakow.pl
[2] Department of Computer Science, Cracow University of Economics, Kraków, Poland
{Piotr.Soja,Grazyna.Paliwoda-Pekosz}@uek.krakow.pl

Abstract. The current study aims at investigating the role of employees' age in the perception of problems and related solutions during an enterprise system (ES) implementation. On the basis of empirical data gathered from Polish ES practitioners and following grounded theory approach, the taxonomies of problems and solutions to these problems have been developed. Next, an analysis into the differences of problem and solution perceptions depending on respondents age has been conducted. The age-based analysis illustrated the need for cooperation between the youngest and the oldest employees in order to work out effective solutions. The main findings suggest that older employees are able to accurately indicate general problems, while younger workers may work out detailed and effective solutions to these problems. The results also suggest that the middle-aged employees have the potential to be the driving force of the implementation project.

Keywords: Enterprise systems · Adoption · Problems · Solutions · Labor force age · Ageing · Poland

1 Introduction

Enterprise systems (ES) are very complex IT-related systems that support the management and integration of the whole company and offer inter-organizational integration with company's clients and suppliers [34]. ES implementations may bring the adopting companies a number of benefits (e.g. [7]). However, the implementation of ES systems is a challenge to an organization, since during this process a considerable variety of problems tend to appear that need to be addressed. The awareness of these problems may allow the practitioners to take remedial measures in order to prevent difficulties to occur. Therefore, investigating difficulties and their solutions during ES adoption and use appears an important and promising research topic.

ES adoptions involve multiple stakeholders both from within the company and external organizations [21]. The complexity of the ES implementation resulting from the advanced technology and interpersonal relationships [4] requires different skills and competences from employees, whose work capacity may depend on age [11, 12, 19]. In the case of older employees, soft (interpersonal) skills grow, but also attitudes toward

S. Wrycza (Ed.): SIGSAND/PLAIS 2016, LNBIP 264, pp. 131–143, 2016.
DOI: 10.1007/978-3-319-46642-2_9

computers tend to be more negative and technology anxiety increases, whereas younger employees tend to reveal more willingness to changes and to learn new skills and to adapt to new technologies (e.g. [11, 35]). Employers tend to associate an ageing staff with a higher knowledge base, but also with higher costs and lower productivity levels (e.g. [8, 26, 33]).

In view of widely reported issue of work force ageing we would like to investigate whether employees' age matters in the perception of problems and related solutions during ES implementation. Specifically, we would like to answer the following research questions:

1. What problems and solutions to the problems were encountered during ES adoption?
2. Did employees' age play any role in an attitude to solving the problems?

The paper is organized as follows. In the next section we present research background concerning implications of ageing and problems and solutions that might occur during ES adoption and use. Next, we describe our research method, which is followed by the presentation of results. We then discuss our findings, explain implications, and close the study with concluding remarks.

2   Research Background

Demographers foresee that population ageing is inevitable and will be deepening in the future. Decrease in fertility and its values remaining below the replacement level lead to the decreasing number of people in younger age groups. At the same time, there are gains in life expectancy related to decrease in mortality. This situation results in a change in the structure of the population in developed countries (e.g. [3, 17, 22, 23]).

According to demographic projections ([32], medium scenario), the percentage of people at age 65 and above will increase and the percentage of population aged 0–19 will decrease. The middle group in age 20–64 is of special importance as it defines the potential labor force. The share of potential working age population will decrease from about 62 % in 2015 to 53 % in 2045 (decline by 60 784 thousands) in Europe and respectively in Poland from about 64 % to 56 % (decline by 3 637 thousands). At the same time, the population in age 20–64 years will gradually age. Median age in this group will rise from 42.8 in 2015 to 43.3 years in 2045 in Europe and respectively in Poland from 41.8 to 46.4 years.

As a result, adapting to progressive population ageing will be the most important challenge for companies (e.g. [5, 18]). The organizations will have to cope with a wide range of difficulties in the future and their success depends on abilities to adjust to demands of ageing societies. In particular, older employees have to adapt to the rapid changes in the contemporary world and the widespread use of information and communications technology (ICT). They have to deal with technology and ICT systems being implemented and operating in the company, such as enterprise systems, which are widely used by various organizations.

In the context of an organization's adjustment to demographic changes, it is important to take into consideration that work capacity changes with age (e.g. [2, 8, 11, 30]). Both researchers and practitioners indicate that some abilities to perform different tasks tend to deteriorate with age (we perceive them as the weak points of the older workers), while other elements are likely to improve (the strong points of the older workers). The most often indicated weak points include: decline in physical abilities, decreased perception and work pace, limited resistance to physical and psychological burdens, lower new technology skills, and lower flexibility as compared to younger workers (e.g. related to technological changes). The strong points involve: know-how and experience, ability to comprehend the whole, awareness of one's own limitations and strong points, greater "soft skills" (e.g. interpersonal skills), reason in solving problems and dealing with co-workers and clients, stronger commitment to work, and loyalty and faithfulness to the employer [11, 19, 26, 33].

The process of ES implementation in a company is very complex, risky, and related to numerous problems and barriers. These impediments might refer to people involved in and affected by the project, the implementation process run, and technology being used. The people-related problems might refer to lack of users' acceptance and involvement, inadequate knowledge of participants, and people's resistance to changes and the new system. Difficulties related to an implementation process include inadequate provider support, poor company's organization and resources, problems with business process reengineering, time over-run, and difficulties with trainings. The technology-related problems boil down to system drawbacks and inadequate infrastructure (e.g. [13–15, 20]).

The variety of impediments experienced by ES adoption projects suggests a vital need to look for recommendations how to improve ES implementations and overcome the problems being encountered. In doing so, there is a need to take into consideration the perspective of various stakeholders of ES adoptions. Although such an approach was employed by some prior research (e.g. [13, 25, 28]), to the best of our knowledge, there is a gap in ES research related to the lack of an in-depth examination of employees' age and demographic background. Such an investigation is, in our opinion, interesting and worth studying since many ES adoption considerations are people-related and also because older employees are more and more significant employee group in companies due to labor force ageing.

3   Research Method

In order to answer our research questions we turned to practitioners to investigate their viewpoints about problems and solutions encountered during ES implementation. In doing so, we applied a qualitative research approach based on grounded theory [6, 9, 10]. The respondents were asked to answer open-ended questions concerning difficulties during ES adoption and use and solutions that were undertaken to overcome these difficulties.

In consequence of the data gathering process, respondent opinions expressed in natural language have been collected. Following the grounded theory approach, we then performed the process of open and axial coding [9], separately for problems and solutions. In the first step we analyzed and compared the respondent opinions in search of similarities and differences. Consequently, the respondent statements were given conceptual labels and categories and subcategories were created. Next, the process of axial coding was performed, during which the relationships between categories and subcategories which emerged during the process of open coding were tested against data and verified. As a result, the categorizations of the reported problems and solutions were worked out and agreed upon by the authors.

The next step of the data analysis process was the age-related analysis. In labor market-related research chronological (demographic) age is most often used and enables us to define the potential of an individual (e.g. [1, 31]). According to Ilmarinen, functional capacities, mainly physical, have declining trend after the age of 30 years, and the trend can become critical after the next 15–20 years if the physical demands of work do not decline. On the other hand, workers' perceptions of their ability to work indicate that some of them reach their peak before the age of 50 years, and five years later about 15–25 % report that they have a poor ability to work, mainly those workers in physically demanding jobs but also those in some mentally demanding positions [11]. Employers most often define older employees as people older than 45–50 years (e.g. [9, 26, 31]). In the comparative analysis related to the perception of younger and older employees by the employers in 8 European countries, Conen et al. [8] defined older workers as people at age 50 years and more and younger workers as those not older than 35 years. Therefore, drawing from prior studies we adopted 50 years as the starting age for the definition of the older employees. We finally divided our respondents into three age groups: the younger (less than 35 years old), the middle-aged (between 35 and 50), and the older (50+). During the age-related analysis, we analyzed the distribution of investigated categories across the defined age ranges. In the final step of the age-related investigation we analyzed the distribution of solution categories across the indicated problems taking into consideration respondent's age.

As a result of the data gathering process, 185 respondents from 157 Polish companies expressed their opinions about problems and solutions to these problems experienced during ES adoption and use. The inquired respondents represented different organizational positions and played various roles during the implementation process. 102 respondents (55 %) belonged to the group "the younger", the middle-aged group consisted of 59 respondents (32 %), and the older group was represented by 24 people (13 %).

4   Data Analysis and Results

On the basis of the empirical data analysis we identified three problem categories perceived by respondents during ES implementation. These categories cover a group of issues of broadly defined implementation process (category Process), a group of issues related to technology (category Technology), and a group of issues relating generally to the attitudes and skills of employees (category People).

In the case of perceived solutions we distinguished eight categories (System, Training, Employees, Implementation process, Infrastructure, Unsolved, Company, and Provider). A relatively large number of the categories are caused by very detailed solutions reported by respondents that may be related to different problem groups.

In discussing separately the results of problems and solutions categorization we took into account their distribution according to respondents' age (Tables 1 and 2). The bullets in the tables were defined on the basis of the percentage of responses provided by the respondents from an individual age group declaring a given problem or solution.

Table 1. Problems by respondent age

Problem category \ Age group	Younger	Middle-aged	Older
Process			
system replacement	◕	◔	
project definition	◑	◑	◔
company's condition and organization	◔	◑	◕
training	◔	◕	◕
provider	◕	◕	◕
schedule	◕	◕	◔
project management	◕	◕	
company's finance	◕	◕	◕
Technology			
system quality	●	●	●
system fit to company's needs	◕	◔	◔
infrastructure	◑	◑	◕
People			
attitudes	◕	◔	●
competence	◑	◕	◕
adjustment and habits	◕	◕	
employees	◕	◕	◕
management personnel	◕	◕	

4.1 Perceived Problems

The first category called Process contains eight problem subcategories. This is the most numerous problem category, including 38 % of all reported problems. The most important problems in this category are the barriers associated with the system replacement (e.g. problems with data import, a smooth transition from the legacy systems), the project definition (e.g. the lack of needs' analysis, faulty planning), company's condition and organization (e.g. problems with carrying out changes) and training (e.g. lack of training, time and quality of training). Less frequently were reported problems related to the provider (e.g. cooperation with and expertise of consultants), schedule (e.g. delays,

Table 2. Solutions during ES adoption by respondent age

Solution category \ Age group	Younger	Middle-aged	Older
System			
functionality and flexibility	●	◕	◑
adjustment to company's needs	◕	◑	◕
database	◕	◑	◑
bug fixing	◑	◑	
testing	◔	◔	
Training			
training/self-study	●	●	●
additional	◕	◑	◑
explaining benefits	◔	◑	
continuous	◔	◔	◑
trainers' training	◔	◔	◑
time for training	◔		
Employees			
cooperation and involvement	◑	◑	◕
project team	◔	◕	◑
incentive system	◑	◔	◑
top management involvement	◑	◔	◔
informing	◑	◔	
Implementation process			
analysis	◑	◑	
schedule	◔	◑	●
methodology	◔	◑	
goal definition	◔	◔	
external partner	◔	◔	
Infrastructure			
equipment modernization and purchase	◑	◕	◕
network modernization	◑	◕	◑
license purchase	◔		
Unsolved			
unsolved	◕	◑	◑
problem acceptance	◔		◔
Company			
reorganization	◑	◕	◑
new and changed jobs	◔		◔
finance	◔		◔
alternative solutions		◔	◔
Provider			
cooperation	◑	◔	◑
consultants	◔	◔	◑
agreement	◔	◔	

meeting deadlines), project management (e.g. change of requirements, communication), and company's finance.

In general, perceptions of problems at the Process category level slightly decrease with respondents' age. However, the essential differences are visible at the level of the subcategories. The older do not notice at all problems associated with the system replacement and project management. On the other hand, to a greater extent than the younger employees they perceive problems with training and schedule. It should also be noted that the middle-aged respondents hardly pay any attention to the problems related to the training.

The second category called Technology contains three problem subcategories. It encompasses 36 % of all reported problems. The greatest number of problems in this category concerns system quality (e.g. system errors, problems with the communication between modules and system efficiency). Then, problems with system fit to company's need were reported. They were next followed by somewhat fewer indications of problems with infrastructure (e.g. network condition and problems with hardware).

Problems belonging to the Technology category are the most emphasized by the youngest, which is visible in the frequency of reported problems connected with system fit to company's needs. The older more often than the others pay attention to problems with hardware. The perception of problems related to the system quality was at the same level in all age groups. However, the older tend to describe problems in more general terms whereas the younger and the middle-aged used a more specialized digital technology vocabulary.

The last category called People mainly includes issues relating to the attitudes and competencies of employees involved in the implementation process (24 % of all reported problems). The most frequently perceived problems from this category are those connected with employees' reluctance towards the new system, lack of system acceptance, resistance to and fear of changes, shortage of skills in system operating and ICT literacy, and lack of specialist knowledge and experience.

The category People is perceived by the respondents from each age group at the similar level. However, differences occurred within the subcategories. The older perceived to the greatest extent problems associated with attitudes, whereas problems with competence are more likely to be indicated by the younger and the middle-aged respondents.

4.2 Perceived Solutions

Solutions belonging to the categories System and Training are among the most frequently reported by the respondents (24 %, 22 %). The suggested solutions in the System category encompass mainly issues concerning the system functionality and flexibility (e.g. configuration improvement, installation of new modules, the possibility of continuous update), adjustment to company's needs (e.g. customization, modifications and improvements), database optimization, and data migration. The category Training includes various types of training (general, additional, continuous), as well as specific ways of training (e.g. training of trainers, self-studying).

Perceptions of solutions within the category System decrease with age. This is particularly illustrated by the differences between the youngest respondents and the other two age groups. The youngest are much more likely to point to the solutions related to advanced information technology than other respondents. Moreover, the older describe solutions in more general terms, whereas the youngest tend to use more specialized vocabulary, which was also observed in reported problems from the Technology category. Solutions concerning training are slightly more often indicated by the youngest and the oldest respondents. Differences are strongly visible within the subcategories. The older strongly emphasize the importance of continuous training and training of the trainers. In contrast, only younger respondents (e.g. from the middle-aged and younger age groups) indicate the importance of training in the context of explaining the implementation benefits.

The second group of solution categories in terms of the intensity of occurrences includes three categories: Employees, Implementation process, and Infrastructure (15 %, 11 %, 11 %). The solution category Employees includes problems related to increasing employees' cooperation and involvement, selection of a suitable project team, employing an incentive system, and informing employees about the benefits of the ES implementation. In the category Implementation process the most important solutions include: conducting various analyses, introducing changes in the schedule (e.g. extending project duration, fine-tuning plans), and employing an appropriate implementation methodology (e.g. phased or parallel approach). Solutions in the Infrastructure category boil down to the modernization of network and computer equipment.

Solutions from the Employees category are perceived by the older to a slightly greater extent as compared to the other age groups. Greater differences are visible inside the category. In particular, the older emphasize the importance of the cooperation, involvement, and incentive system. For the middle-aged group the most important is an improvement in the implementation team as well as employees' involvement. The younger, in relation to the others, more strongly emphasize the importance of the top management involvement and informing employees about the benefits from the implemented system. The middle-aged respondents more often than the others reported solutions related to the Implementation process in the majority of sub-categories. In this category, the older perceived only solutions related to the schedule. In the case of the category Infrastructure, the solution perceptions do not differ with respect to respondents' age. However, the older strongly perceived more basic solutions, whereas the younger suggested solutions requiring greater awareness of information technology.

Solutions belonging to Company and Provider categories are among the least frequently reported issues (6 % and 5 % respectively). The most important solutions are associated with the reorganization of company activities, increased cooperation with the provider, and acquiring additional or more competent consultants. In general, the older respondents attach the strongest importance to solutions belonging to the Company and Provider categories. These solutions concern activities that do not require advanced knowledge of computer technology, but involve more experience, comprehensive knowledge about company, and interpersonal skills.

The solution categories also include the category named Unsolved which encompasses issues left unresolved or problems to be waited out (acceptance of the problem). Lack of solutions was noticed mainly by the younger, and then by the older respondents.

5   Discussion of Findings and Implications

On the basis of the age-based analysis of the perceptions of problem and solution categories, the following conclusions may be drawn (see Table 3):

1. Solutions perceived in the context of problems with implementation process (i.e. problem category Process) seem the most diversified as regards to the respondent age group. The most frequently reported solutions in this category, in every age group, belong to different categories:

    * The youngest respondents prefer solutions concerning System (improvement of functionality and flexibility and better adjustment to company needs), which can be explained by the young employees' experience and competence in IT.
    * The middle-aged point out solutions from Implementation process category (more analysis and proper implementation methodology). It seems that this group of respondents is more focused on actions directly concentrated on implementation. It appears that the middle-aged combine IT- and BPR-related knowledge with previously gained experience.
    * The older attach the greatest importance to solutions belonging to the Employees category (greater cooperation and involvement, adequate implementation team, and incentive system). It seems that this might be explained by their long professional experience (positive and negative experience with cooperation), as well as a greater fear of changes (the importance of support in difficult situations).

2. In the case of the most strongly perceived solutions regarding problems from the Technology category, there is a difference between younger (the younger and middle-aged groups) and the oldest respondents (the older group). Younger respondents indicate firstly solutions belonging to the System category, while older respondents attach the same importance to solutions related to System and Infrastructure. It seems that this is due to the fact that the older perceive solutions from these categories on the basis of their rather rudimentary IT knowledge (e.g. adaptation to the needs, purchase of equipment); while the younger notice a greater variety of detailed system solutions that require advanced IT knowledge.

3. In the case of problems with people the most strongly perceived solutions are related to trainings. However, it should be noted that the older notice mainly problems concerning employees' attitudes, whereas the younger notice problems with both attitudes and lack of competence. Perhaps younger respondents, while working with older employees, notice their shortcomings in the IT domain (competence) and see their reluctance to change (attitudes). The older also perceive and report problems concerning attitudes. However, they perceive lack of IT skills as more of a problem with the training (as part of the implementation process). Therefore, it appears that in their opinions the origin of this problem is attributable to the company, not the employee. Problems with employees' attitudes sometimes boil down to resistance,

which might occur when the expected consequences of the project are threatening [16]. To address such a problem special care should be taken in the case of older employees who, due to their limited IT skills, might especially anticipate unfavorable results of the implementation project.

Table 3. Solutions to problems during ES adoption by respondent age

Solution category	People			Technology			Process		
	Younger	Middle-aged	Older	Younger	Middle-aged	Older	Younger	Middle-aged	Older
System	◔			●	●	◕	◕	◑	◑
Training	●	●	●	◔	◔	◔	◑	◔	◑
Employees	◑	◑	◔	◔		◔	◑	◑	●
Implementation process	◔	◔	◔	◔	◔		◑	●	◑
Infrastructure				◕	◕	◕	◔		
Unsolved	◔		◔	◑	◔	◔	◔	◔	
Company	◔	◔		◔	◔	◑	◔	◑	◔
Provider	◔	◔	◔	◔	◔	◔	◔	◔	◑

In previous studies the importance of implementation team composition for the quality of implementation was emphasized (e.g. [27]). In connection with inevitable labor force ageing, research into the team composition in the context of age becomes of utmost importance. In addition, in light of the constant progress and knowledge and technology becoming obsolete, it becomes necessary to develop effective ways of retraining workers and fostering mutual cooperation among them.

Relationships between perceived problems and solutions and the respondents' age allow us to point out some opportunities for cooperation between the youngest and oldest employees. The basis for such cooperation covers mainly the area of widely understood customization (the company's needs, adaptation to needs) and engages the strengths of both older and younger workers. The older, possessing profound general knowledge and experience can accurately indicate the important needs of the enterprise, while the younger, revealing up-to-date knowledge of IT, may indicate more detailed, effective solutions to these problems.

The middle-aged have the potential to be the driving force of the implementation process, as they are appropriately educated about modern management techniques and possess substantial experience. Besides, they are oriented towards activities related to the implementation process which might be due to their accumulated experience and more up-to-date IT knowledge.

The problem of effective training of the elderly is associated with proper support. Prior studies show that an important determinant of high satisfaction with work is related to support in difficult situations (e.g. [24]). In this context, it seems that the middle-aged group could offer good support for the elderly. However, the interrelations between these two employee groups should be better investigated. It is not clear whether the middle-aged actually understand the problems of the elderly. On the one hand they indicate training as a solution to problems with employees' competences and perceive the need of making them aware of the benefits of ES implementation. However, on the other hand, they do not see the problem with training during the implementation. In order to better understand these interrelations further research should be conducted into a mutual trust and competition among employees and the role of their job positions. The notion of trust is especially important in the context of the current study research setting, i.e. Poland, as prior research suggests low level of trust in relationships in such transition economies [29].

The study's results provide valuable insights into an ES implementation process that can result in the following implications for practice:

- Employers should benefit from diversified work force: the experience of older employees having long work experience can help them to foresee future problems, whereas the potential of up-to-date knowledge and skills of younger employees might be used to solve technical problems connected with new technology.
- Companies should elaborate a systematic training schedule for middle-aged and older employees who need to update their professional knowledge and acquire skills needed to reap the benefits from technological progress.
- Special attention should be paid to creating a favorable cooperative environment that enables knowledge and experience transfer between different age groups of employees. In such an environment younger employees can learn from older coworkers and vice versa.
- Older consultants might be especially useful in projects that involve older employees from an adopter company since they possess good communications skills and can understand better older employees. This situation will occur more often in view of ageing labor force.

6 Conclusion

The current study examined the role of employee age in the perception of problems and solutions to problems during an enterprise system implementation and use. The study builds on the experience of ES practitioners from Poland. Using data-driven approach, the discovered problems were divided into three main categories: People, Process, and Technology. Solutions to the problems, in turn, were categorized into eight main categories: System, Training, Employees, Implementation process, Infrastructure, Unsolved, Company, and Provider. In order to investigate the role of respondent age in barrier perception, we identified the following age groups: the young, the middle-aged, and the older. The results of the analysis suggest that during ES implementation both parties involved, i.e. adopter and provider, should take into consideration employees' age structure. The findings indicate that perceived problems and solutions are related to employees' age. Older employees, thanks to their experience, awareness of one's own limitations and strong points, and comprehensive knowledge about the company, especially point to people-related problems and related solutions (e.g. training, cooperation, involvement). They are also capable of perceiving some other general and significant problems occurring during ES implementations. The youngest employees emphasize the importance of problems and solutions in the context of their strong points associated with ICT-related skills and knowledge. Solutions perceived by them seem more detailed and adjusted to specific problems. For the middle-aged employees, possessing both substantial job experience and up-to-date ICT- and BPR-related knowledge, issues directly related to an implementation process (analysis, implementation methodology) appear the most significant. They also perceive people-related problems from the perspective of implementation project needs (project team, competence).

Acknowledgments. This research has been financed by the funds granted to the Faculty of Management, Cracow University of Economics, Poland, within the subsidy for maintaining research potential.

References

1. Ashon, K., Bass, M.: Past it at 40? The Policy Press, Bristol (2002)
2. Baltes, P., Staudinger, U., Lindenberger, U.: Lifespan psychology: theory and application to intellectual functioning. Annu. Rev. Psychol. **50**, 471–507 (1999)
3. Basten, S., Lutz, W., Scherbov, S.: Very long range global population scenarios to 2300 and the implications of sustained low fertility. Demographic Res. **28**(39), 1145–1166 (2013)
4. Bingi, P., Sharma, M.K., Godla, J.K.: Critical issues affecting an ERP implementation. Inf. Syst. Manag. **16**(3), 7–14 (1999)
5. Boersch-Supan, A.: The impact of global ageing on labour, product and capital markets. In: Cabrera, M., Malanowski, N. (eds.) Information and Communication Technologies for Active Ageing, pp. 7–34. IOS Press, Amsterdam (2008)
6. Charmaz, K.: Constructing Grounded Theory. A Practical Guide Through Qualitative Analysis. Sage, London (2006)
7. Chou, S.-W., Chang, Y.-C.: The implementation factors that influence the ERP (enterprise resource planning) benefits. Decis. Support Syst. **46**, 149–157 (2008)
8. Conen, W., van Dalen, H., Henkens, K., Schippers, J.J.: Activating Senior Potential in Ageing Europe: an Employers' Perspective. Netherlands Interdisciplinary Demographic Institute (NIDI), The Hague (2011)
9. Corbin, J., Strauss, A.: Grounded theory research procedures, canons, and evaluative criteria. Qual. Sociol. **13**(1), 3–21 (1990)
10. Glaser, B., Strauss, A.L.: Discovery of Grounded Theory: Strategies for Qualitative Research. Aldine, Chicago (1967)
11. Ilmarinen, J.: Ageing workers. Occup. Environ. Med. **58**, 546–552 (2001)
12. Ilmarinen, J., Tuomi, K.: Past, present and future of work ability. In: Ilmarinen, J., Lehtinen, S. (eds.) Past, Present and Future of Work Ability. People and Work Research Reports 65, pp. 1–25. Finnish Institute of Occupational Health, Helsinki (2004)
13. Kamhawi, E.M.: Enterprise resource-planning systems adoption in Bahrain: motives, benefits, and barriers. J. Enterp. Inf. Manag. **21**(3), 310–334 (2008)
14. Kim, Y., Lee, Z., Gosain, S.: Impediments to successful ERP implementation process. Bus. Process Manag. J. **11**(2), 158–170 (2005)
15. Kumar, V., Maheshwari, B., Kumar, U.: ERP systems implementation: best practices in Canadian government organizations. Gov. Inf. Q. **19**(2), 147–172 (2002)

16. Lapointe, L., Rivard, S.: A multilevel model of resistance to information technology implementation. MIS Q. **29**(3), 461–491 (2005)
17. McMichael, A.J., McKee, M., Shkolnikov, V., Valkonen, T.: Mortality trends and setbacks: global convergence or divergence. The Lancet **363**, 1155–1159 (2004). Public Health
18. McMorrow, K., Roeger, W.: The Economic and Financial Market Consequences of Global Ageing. Springer, Heidelberg (2004)
19. Reday-Mulvey, G.: Working Beyond 60. Key Policies and Practices in Europe. Palgrave Macmillan, London (2005)
20. Saatcioglu, O.Y.: What determines user satisfaction in ERP projects: benefits, barriers or risks? J. Enterp. Inf. Manag. **22**(6), 690–708 (2009)
21. Soh, C., Chua, C.E.H., Singh, H.: Managing diverse stakeholders in enterprise systems projects: a control portfolio approach. J. Inf. Technol. **26**(10), 16–31 (2011)
22. Soja, E.: Konwergencja płodności krajów europejskich. Studia Ekonomiczne: Zeszyty Naukowe Uniwersytetu Ekonomicznego w Katowicach **95**, 13–19 (2011)
23. Soja, E.: Convergence or divergence? Mortality in Central Eastern and Western European Countries. In: Pociecha, J. (ed.) Quantitative Methods for the Analysis of the Economic and Social Consequences of Transition Processes in Central-East European Countries, pp. 232–246. Cracow University of Economics Press, Krakow (2013)
24. Soja, E.: Uwarunkowania satysfakcji zawodowej starszych pracowników w Polsce. Stud. Demograficzne **2**(168), 3–24 (2015)
25. Soja, E., Paliwoda-Pękosz, G., Soja, P.: Perception of difficulties during enterprise system adoption and use: the role of employees age. In: Proceedings of the 10th International Conference Accounting and Management Information Systems AMIS 2015, Bucharest, Romania, 10–11 June, pp. 50–65. The Bucharest University of Economic Studies (2015)
26. Soja, E., Stonawski, M.: Zmiany demograficzne a starsi pracownicy w Polsce z perspektywy podmiotów gospodarczych. In: Kurkiewicz, J. (ed.) Demograficzne uwarunkowania i wybrane społeczno-ekonomiczne konsekwencje starzenia się ludności w krajach europejskich, pp. 173–210. Wydawnictwo Uniwersytetu Ekonomicznego w Krakowie, Kraków (2012)
27. Soja, P.: Building project teams in enterprise system adoption: the need for the incorporation of the project type. In: Wrycza, S. (ed.) SIGSAND/PLAIS 2011. LNBIP, vol. 93, pp. 51–65. Springer, Heidelberg (2011)
28. Soja, P.: A stakeholder analysis of barriers to enterprise system adoption: the case of a transition economy. Inf. Technol. Manag. **16**(3), 253–271 (2015)
29. Soja, P., Cunha, P.R.: ICT in transition economies: narrowing the research gap to developed countries. Inf. Technol. Dev. **21**(3), 323–329 (2015)
30. Stonawski, M.: Kapitał ludzki w warunkach starzenia się ludności a wzrost gospodarczy. Wydawnictwo Uniwersytetu Ekonomicznego w Krakowie, Kraków (2014)
31. Stypińska, J.: Starszy pracownik na rynku pracy w Polsce: 40+? 50+? Czy tylko "plus"? Stud. Socjologiczne **217**(2), 143–165 (2015)
32. United Nations: World Population Prospects: The 2015 Revision. Department of Economic and Social Affairs, Population Division (2015)
33. Van Dalen, H.P., Henkens, K., Schippers, J.: Productivity of older workers: perceptions of employers and employees. Popul. Dev. Rev. **36**(3), 309–330 (2010)
34. Volkoff, O., Strong, D.M., Elmes, M.: Understanding enterprise systems-enabled integration. Eur. J. Inf. Syst. **14**, 110–120 (2005)
35. Wagner, N., Hassanein, K., Head, M.: Computer use by older adults: a multi-disciplinary review. Comput. Hum. Behav. **26**, 870–882 (2010)

Project Management in International IT Ventures – Does the Practice Go Hand in Hand with Theory?

Bartosz Marcinkowski[✉] and Bartłomiej Gawin

Department of Business Informatics, University of Gdansk,
Piaskowa 9, 81-864 Sopot, Poland
{bartosz.marcinkowski,bartlomiej.gawin}@ug.edu.pl

Abstract. IT solutions provide international and global businesses with effective means of coordinating local operations and facilitating flow of essential information and knowledge across national borders. The paper focuses on project management challenges regarding development of proprietary IT solution by a multinational facility management company – SESCOM Group. The goal of the paper is to establish inefficiencies regarding development sub-cycles of the solutions within the Agile Business Process Management Model introduced in SESCOM Group. Research incorporates Participatory Action Research (PAR) approach, providing insight into current situation of the company as depicted by all stakeholders involved in the research process at baseline analysis stage and highlights discrepancies between practice and theory.

Keywords: IT project management · Global information system · Agile · Participatory Action Research

1 Introduction

Information Technology (IT) serves as a vital component for more and more businesses. Information and communication technology prove to have a significant impact on manufacturing enterprises' performance as well as on the service industry (Kiiza and Pederson 2012; Mirbaha 2008; Mohamed and Kaur 2012). IDC forecasts increase in worldwide IT spending from $2.46 trillion in 2015 to more than $2.8 trillion in 2019 – while business classified as medium (100–499 employees) and large (500–999 employees) will see the fastest growth in IT spending, with compound annual growth rate of 4.4 % and 4.8 % respectively (International Data Corporation 2016). According to McKinsey, IT was most effective when tailored to sector-specific business processes, deployed sequentially to build capabilities over time, and co-evolved with managerial and technical innovations incrementally (Farrell et al. 2002).

Information Technologies may be considered a backbone of organization that, owing to their growth, begins to provide services across national borders – acquiring new markets and resources in the process of internationalization and globalization. Multinational enterprises transfer key abilities, resources and skills to foreign organizational units within the same group, while marketing strategies, sale channels and customer cooperation style stay local. Global company treats the whole world as a single market,

S. Wrycza (Ed.): SIGSAND/PLAIS 2016, LNBIP 264, pp. 144–152, 2016.
DOI: 10.1007/978-3-319-46642-2_10

where the operation and marketing strategy becomes single worldwide strategic entity (Tallman and Fladmoe-Lindquist 2002). In both cases, IT is vital to coordinate operations, share information and facilitate the flow of knowledge and expertise exchange across international organizational units as well as support employees as they move back and forth across countries in their work (Trang et al. 2014).

IT project management-oriented research was launched as a joint research initiative together with extensive study regarding transition from domestic into international/ global information systems within Facility Management domain. The domain is represented by SESCOM Group, being a multinational company with headquarters located in Poland and delivering premises maintenance and technical service solutions to customers across many countries in Europe. It was confronting SESCOM's proprietary IT solution named SES Support with project management body of knowledge was the main motivation for the research. The SES Support platform combines functionalities of EPR, CRM and workflow solutions to manage core business processes.

The goal of the paper is to establish inefficiencies regarding SES Platform development sub-cycles within the Agile Business Process Management Model introduced in SESCOM Group in order to develop best practices for requirements elicitation/analysis, Scrum-based methodological improvements as well as system architecture within further research stages. The Agile Business Process Management (ABPM) model (Gawin and Marcinkowski 2014) functions as a general framework for modern company management, clarifying the relations between Deming cycle (Teague 2005; Hammar 2016) and Agile Methods implemented in companies that act in an agile way but are process-oriented in nature – and for which the processes constitute the core business. For SESCOM, adapting the ABPM means perceiving its IT resources as adaptively-improved infrastructure with catalog of functionalities enabling composition of business processes and enables analysis of main factors regarding IT and business mismatch.

After the Introduction, Sect. 2 provides an overview of related work addressing both organizational and technical challenges regarding development of international/global IT solutions. Research design is discussed in Sect. 3, while preliminary results – in Sect. 4. The paper is concluded with a summary and outline of future work.

2   Related Work

Development of IT solutions capable of supporting international/global company in a highly flexible environment invariably involves a number of challenges, in particular when requirement engineering process or development process is distributed (see Fig. 1). Target product itself must as well address cultural and national differences, data collection issues among companies within the group, face issues related to international data flows, and – what is crucial – be delivered fast enough to provide a strategic advantage (Gray 1999). As stated by Akmanligil and Palvia (2004), classifying global system development projects as simply larger versions of their domestic counterparts is an oversimplification. In fact a number of strategies for developing global information systems are discussed in the literature: development with a multinational design team; parallel development; central development; core versus local development; best-in-firm software adoption; outsourced custom development; unmodified package software acquisition; modified package software acquisition as well as joint development with vendor (Janz et al. 2002; Akmanligil and Palvia 2004).

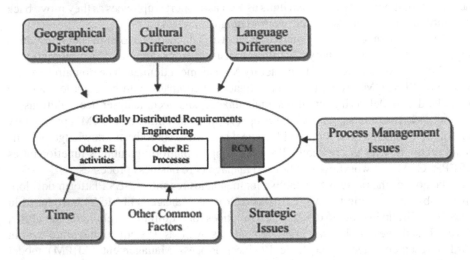

Fig. 1. Factors influencing globally distributed requirements engineering. Source: (Hussain, 2010).

Regardless of strategy adopted, development pace dictated by continuously changing environment and high value of flexibility (as fostered by ABPM model) question the avail of traditional project management approach. Methodologies such as Prince2 (Projects In Controlled Environments), PMBOK (Project Management Body of Knowledge) or Six Sigma rely heavily on waterfall lifecycle, where particular stages – including analysis, design, development, integration, testing and implementation – are realized in sequential manner. Traditional project management approach finds its merits in project that are static in nature (Mikoluk 2013; Lotz 2013); in particular while utilized by large organizations responsible for quality assurance and certification (comp. Fredriksson and Ljung 2011) such as PMI (Project Management Institute) or IPMA (International Project Management Association). On the other hand, challenges related to dealing with only partially discovered and fluctuating requirements, documentation-oriented nature and no built-in support for orchestrating interoperable services contribute to the high share of projects classified as failed (Hoehle and Venkatesh 2015) and favor agile project management approach. In fact, almost 87 % of companies claim that implementing the latter contributes to rising profits (Actuation Consulting 2013). The agile concept assumes that requirement engineering continues through the lifetime of a system (Bernhaupt et al. 2015), thus enabling modifying the requirements of a system under development during the course of a project to consistently reflect the current expectations of the client and users (Chin 2004). Specific methods of agile project management include Adaptive Software Development (ASD), Agile Modeling, Dynamic Systems Development Method (DSDM), Agile Project Management (AgilePM), Extreme Programming (XP), Feature-Driven Development (FDD), Kanban,

Lean Software Development, Crystal family of methodologies and Scrum. Most of the companies that switch to the agile project management choose Scrum (Scrum Alliance 2011), making it the most popular agile project management approach applied for IT projects (Overhage and Schlauderer 2012).

It should be noted that Scrum values interpersonal communication between all team members (Hummel et al. 2015) that often takes shape of daily standups, real-time video, always available phone communication or frequent travels (comp. Lacey 2012). Effective communication is listed as one of the major success factors of system implementation, holding organizational culture together (Vaughan 2001) and – supported by appropriate collaboration and communication tools – helping to limit scope creep (Katcherovski 2010). Unchecked scope creep inevitably causes downstream issues in project cost, time or quality (comp. Kerton 2011), especially taking into account that different companies within the group tend to have conflicting demands regarding IT solutions.

In contrast to functional requirements, non-functional ones were found to be often elicited only by architects themselves in an iterative process with minimum documentation and only partial validation (Ameller et al. 2012). On the other hand, IT projects that applied NFR verification techniques relatively early in development were more successful on average than IT projects that did not apply verification techniques or applied it relatively late in development (Poort et al. 2012). In order to discover nonfunctional requirements not explicitly stated in formal specifications, automated natural language processing may be used (Slankas and Williams 2013).

Flexibility in managing requirements provided by agile project management approach raises the issue of requirement traceability; in particular regarding non-functional requirements (Mirakhorli and Cleland-Huang 2012). As stated in (Gotel and Finklestein 1994), requirements traceability refers to the ability to describe and follow the life of a requirement, in both forwards and backwards direction (i.e. from its origins, through its development and specification, to its subsequent deployment and use, and through all periods of on-going refinement and iteration in any of these phases. Similarly to efficient communication among team members, traceability can be hard to do without proper tools – simple traceability within small IT projects can be reasonably managed with spreadsheets (Kerton 2011), but in larger projects dedicated software provides added value. Depending on the scope of documentation required, modeling capability of the tool may become a factor – both the opinions regarding irrelevance of modelling while following an Agile process (Quatrani 2010) as well as incorporating Agile being the reason itself to shelf standards such as Unified Modelling Language (Verhas 2013) have been challenged.

3   Research Design

Research process carried out involved a number of employees representing different countries, departments and levels of SESCOM Group. Participatory Action Research (PAR) was the research method selected (Baskerville 1999; Eden and Huxham 1996), as it enables solving real-life problems while expanding scientific knowledge and provides one potential method of improving the practical relevance of IS research. 17 separate interview sessions were completed. Qualitative data was gathered. Each of the sessions was about two-hour long and involved tape-recording. Voice source material was transcribed, and target dataset was subsequently subjected to coding using NVivo software (v11) and the further analysis involving seeking common themes. Employees taking part in research represented diverse European countries (i.e. Austria, Czech Republic, Germany, Hungary, Italy, Poland, Romania, Russian Federation and Switzerland) as well as a number of SESCOM departments (i.e. Finance, IT, Logistics, Marketing, Services, Services Management and Technical).

Questionnaire survey was structured appropriately to support two inter-related research tracks: IT project management and transition from domestic into international/global information systems within Facility Management domain. Research plan involved three stages that consequently recognized five PAR-specific research steps, i.e. action planning, action taking, evaluating, learning as well as diagnosis. The stages included:

- Baseline Analysis stage, aimed at understanding the current situation of the company and mapping it in respect of technical and business aspects of business internationalization;
- Global IS Aspects Improvement stage, devoted to planning a common business strategy describing desired state;
- Requirements Specification stage, involving elaborating a target document including recommendations, specifications, best practices as well as implementation plans.

Table 1. Baseline analysis stage – IT project management-related questions.

No.	Question
1	Was more formalized approach that involved documents, forms or diagrams used in case of developing international/global systems? Or was it rather based on discussions and informal knowledge flows?
2	Were there regular meetings with stakeholders held regarding system requirements? What form did such meetings have?
3	In what way and in what form were system requirements submitted?
4	Were functional requirements strictly prioritized or were there discussions regarding non-functional requirements – such as performance-, reliability- or security-related ones?
5	Were there either project management or requirement management IT tools used?
6	Were there specific IT project risks arising from the internationalization and how such risks were managed?
7	Did the system development process have an impact on the on-going management of business processes and how the potential conflicts of business practices with the proposed IT solutions were resolved?
8	Did the project take into account the cultural specificity of countries being involved in the system deployment? Or was there unification of functionality regardless of local needs attempted?
9	Was the budget allocated to individual countries in case of international/global systems? Or were there no such constraints?

Specific questions covering the Baseline Analysis stage within IT project management research track are included in Table 1. The main focus was placed on practices for gathering and documenting system requirements as well as modeling artifacts that elaborate the requirements – including the potential tool support it in this regard. This is due to the specificity of IT projects, where a significant proportion tends to fail just because requirements specification discipline is not carried out properly. Risks associated with development of corporate IT solutions that matches the internationalization of the business itself, in turn, justify a more detailed analysis of how the management addresses such risks.

4   Preliminary Results

Baseline analysis stage provides insight into current situation of the company as depicted by all stakeholders involved in the research process. The nature of ABPM model, constituting the framework for continuous company improvement, is keeping both process design and IT system development adaptive. Ipso facto, while signing a contract with a new customer, rich portfolio of IT services enables addressing specific customer requirements by assembling processes based on digital options. While sooner or later a thorough improvement of business processes is expected – what involves thorough overhaul of IT and (re-)development of complex features – minor requirements are supposed to be addressed and target products included in the digital options repository on an on-going basis. Reality of organization just learning to act in such and coping with limited IT resources means focusing on bug-fixing and putting continuous buildup of digital options aside (see Fig. 2). This may lead to limiting the role of company's task management software, and even worse, to a substantial part of tasks reported in such system getting outdated. In such case, the companies within group that require more intensive services development or more extensive interfacing with external systems tend to put considerable pressure on IT department and monopolize common IT solution to a certain extent. Research revealed that a considerable responsibility rests on IT to prioritize ideas, which numerous companies within the group might benefit from. This requires support from the management and is associated with the development of analytical competence among technical staff.

While organizational issues tend to dominate, one must not overlook technical ones. Thus, limited effort regarding planning IT tool repository tends to result in maintaining licenses of a few tools that prove to be redundant to a degree or lack reliable functional/model interchange features. Since it is a challenge to select a tool that fulfills both the demands of IT staff and the other stakeholders, parallel IT solutions are used – for instance, while one tool is used to gather new requirements from employees, another is dedicated to their future analysis and management. This may result in additional workflows (should model interchange be absent/unreliable) and additional risk regarding lack of proper feedback to the original requirements' authors (since IT staff concentrates on maintaining data within in-house solution). Research revealed as well that while functional requirements were given a proper

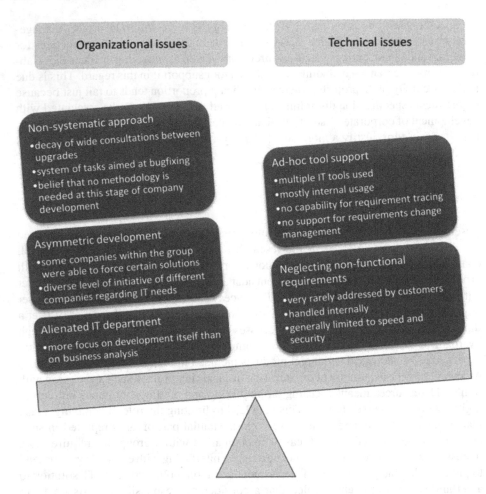

Fig. 2. Baseline analysis stage – issues identified.

consideration, non-functional ones were rarely brought up by the stakeholders and it was mostly up to IT staff initiative to take such requirements into account.

5   Summary and Future Work

The paper addresses selected project management challenges regarding development of proprietary IT solution supporting multinational business based on experiences of SESCOM Group. Participatory Action Research approach is used to execute baseline analysis, thus providing insight into current situation of the company as depicted by all stakeholders involved in the research process. Issues identified are of both organizational and technical nature.

Feedback gathered during baseline analysis stage enabled successful launch of succeeding research stages, i.e. global IS aspects improvement stage and requirements specification stage. In order to counter issues identified while running IT operations in accordance with the ABPM model, both the Scrum-based methodology tailored to specific needs of the company as well as proposal for restructuring IT tool repository are expected to be elaborated. Study completed additionally provides a basis for conducting research regarding target architecture of IT solution for an international/ global company.

References

Actuation Consulting: The study of product team performance (2013). http://www.actuation consulting.com/whitepaper_request_2013.php

Akmanligil, M., Palvia, P.: Strategies for global information systems development. Inf. Manag. **42**(1), 45–59 (2004)

Ameller, D., Ayala, C., Cabot, J., Franch, X.: Non-functional requirements in architectural decision making. IEEE Softw. **30**(2), 61–67 (2012)

Baskerville, R.: Investigating information systems with action research. Commun. Assoc. Inf. Syst. **2**(19), 1–32 (1999)

Bernhaupt, R., Manciet, F., Pirker, M.: User experience centered engineering: a process model inspired by games development. In: Proceedings of 15th IFIP TC.13 International Conference on Human-Computer Interaction, INTERACT 2015 Adjunct, University of Bamberg Press (2015)

Chin, G.: Agile Project Management: How to Succeed in the Dace of Changing Project Requirements. AMACON, New York (2004)

Eden, C., Huxham, C.: Action research for management research. Br. J. Manag. **7**(1), 75–86 (1996)

Farrell, D., Mendonca, L., Nevens, M., Manyika, J., Lal, S., Roberts, R., Baily, M., Terwilliger, T., Webb, A., Kale, A., Ramaratnam, M., Rzepniewski, E., Santhanam, N., Cho, M.: How IT enables productivity growth (2002). http://www.mckinsey.com/business-functions/business-technology/our-insights/how-it-enables-productivity-growth

Fredriksson, O., Ljung, L.: Modern enterprise systems as enablers of Agile development. In: Song, W., Xu, S., Wan, Ch., Zhong, Y., Wojtkowski, W., Wojtkowski, G., Linger, H. (eds.) Information Systems Development. Asian Experiences. Springer-Verlag, New York (2011)

Gawin, B., Marcinkowski, B.: Do the adaptive methods of business processes management allow for achieving competitive advantage? (in Polish). E-mentor **57**, 62–73 (2014)

Gotel, O.C.Z., Finklestein, A.C.W.: An analysis of the requirements traceability problem. In: Proceedings of 1st International Conference on Requirements Engineering on ICRE 1994. IEEE CS Press, Colorado Springs (1994)

Gray, K.R.: Information system development in a global environment. J. Teach. Int. Bus. **10** (3–4), 113–128 (1999)

Hammar, M.: Plan-Do-Check-Act in the ISO 9001 Standard (2016). http://advisera.com/9001academy/knowledgebase/plan-do-check-act-in-the-iso-9001-standard

Hoehle, H., Venkatesh, V.: Mobile application usability: conceptualization and instrument development. MIS Q. **39**(2), 435–472 (2015)

Hummel, M., Rosenkranz, C., Holten, R.: The role of social Agile practices for direct and indirect communication in information systems development teams. Commun. AIS **36**, 273–300 (2015)

Hussain, W.: Requirements change management in global software development: a case study in Pakistan (2010). http://www.diva-portal.org/smash/get/diva2:323787/FULLTEXT01.pdf

International Data Corporation (2016). https://www.idc.com/getdoc.jsp?containerId=prUS 41006516

Janz, B.D., Vitalari, N.P., Wetherbe, J.C.: Emerging best practices in global systems development. In: Palvia, P., Palvia, S., Roche, E. (eds.) Global Information Technology and Electronic Commerce. Ivy League Publishing, Marietta (2002)

Katcherovski, V.: 3 Tips for managing requirement changes (2010). https://esj.com/Articles/2010/10/05/Managing-Requirement-Changes.aspx

Kerton, B.: Requirements traceability: why bother (2011). http://blog.smartbear.com/sqc/requirements-traceability-why-bother

Kiiza, B., Pederson, G.: ICT-based market information and adoption of agricultural seed technologies: insights from Uganda. Telecommun. Policy 36(4), 253–259 (2012)

Lacey, M.G.: The Scrum Field Guide: Practical Advice for Your First Year. Addison-Wesley, Upper Saddle River (2012)

Lotz, M.: Waterfall vs. Agile: which is the right development methodology for your project? (2013). http://www.seguetech.com/blog/2013/07/05/waterfall-vs-agile-right-development-methodology

Mikoluk, K.: Agile vs. Waterfall: evaluating the Pros and Cons (2013). https://www.udemy.com/blog/agile-vs-waterfall

Mirakhorli, M., Cleland-Huang, J.: Tracing non-functional requirements. In: Cleland-Huang, J., Gotel, O., Zisman, A. (eds.) Software and Systems Traceability, pp. 299–320. Springer, London (2012)

Mirbaha, M.: IT Governance in Financial Services and Manufacturing: Comparing the Two Sectors Using COBIT 4.1 as Framework. KTH Electrical Engineering, Stockholm (2008)

Mohamed, N., Kaur, J.: A conceptual framework for information technology governance effectiveness in private organizations. Inf. Manag. Comput. Secur. 20(2), 88–106 (2012)

Overhage, S., Schlauderer, S.: How sustainable are Agile methodologies? Acceptance factors and developer perceptions in Scrum Projects. In: Proceedings of ECIS 2012. Association for Information Systems (2012)

Poort, E.R., Martens, N., van de Weerd, I., van Vliet, H.: How architects see non-functional requirements: beware of modifiability. In: Regnell, B., Damian, D. (eds.) REFSQ 2011. LNCS, vol. 7195, pp. 37–51. Springer, Heidelberg (2012)

Quatrani, T.: The truth about Agile modeling (2010). https://www.ibm.com/developerworks/mydeveloperworks/blogs/invisiblethread/entry/truthaboutagile?oldlang=en&lang=en

Scrum Alliance: Who uses Scrum and why? (2011). https://www.scrumalliance.org/why-scrum/who-uses-scrum

Slankas, J., Williams, L.: Automated extraction of non-functional requirements in available documentation. In: 2013 1st International Workshop on Natural Language Analysis in Software Engineering (NaturaLiSE), San Francisco. IEEE (2013)

Tallman, S., Fladmoe-Lindquist, K.: Internationalization, globalization, and capability-based strategy. Calif. Manag. Rev. 45(1), 116–135 (2002)

Teague, N.R.: Quality Toolbox, 2nd edn. American Society for Quality, Quality Press, Milwaukee (2005)

Trang, S., Zander, S., Kolbe, L.M.: Dimensions of trust in the acceptance of inter-organizational information systems in networks: towards a socio-technical perspective. In: Proceedings of the 18th Pacific Asia Conference on Information Systems, Chengdu, China (2014)

Vaughan, P.J.: System implementation success factors; it's not just the technology. In: CUMREC Conference (2001)

Verhas, P.: We do not use UML, we are Agile (2013). https://dzone.com/articles/we-do-not-use-uml-we-are-agile

Information Systems Learning

Students Acceptance of m-Learning for Higher Education – UTAUT Model Validation

Michał Kuciapski[✉]

Department of Business Informatics, University of Gdansk, Gdańsk, Poland
m.kuciapski@univ.gda.pl

Abstract. This study investigated how students perceive the use of mobile technologies during studying process. Although mobile devices are ubiquitous among students, their awareness and readiness to use mobile technologies for studying is still not enough widespread and thus should still be explored especially in various cultural context. Therefore proper study was based on the Unified Theory of Technology Acceptance (UTAUT) to explain determinants impacting students' intention to use mobile devices and software for studying. Structural equation modelling was used to analyze data collected from 370 students from two universities in Poland. Additionally study allowed to verify the correctness of UTAUT model in this context. The findings showed that the UTAUT model extended with no existing in it connections between Facilitating conditions (FC) and Behavioral intention to use (BI) explains students' acceptance of m-learning for higher education reasonably well. As a result elaborated model provides a valuable solution with practical implications for increasing mobile technologies acceptance for studying process. More specifically Facilitating conditions occurred to have both impact on Behavioral intention to use and Effort expectancy. This highlights that in contrast to UTAUT model FC does not have to be exclusively associated with Use behavior. Moreover a connection between other UTAUT variables as Effort expectancy and Performance expectancy has been confirmed. Therefore research results showed that UTAUT model can be extended not only with new variables but also with new connections between existing ones.

Keywords: Mobile learning · m-Learning · Higher education · Interactive learning environments · Student perception · Technology acceptance · UTAUT

1 Introduction

Providing quick and permanent access to professional knowledge and competences necessitates the use of digital materials and mobile devices. Such a form of learning is called mobile learning (m-learning), and can be defined as the acquisition of any knowledge and skills through the use of mobile technologies, anywhere, and anytime with strong social interactions [10]. Thus m-learning is unique in terms of time flexibility and location [27] and is treated as a new and independent part of e-learning [7]. As e-learning took learning away from the classroom, m-learning takes learning away from a fixed location.

S. Wrycza (Ed.): SIGSAND/PLAIS 2016, LNBIP 264, pp. 155–166, 2016.
DOI: 10.1007/978-3-319-46642-2_11

In the m-learning approach, studying is highly associated with the use of mobile systems which are extremely beneficial to learners' knowledge and competency development [6]. The purpose of such systems is to build m-learning solutions that could assist learners in: searching for, retrieving, creating their own, sharing, and managing knowledge [31]. With the proliferation of mobile computing technology, mobile learning will play a vital role in the rapidly growing electronic learning market.

Finding a way to successfully transform ordinary e-learning to m-learning is necessary in order to enhance learning effectiveness. Especially as m-learning stimulates collaborative learning often in informal students groups. Informal knowledge is often published on blogs or wikis. In addition, mobile technologies contribute to improving the accessibility, interoperability and reusability of educational resources, and to enhance the interactivity and flexibility of learning at convenient times and places [21].

The characteristics of mobile devices used for m-learning are three fold [8, 15]:

- portability - mobile devices can be taken to different locations,
- instant connectivity - mobile devices can be used to access a variety of information anytime and anywhere,
- context sensitivity - mobile devices can be used to find and gather real or simulated data.

These three idiosyncratic features of m-learning can constitute a unique learning experience [33, 34]. Mobile devices have already become very popular among teenagers that should result in the ubiquitous idea of learning [12]. As the usage of mobile phones become increasingly pervasive, people carry their devices almost anywhere [17]. Tablets, smartphones, fablets (phone and tablet) and e-book readers enable access to training materials and interactive communication from a wide spectrum of locations, in particular public transport [19]. Thus students can broaden their knowledge and skills in a more convenient way. Compared with traditional instruction or information from textbooks, mobile learning seems to be a more attractive way of learning that can trigger the interest and motivation of the learners [14].

The usefulness aspect is paramount when users want to obtain some advantages from content provided by specific services or systems [4]. Unfortunately, m-learning has many barriers which stand in the way of its convenient use. These are connected with technical, psychological, pedagogical and financial issues. Technical issues include small screens with low resolution, inadequate memory, slow networks speeds, and lack of standardization and compatibility [16, 26]. Psychological limitations mean that students are more likely to use mobile devices for fun activities such as texting with friends, listening to music, and checking social network services, rather than for instructional purposes [26]. Pedagogical problems concern the distraction of students and the interruption of class progress through the use of mobile devices [11, 14]. Financial issues of using m-learning relate to cost of internet connection, in particular while abroad.

Since the capabilities of mobile devices change over time, their role in terms of access to information and communication is increasing, and there are various contexts for their utilization. The extension of e-learning systems to include mobile devices for managing learning activities is an important issue [5]; [23] with integrating mobile social networking technologies that are being rapidly developed to meet recent user trends [3].

Highlighted, constantly occurring changes in technical capabilities of mobile devices also justifies the necessity for conducting research in the field of mobile technologies acceptance for various areas. Moreover, we should agree with [18] that despite the high recognition of acceptance models like UTAUT, their validity in the information system context needs further testing, which has been conducted in this study. Study conducted by Park, Nam and Seung-Bong [26] confirmed that in different countries for miscellaneous technologies and various target groups such as students or academicians, technology acceptance determinants can be different.

Therefore the aim of the study is to investigate determinants of mobile learning acceptance by students in Poland with simultaneous validation of UTAUT model. Gained results would fill the research gap in studying technology acceptance in Poland especially from m-learning perspective, where no studies have not been conducted. The second point of the paper contains research methodology and stated hypotheses in the area of m-learning. Research results are presented in the third part of the article. The article finishes with discussion and conclusions.

2   Research Methodology

UTAUT was chosen as the research model as being widely accepted and used in many studies. It is capable to predict technology acceptance in 70 % [30] that is much higher rate than for TAM (30 %) or TAM2 (40 %) [24] UTAUT2 and TAM3 have not been chosen as perceived as too much complicated as giving similar prediction level. The model, analogically to most of the studies that utilize UTAUT as a basic solution omits moderators included in this theory: age, gender, experience and voluntariness of use.

As a result model contains independent variables as: Performance expectancy (PE), Effort expectancy (EE) and Social influence (SI); and dependent variable of Behavioral intention to use (BI). PE included in model and existing in UTAUT measures the degree to which an individual believes that using the m-learning will help him or her to attain gains in studying process performance. Improving a student's performance expectancy towards wiki technology usage was essential to the student's level of intent to adopt the wiki for individual and collaborative learning [38]. EE in model indicates the students perceived ease of utilizing mobile technologies for learning. SI measures the degree to which an individual perceives that important others believe he or she should use the m-learning. For the m-learning usage, other students or faculty board can encourage students to use m-learning solutions for developing knowledge and skills. FC in model reports perceived by students support from the organization in order to adopt m-learning successfully for studying process. As presented in UTAUT, FC is connected only with use behavior and thus not have impact on behavior intension to use technology [34]. BI variable in model represents intention to use m-learning technologies for learning.

Connections between UTAUT model variables, both dependent and independent have been extended in accordance to subject matter literature. In a few studies, authors indicate the potentially important role of available infrastructure on technology acceptance [22, 25]. Thus verification of the Facilitating conditions (FC) role in mobile technologies acceptance should be conducted along with the variable connection with

BI or other variables included in UTAUT model. As m-learning acceptance seems to be highly influenced by mobile devices restrictions it is reasonable that Facilitating conditions (FC) may influence perceived Effort expectancy. Such new connection has been introduced. Studies of Sumak, Polancic and Hericko [32] as well as Alrawashdeh, Muhairat and Alqatawnah [1] indicated that ease of use (EoU), similar to EE, affects usefulness, with a meaning convergent with PE. Thus such connection was also included in model. Extended UTAUT model of acceptance of mobile learning by students for higher education is presented in Fig. 1.

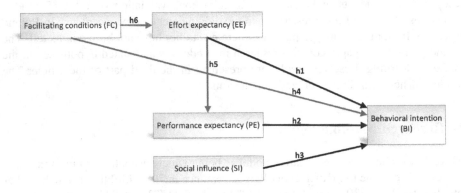

Fig. 1. Mobile learning acceptance by students for higher education

According to the model in Fig. 1 six hypotheses are formulated and presented in Table 1. They are strictly related to the assumed relationships between the variables.

The research data was collected via a survey. Because of the lack of a reliable sampling frame, it is difficult to conduct a random sampling for all potential mobile technologies users. Similar to [36] this study adopted a nonrandom sampling technique (i.e. convenience sampling) to collect the sample data. To be able to generalize the results, the survey data was collected from students studying face-to-face programs on various specializations, mainly connected with computer science or management. The survey was conducted among 423 students from two universities in Poland, who knew how to use mobile devices, applications and services, and thus were able to report on their experience. The use of m-learning during studying process by students was voluntary. Data was collected in a five months period starting from May 2015. Eventually, 370 students filled in the questionnaire, giving a response rate of 87 %. The questionnaire began with an explanation of key concepts of mobile devices and m-learning. The first section of the questionnaire consisted of classification data. Survey participants represented wide spectrum of characteristics:

- age from below 21 to over 40;
- studying for bachelor's degree or master's degree;
- all studying years.

Table 1. Research hypotheses

Hypothesis number	Connection	Description
H1	EE ●—+→ BI	Effort expectancy has a direct effect on the perceived Behavioral intention to use mobile learning during studying process.
H2	PE ●—+→ BI	Performance expectancy has a direct effect on the perceived Behavioral intention to use mobile learning during studying process.
H3	SI ●—+→ BI	Social influence has a direct effect on the perceived Behavioral intention to use mobile learning during studying process.
H4	FC ●—+→ BI	Facilitating conditions have a direct effect on perceived Effort expectancy of using mobile learning during studying process.
H5	EE ●—+→ PE	Effort expectancy has a direct effect on perceived Performance expectancy of using mobile learning during studying process.
H6	FC ●—+→ EE	Facilitating conditions have a direct effect on Perceived effort expectancy of using mobile learning during studying process.

What is more important, the survey participants represented a range of experience in using mobile devices and services – from low experienced to seasoned practitioners. This allows to generalize the survey results.

The crucial second part of the survey included 16 statements assertions formulated in accordance with acceptance questionnaires rules – 3–4 statements for each variable. Each question was measured using the 7-point Likert scale. The assertion statements in the survey were created and connected to all variables included in the developed model. Standard UTAUT's assertion statements have been used with taking into account m-learning and students context.

The study used structural equation modelling (SEM) for data collected via the survey, to validate the model. SEM was used due to both its popularity and the fact that it has also been tested in the field of technology acceptance. The advantage of SEM is that it considers the evaluation of the measurement model and the estimation of the structural coefficient at the same time. A two-step modelling approach, recommended by Anderson and Gerbing [2] as well as McDonald and Ho [20] was followed such that the confirmatory factor analysis (CFA) was carried out first to provide an assessment of convergent and discriminant validity, and then SEM was carried out to provide the path coefficients with significance tests allowing for stated hypotheses verification. Such research methodology ensures the correctness of a given model.

IBM SPSS Statistics 21 was applied while calculating the reliability coefficients and the explanatory factor analysis. Data validity tests showed that all 370 questionnaires were valid. The validity test was performed to reduce the possibility of receiving incorrect answers during the data collection period [29]. Inter-construct correlation coefficient estimates were examined along with a particular item's internal consistency reliability, by using Cronbach's alpha coefficient estimates [9]. Table 2 includes the relevant results.

Table 2. Data reliability

Variable	Cronbach's Alpha	Cronbach's Alpha based on standardized items
PE	0,935	0,935
EE	0,768	0,772
SI	0,798	0,801
FC	0,806	0,806
BI	0,901	0,902

Reliability values greater than 0,6 are considered acceptable in technology acceptance literature [39]. All items significantly exceeded the recommended level. The research instrument confirmed that the data is internally consistent and acceptable, with a total reliability equal to 0,798.

The validity of elaborated model of m-learning acceptance by students was checked through CFA - an integral part of SEM. Consequently, the model meets accuracy requirements of the fit measures presented in Table 3.

Table 3. Fit indices of model

Fit indices	Recommended value	Result
χ^2/d.f.	<3	2,828
GFI (Goodness of Fit Index)	>0,8	0,888
CFI (Comparative Fit Index)	>0,9	0,901
AGFI (Adjusted Goodness of Fit Index)	>0,8	0,844
RMSEA (Root Mean Square Error of Approximation)	<0,08	0,078
NFI (Normed fit index)	>0,8	0,878

Six fit indices satisfied by elaborated model confirm its validity and enable through regression analysis to verify stated hypotheses, given in Table 1 and included in Fig. 1.

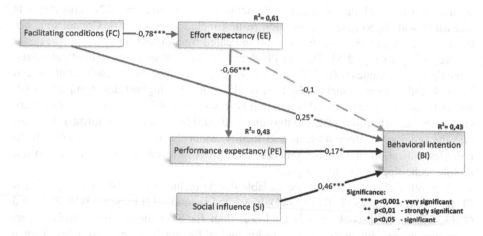

Fig. 2. Mobile learning acceptance by students for higher education - validation results

3 Research Results and Discussion

The confirmation of the stated hypotheses was examined with SEM through significance levels. In accordance with statistics rules, paths with $p < 0,05$ were accepted. Table 4 shows the overall results of the hypotheses' verification.

Table 4. Hypotheses verification results

Hypothesis number	Path	Standardized β-coefficient	Significance (p)	Verification result
H1	EE ●⁻→ BI	-0,097	0,439	REJECTED
H2	PE ●⁺→ BI	0,174	0,011	Accepted
H3	SI ●⁺→ BI	0,464	< 0,001	Accepted
H4	FC ●⁺→ BI	0,254	0,016	Accepted
H5	EE ●⁺→ PE	-0,656	< 0,001	Accepted
H6	FC ●⁺→ EE	-0,784	< 0,001	Accepted

As presented in Table 4, all hypotheses except for the first one ($p > 0,05$) were accepted, and detailed implications are explained later in this section. Figure 2 presents the created structural model of mobile learning by students in with path coefficients (β), significance (p) and the adjusted coefficients of determination (R2) scores that is consistent with hypotheses' verification results included in Table 4. Connections not confirmed by hypotheses verification are indicated by a dotted line.

According to Fig. 2 SI, FC and PE determinants' influence BI with standardized β-coefficients of values 0,46, 025, and 0,17 respectively. The study results contained in Table 4 lead to many conclusions. First of all, SI has the highest direct impact on BI, that is 0,464. As p-value for this variable is less than 0,001 (***) there exists a very significant impact of SI on BI, and thus the third (H3) hypothesis is confirmed. It means that the opinion of other students and faculty about the importance of mobile technologies utilization in studying process has a great influence on the intention to use mobile technologies for this purpose.

Also other classical acceptance variable that is included in UTAUT model, that is PE has a direct impact on BI (0,174*), hence the second (H2) hypothesis is supported (Table 4). As the β-coefficient is far lower than for SI it means that perceived performance gained by using mobile technologies for studying process does have a moderate influence on the intention to use m-learning.

Interestingly, the first hypothesis (H1) related to other UTAUT variable, revealed that EE does not have a direct effect on the students intention to use m-learning (Table 4). This hypothesis was rejected, since the statistical result showed that there is no significant relationship (p > 0,05) between the EE and the students' intention to use mobile technologies during studying process (Fig. 2). This result is contrary to the basic UTAUT model [34] in which the connection between EE and BI is an integral part. On the other hand, it is consistent with the findings of a previous study of Yong, Hongxiu and Carlssont [37]. This means that the existence of EE impact on BI may depend on the country of research. Moreover, the target group and technology usage area are also important. As a contribution for studying the EE variable role in technology acceptance, hypotheses rejection indicates that how students perceive the level of effort needed to use mobile devices and services for studying does not influence their decision whether or not to accept m-learning.

With the fourth hypothesis (H4), the impact of FC on BI was examined, that does not exist in UTAUT model. The hypothesis was confirmed and highlighted the existence of the important impact (β = − 0,254*) of FC on BI. Thus the conditions and the level of support provided for mobile application have significant influence on intention to use m-learning during studying process. Such relationship is consistent with Nassuora study [22] that confirmed that FC may have an impact on BI, in particular in the m-learning context.

In accordance with this result as stated in the sixth hypothesis (H6), the impact of FC on EE was examined. Such a relationship seemed to be quite natural, and was not noticed in the reviewed subject matter literature. The sixth hypothesis was confirmed and highlighted the existence of the very strong impact (β = − 0,784) and significance (p < 0,001) of FC on EE. Thus the conditions and the level of support provided for mobile technologies very highly influence the effort, as perceived by students, needed to use mobile devices and software for m-learning. With confirmed fourth hypothesis it highlights that universities should focus on ensuring very comfortable technical conditions and convenient support for using mobile technologies during studying process. Moreover, it highlights that classical UTAUT relationships between variables are not sufficient to explain the behavioral intention to use particular technology. This confirms the results of the other studies that general acceptance models like TAM and UTAUT should be continuously extended as acceptance determinants and relations between them depend on: technology, target group, country, application area and others.

The confirmed fifth hypothesis (H5) proves that EE very strongly impacts on PE ($-0{,}656^{**}$) and this is consistent to many studies concerned e-learning acceptance who indicated that ease of use, similar to EE, affects usefulness, with a meaning convergent with PE [1, 32]. This highlights that the effort, as perceived by students, needed to use mobile devices and software affects the expected increase in the efficiency of studying thanks to the use of m-learning. The minus sign for the β-coefficient points out that the higher the level of effort required, the lower the perceived PE. As a result mobile systems designers for m-learning should provide easy to learn and intuitive interfaces for applications. As direct impact of EE on BI was not confirmed ($p > 0{,}05$) this should not be the most significant issue. Far more important, as a result of confirmed H3 and H4 hypotheses is the impact of the SI and FC variables on BI. This means that for developing highly accepted m-learning systems it is crucial to create students' community for application, where there are already many other users, that is the typical case for social services like Facebook or Twitter. Students seem to use the tools as the other already do it. Secondly providing on a very high level facilitating conditions is also very important, meaning fast support and same use and possibilities on all mobile platforms. It indicates that students expect the possibility to comfortable use m-learning in relation to alternative solutions like: e-learning, traditional classroom learning or f-2-f workshop meetings.

Elaborated model explains in the 43 % (R2) behavioral intention of students to use mobile technologies during studying process (Fig. 2). Thus, it provides a valuable solution with practical implications for increasing mobile technologies acceptance for m-learning utilization. R2 value highlights that there is a need to further explore for new variables that will enable to better explain behavioral intention of students to utilize m-learning. Further research should also take into account moderators, especially new ones not included in technology acceptance theories, like combining studying and working.

4   Conclusions

Based on the UTAUT model this study investigated determinants affecting the intention of students to use m-learning for studying process. Elaborated model explains in 43 % behavioral intention to use m-learning for higher education by students. As a result, this study has contributed both to mobile technologies acceptance and general acceptance theories.

First of all, the proposed and validated model, verified the UTAUT in mobile technologies context. As a result, it turned out that all UTAUT variables apart from effort expectancy (EE) directly influence students' intention to use mobile technologies for learning. Social influence (SI) occurred to be the UTUAT variable that has the largest overall impact on behavioral intention (BI) to use m-learning. Therefore the opinion of other students about the importance of mobile technologies utilization in studying process is crucial when deciding to use mobile technologies for this purpose. This means that for developing highly accepted m-learning systems it is crucial to create students' community for application, where there are already many other users, what is the typical case for social services.

Another important study outcome is that Facilitating conditions (FC) variable existing in UTUAT model has moderate significant impact on the intention to use mobile technologies by students for studying. Thus the conditions and the level of support provided for mobile application influence intention to use m-learning during studying process. Such connection does not in UTAUT model.

Study also confirmed other connections not existing in UTAUT model. First one between Facilitating conditions and Effort expectancy shows that the conditions and the level of support provided for mobile technologies very highly influence the effort, as perceived by students, needed to use mobile devices and software for m-learning. Second one between Effort expectancy and Performance expectancy was also confirmed in many other studies presented in subject matter literature. It highlights that the effort, as perceived by students, needed to use mobile devices and software affects the expected increase in the efficiency of studying thanks to the use of m-learning.

Confirmation of existing new connections between UTAUT model variables points out that classical UTAUT relationships between variables are not sufficient to explain the behavioral intention to use particular technology. Therefore general acceptance models like TAM and UTAUT should be continuously extended not from new variables exploration perspective but also with better understanding of relations between actual ones.

References

1. Alrawashdeh, T., Muhairat, M., Alqatawnah, S.: Factors affecting acceptance of web-based training system: using extended UTAUT and structural equation modeling. Int. J. Comput. Sci. Eng. Inf. Technol. (IJCSEIT), 2(2) (2012)
2. Anderson, J.C., Gerbing, D.W.: Structural equation modeling in practice: a review and recommended two-step approach. Psychol. Bull. 103, 411–423 (1988)
3. Barker, V.: Older adolescents' motivations for social network site use. Cyberpsychol. Behav. 10(3), 478–481 (2009)
4. Bourgonjon, J., Valcke, M., Soetaert, R., Schellens, T.: Students' perceptions about the use of video games in the classroom. Comput. Educ. 54(4), 1145–1156 (2010)
5. Chen, N.S., Kinshuk Wei, C.W., Yang, S.J.H.: Designing a self-contained group area network for ubiquitous learning. Educ. Technol. Soc. 11(2), 16–26 (2008)
6. Chen, R.S., Hsiang, C.H.: A study on the critical success factors for corporations embarking on knowledge community-based e-learning. Inf. Sci. 177, 570–586 (2007)
7. Cho, S.K.: Current status and future of MALL. Multimed. Assist. Lang. Learn. 10(3), 197–211 (2007)
8. Churchill, D., Churchill, N.: Educational affordances of PDAs: a study of a teacher's exploration of this technology. Comput. Educ. 50(4), 1439–1450 (2008)
9. Cronbach, L.J., Shavelson, R.J.: My current thoughts on coefficient alpha and successor procedures. Educ. Psychol. Meas. 64(3), 391–418 (2004)

10. Crompton, H.: A historical overview of m-learning. Toward learner-centered educaton. In: Berge, Z.L., Muilenburg, L. (eds.) Handbook of Mobile Learning, pp. 3–4. Routledge (2013)
11. Gu, X., Gu, F., Laffey, J.M.: Designing a mobile system for lifelong learning on the move. J. Comput. Assist. Learn. **27**(3), 204–215 (2011)
12. Habboush, A., Nassuora, A., Hussein, A.R.: Acceptance of mobile learning by university students. Am. J. Sci. Res. **22**, 119–122 (2011)
13. Hsu, C.K., Hwang, G.J., Chang, C.K.: Development of a reading material recommendation system based on a knowledge engineering approach. Comput. Educ. **55**, 76–83 (2010)
14. Hwang, G., Chang, H.-F.: A formative assessment-based mobile learning approach to improving the learning attitudes and achievements of students. Comput. Educ. **56**, 1023–1031 (2011)
15. Klopfer, E., Squire, K., Jenkins, H.: Environmental detectives: PDAs as a window into a virtual simulated world. In: Proceedings of IEEE International Workshop on Wireless and Mobile Technologies in Education, pp. 95–98. IEEE Computer Society, Vaxjo (2002)
16. Lowenthal, J.: Using mobile learning: determinates impacting behavioral intention. Am. J. Dist. Educ. **24**(4), 195–206 (2010)
17. Mallat, N., Rossi, M., Tuunainen, V.K., Öörni, A.: The impact of use context on mobile services acceptance: The case of mobile ticketing. Inf. Manage. **46**(3), 190–195 (2009)
18. Marchewka, J., Liu, C., Kostiwa, K.: An application of the UTAUT model for understanding student perceptions using course management software. Commun. IIMA **7**, 93–104 (2007)
19. McConatha, D., Praul, M.: Mobile learning in higher education: an empirical assessment of a new educational tool. Turk. Online J. Educ. Technol. **7**(3), 15–21 (2008)
20. McDonald, R.P., Ho, M.H.: Principles and practice in reporting structural equation analysis. Psychol. Meth. **7**(1), 64–82 (2002)
21. Murphy, A.: Mobile learning in a global context: a training analysis. In: Proceedings of the International Conference on Networking. International Conference on Systems and International Conference on Mobile Communications and Learning Technologies, Morne, Mauritius (2006)
22. Nassuora, A.B.: Students acceptance of mobile learning for higher education in Saudi Arabia. Int. J. Learn. Manage. Syst. **1**, 1–9 (2013)
23. Ogata, H., Saito, N.A., Paredes, R.G., Martin, G.A.S., Yano, Y.: Supporting classroom activities with the BSUL system. Educ. Technol. Soc. **11**(1), 1–16 (2008)
24. Oye, N.D., Iahad, A.N., Rahim, N.A.: A comparative study of acceptance and use of ICT among university academic staff of ADSU and LASU: Nigeria. Int. J. Sci. Technol. **1**(1), 40–52 (2012)
25. Park, S.Y., Nam, M.-W., Seung-Bong, C.: University students' behavioral intention to use mobile learning: Evaluating the technology acceptance model. Br. J. Educ. Technol. **43**(4), 592–605 (2012)
26. Park, Y.: A pedagogical framework for mobile learning: categorizing educational applications of mobile technologies into four types. Int. Rev. Res. Open Dist. Learn. **12**(2), 78–102 (2011)
27. Peters, K.: M-learning: positioning educators for a mobile, connected future. Int. Rev. Res. Open Dist. Learn. **8**(2), 1–17 (2007)
28. Sarala, R.M.: The impact of cultural differences and acculturation factors on post-acquisition conflict. Scand. J. Manage. **26**(1), 38–56 (2010)
29. Sekaran, U.: Research Methods for Business: A Skill Building Approach, p. 172. Wiley, New York (2003)

30. Shaper, L.K., Pervan, G.P.: ICT and OTS a model of information and communication technology acceptance and utilizations by occupational therapist. Int. J. Med. Inform. **76**(1), 212–221 (2007)
31. Shu-Sheng, L., Hatala, M., Huang, H.-M.: Investigating acceptance toward mobile learning to assist individual knowledge management: based on activity theory approach. Comput. Educ. **54**, 446–454 (2010)
32. Sumak, B., Polancic, G., Hericko, M.: An empirical study of virtual learning environment adoption using UTAUT, pp. 17–22. IEEE (2010)
33. Traxler, J.: Sustaining mobile learning and its institutions. Int. J. Mob. Blended Learn. **2**(4), 58–65 (2010)
34. Venkatesh, V., Morris, M.G., Davis, G.B., Davis, F.D.: User acceptance of information technology: toward a unified view. MIS Q. **27**(3), 425–478 (2003)
35. Wang, S., Higgins, M.: Limitations of mobile phone learning. JALT CALL J. **2**(1), 3–14 (2006)
36. Wang, Y., Wu, M., Wang, H.: Investigating the determinants and age and gender differences in the acceptance of mobile learning. Br. J. Educ. Technol. **40**(1), 92–118 (2009)
37. Yong, L., Hongxiu, L., Carlsson, C.: Factors driving the adoption of m-learning: An empirical study. Comput. Educ. **55**, 1211–1219 (2010)
38. Yueh, H., Huang, J., Chang, C.: Exploring factors affecting students' continued Wiki use for individual and collaborative learning: an extended UTAUT perspective. Australas. J. Educ. Technol. **31**(1), 19 (2015)
39. Zhang, P., Li, N., Sun, H.: Affective quality and cognitive absorption: extending technology acceptance research. In: The Hawaii International Conference on System Sciences (2006)

Computer Science Studies in English from the Perspective of Students and Business

Marek Milosz[✉] and Elzbieta Milosz

Institute of Computer Science, Lublin University of Technology,
Nadbystrzycka 36B, 20-618 Lublin, Poland
{m.milosz,e.milosz}@pollub.pl

Abstract. Software development and the digital services market are currently growing very rapidly and, as most other areas, are subject to processes of globalisation. As a consequence, ICT companies need personnel prepared to work in international environments. This applies especially to developing economies, such as Poland.

In the paper we present the results of research among computer science students and software developing enterprises regarding student preparedness to study in English and the needs of software companies in hiring graduates of such studies. Apart from the desire to study in English and to employ English-speaking graduates, motives of such decisions by students and the benefits offered by employers are examined.

The general conclusions of the research are positive. Both students and employers point to the need for Computer Science studies in English. Unfortunately, students' expectations regarding the benefits of the completion of such studies and the actual benefits offered by employers are divergent.

Keywords: Globalisation of the software industry · Students' readiness to work in international environment · Employers' requirements and rewards

1 Introduction

The ICT sector has been developing for many years now. The arrival of new, emerging technologies such as the Internet of Things, Cloud Computing and Big Data Analytics, combined with the expanding impact of ICT on every aspect of modern life, require huge financial investments and the commitment of a large number of specialists in the area of ICT. According to OECD studies, the most important policy areas regarding the promotion of ICT include [1]:

- ICT specialists,
- government on-line and as a model user,
- digital content creation and access,
- public sector information,
- data use and re-use across the economy, and
- security of information systems and networks.

© Springer International Publishing AG 2016
S. Wrycza (Ed.): SIGSAND/PLAIS 2016, LNBIP 264, pp. 167–178, 2016.
DOI: 10.1007/978-3-319-46642-2_12

ICT specialists account for 3.4 % of the European workforce [3]. However, many reports (e.g. [2, 3]) indicate the growing shortages of ICT professionals, mainly software developers, application programmers and systems analysts/architects. By 2020, these deficiencies can reach nearly 1 million of job vacancies – Fig. 1.

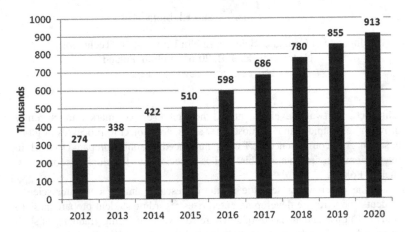

Fig. 1. Number of missing ICT specialists in the EU. Source: own study based on the "EU27 – main forecast scenario" [3].

On the downside, a period of growth in the number of graduates in computer studies is followed by stagnation, even a slight decline (Fig. 2). As a result, more than 38 % of EU enterprises which recruited or tried to recruit ICT specialists in 2014 reported difficulties in filling vacancies [4], the greatest demand applying to software developers [5].

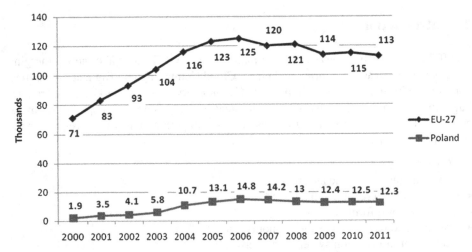

Fig. 2. Tertiary level computer science graduates in the EU and Poland. Source: own study based on [3].

The software industry and the digital services market are rapidly globalising. This process is promoted by a whole range of reasons, such as:

- increased opportunities and reduced cost of remote work [6, 7];
- easy transfer of the manufactured product (software or digital services) from country to country, often bypassing the procedures and customs duties [8–10];
- differences in the levels of wages and productivity of ICT specialists in different countries and even regions of one country [11–13];
- access to a large skilled labour pool, particularly important for fast-growing regions of the world [11];
- dissemination of the English language in the ICT industry.

The consequences of market globalisation are the growth strategies of ICT companies and the demand for ICT professionals with specific competences that enable them to work in an international environment.

2 Definition of the Research Problem and Hypotheses

One of the markets that derive significant profits from the trend of globalisation in the software industry is Poland. Many IT companies in Poland work for external customers by exporting their software products or services. These companies need personnel adequately prepared to work in international teams. Most of the activities of IT companies in the global market are conducted in English.

The Lublin University of Technology is a university that adapts its educational offer to the needs of the local labour market and beyond. These activities are related to the professionalisation of courses in Computer Science [14, 15] by adapting education to the requirements of the IT industry [16–19], and its internationalisation [20, 21]. These actions often result in the implementation of non-standard elements of student education [22, 23]. The article presents a continuation of research activities at the Lublin University of Technology, aimed at improving the educational offer.

The problem of this study is *to compare the willingness of students to study Computer Science in English with the needs of software developing companies in hiring graduates of such studies*.

The analysis looks at the students' ability and willingness to study in English, their causes and the expected benefits after graduation from studies in English.

On the other hand, it analyses the needs of software companies in the graduates of Computer Science studies in English and the additional benefits offered to them by companies.

The *subjects* of the research are students of the Lublin University of Technology (LUT) in Lublin, Poland, and software companies operating in the Lublin region.

In the area of the research problem we formulated the following hypotheses:

H1. LUT students are ready and willing to study in English at Master's level
H2. The primary motive for studying in English is a higher salary at work

H3. Fear of studies in English is the main de-motivator in choosing this option
H4. Software developing companies in the Lublin region are willing to employ graduates of Computer Science studies in English
H5. Software developing companies in the Lublin region offer higher salaries to graduates of Computer Science studies in English

3 The Research Methodology

In order to verify the research problem and hypotheses a survey was conducted among the students of Computer Science at the Lublin University of Technology and representatives of software companies from the Lublin region. The study was conducted in a manner that guarantees the anonymity of respondents.

Two types of questionnaire have been developed to be filled in the traditional manner, i.e. on paper. Most of the questions in the survey were of the closed kind, with the ability to add respondents' own answers. The questionnaires were developed separately for students and employers' representatives from the industry.

Each type of survey showed the following situation: "The Lublin University of Technology wants to expand its teaching and start a Master's degree course in the specialty Computer Science for Poles." This situation applies to the first degree students in Computer Science and their potential future employers.

The questionnaire addressed to the students, apart from a metric, included questions about their self-evaluation of their level of English, willingness to take a Master's degree in English, the causes of the desire to study in English, and the expected benefits. The survey also included a question about the support expected by students from the university and the areas of computer science that the students would like to study at the Master's course.

The questionnaire addressed to the representatives of software companies contained in its metric questions about the size of the company, the areas of its activity (in terms of internationalisation) and the number of vacant IT positions. The main part of the survey included questions about the degree of interest in employing Computer Science in English graduates, the expected benefits to the company and the graduates resulting from such employment, as well as the motivation for taking on graduates in Computer Science in English. The last question concerned the areas of computer science in which graduates were sought by employers.

The answers obtained were subjected to quantitative analysis.

4 Research Results

4.1 The Student Perspective

Surveys among students were conducted in May 2016. The study involved 324 full-time students in Computer Science from semesters 2, 4 and 6. This represents nearly 76 % of all undergraduate students in the academic year 2015–16 in Computer Science.

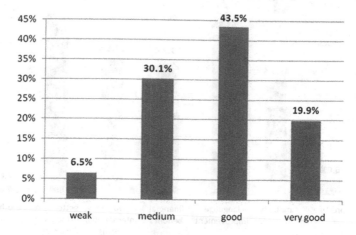

Fig. 3. Knowledge of English as self-assessed by the students

Among the study population women numbered only 11.8 %. This is the norm for Computer Science at the Lublin University of Technology.

A little over 6 % of the students assessed their knowledge of English as poor (Fig. 3). The percentage of such students is greatest in the first year of studies (over 10 %) and constantly decreases (to 4.3 % in three years) in the later years of study. Good and very good knowledge of English was declared by over 63 % of students (Fig. 3).

The interest in graduate studies in English was expressed by 72.8 % of the students surveyed, including a decisive *yes* given by 19.5 %, and a definite *no* by 27.2 %. 53.3 % of students considered the possibility of continuing studies in English. The reasons for the desire to study in English were associated with obtaining (Fig. 4):

- a better start in the labour market – 68.9 % of respondents,
- improving the level of English proficiency – 63.8 %
- wishing to work in international teams – 53.6 %.

Financial benefits after graduation in English were indicated as a motive to study by 53.2 % of students who declared the intention or considered the possibility of studying in English (Fig. 4). A low position in the ranking was taken by the prestige of studying in English (6 %). Among other reasons, students usually gave easier access to working abroad.

Fear (Fig. 5) was the most common cause for which 27.2 % of the respondents did not want to take up a Master's course in English. It was indicated by 58 % of students who wanted to study in English. Further causes were (Fig. 5):

- reluctance of extra effort (31.8 %),
- poor knowledge of English (20.5 %),
- no noticeable benefits (13.6 %).

Among other reasons, the most often cited was the lack of interest in taking up the Master's program in general and the lack of certainty as to the benefits of studying in English. Quite often (3.5 %) the reason for the lack of interest in studies in English at

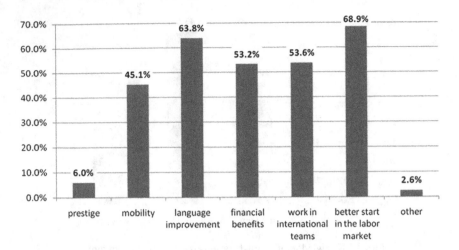

Fig. 4. Reasons for the willingness to study in English

the Lublin University of Technology was given to be the desire to undertake graduate studies abroad.

Students look primarily to the financial benefits resulting from the completion of studies in English (Fig. 6). This was indicated by 64.3 % of students who wanted to study in English. About half of them (57 %) expected priority opportunities to work in international teams and positions requiring frequent international contacts (46.8 %).

Internships in international companies (65.1 %) and foreign practices (59.1 %) were the most frequently cited as the support expected from the Lublin University of Technology in the course of study in English (Fig. 7). The university's help in finding employment, however, was cited the least frequently (Fig. 7). It was expected by only 41.1 % of the students who wanted to study English.

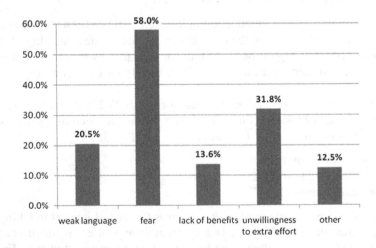

Fig. 5. Reasons for the reluctance to take up studies in English

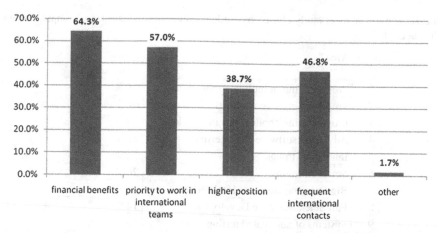

Fig. 6. Benefits expected by the students due to graduation in English

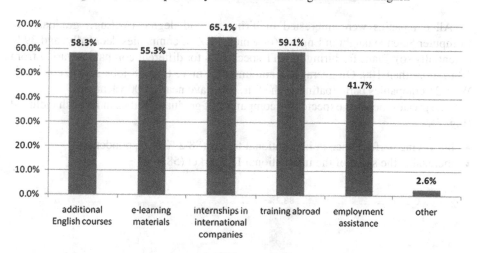

Fig. 7. Expected support while studying in English

Table 1 shows the areas of computer science which students would like to explore during graduate studies in English.

4.2 The Business Perspective

The survey was conducted among employers during job fairs in the area of IT, known as the Lublin IT Day, on 19 April 2016. The fair was participated in by companies from the region that were actively seeking employees in the field of computer science.

The survey was answered by 17 of the 21 companies approached. More than half of the companies belonged to large ones (more than 250 employees). There were also medium-sized companies (35 %), small and micro enterprises. 94 % of companies-respondents have international teams.

Table 1. Top-ten areas of study chosen by students eager to graduate from computer science studies in English

N°	Area	% of respondents
1	Programming of mobile applications	71 %
2	Programming web applications	64 %
3	Programming applications in the cloud	39 %
4	Advanced software engineering	33 %
5	Internet of things	32 %
6	Smart buildings	26 %
7	Big Data and Business Intelligence	16 %
8	Full Stack Software Development	14 %
9	Systems of automated testing	13 %
10	Ergonomics and interfaces	12 %

All companies were interested in hiring second degree (M.Eng.) graduates in Computer Science taught in English (of which 61 % of companies decidedly, and 39 % potentially so). Plans for hiring new IT specialists for different companies varied from 10 to more than 100. On average, it amounted to more than 28 jobs in one company. With 21 companies participating in the fair, this gave nearly 600 vacancies.

The greatest benefits expected by companies of graduate studies in English included (Fig. 8):

- improving performance in international teams (88.2 % of respondents)
- increasing the share of the international IT market (58.8 %),

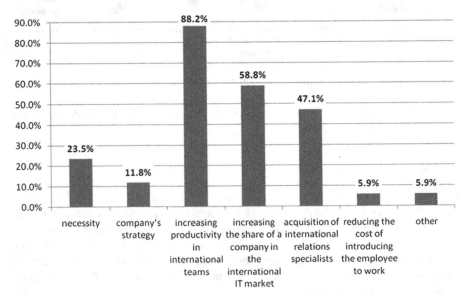

Fig. 8. Benefits perceived by companies from employment of graduates in English

Table 2. The demand for graduates in 2nd degree (M.Eng) computer studies in English – top-ten list

N°	Area	% of respondents
1	Programming web applications	72 %
2	Systems of automated testing	72 %
3	Programming of mobile applications	61 %
4	Advanced Software Engineering	50 %
5	Programming applications in the cloud	50 %
6	Agile project management	50 %
7	Big Data and Business Intelligence	44 %
8	Internet of things	44 %
9	Full Stack Software Development	33 %
10	Ergonomics and interfaces	22 %

- attracting specialists of international relations (47.1 %),
- necessity, resulting from the company's business profile (22.0 %).

Companies wanted to offer graduates of information studies in English employed by them the following benefits (Fig. 9):

- work in positions requiring frequent contacts with a foreign partner (88.2 %),
- priority in employment in international teams (35.3 %).

Reluctantly, companies offered (Fig. 9) increased earnings (only 5.9 % of respondents) or a higher position (0 %).

Computer science specialties whose graduates were of interest to the software companies examined can be found in Table 2.

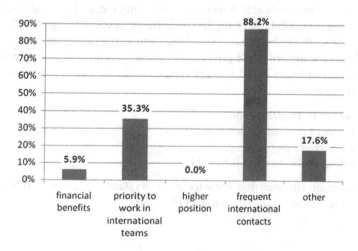

Fig. 9. Benefits offered by employers to graduates in English

5 Discussion

The research results presented in Sect. 4 allow to verify the hypotheses and draw conclusions. Some of the hypotheses have been verified positively, and some not. Especially:

H1. The hypothesis *Students at the LUT are ready and willing to study English at the Master's level* has been verified. Only 27.2 % of students did not want to take up the master's degree in English. Good and very good command of English is claimed by more than 63 % of students, and poor by only 6.5 %.

H2. The hypothesis *The primary motivator for studying in English is a higher salary at work* has only partly been confirmed. Admittedly, the financial benefits were fourth on the list of reasons for the desire to study in English (Fig. 4), but appeared in the first place of the benefits expected by the graduates of studies in English (Fig. 6).

H3. The hypothesis *Fear of studies in English is the main de-motivator in choosing this option* has been fully confirmed. Fear inhibits 58 % of the students from readiness to study in English (Fig. 5). Also, students who would enrol in studies in English expected a broad support during their studies (Fig. 7).

H4. The hypothesis *Software developing companies in the Lublin region are willing to employ graduates of Computer Science studies in English* has been completely confirmed. All respondents from software companies expressed interest in hiring science graduates studying in English. The number of vacancies in the area of software developing was almost 600, which – with the Computer Science students of the Lublin University of Technology numbering about 100–150 – points to a large gap between the needs and the possibilities of their fulfilment by the universities.

H5. The hypothesis *Software developing companies in the Lublin region offer higher salaries to graduates of Computer Science studies in English* has been verified negatively. Such benefits for employed graduates of studies in English were offered by less than 6 % of the companies.

Interesting findings appear as a result of comparing areas of computer science that students want to study (Table 1) with the needs for professionals signalled by software companies (Table 2). On both lists, the top ten were virtually the same areas. Students did not indicate the area of Agile project management (6th on the list of employers – Table 2), while employers failed to mark Smart buildings. Four of the first five areas were on both lists:

- Web applications programming.
- Programming of mobile applications.
- Advanced software engineering.
- Programming applications in the cloud.

Students underestimated the knowledge of Systems of automated testing, and employers were less in need of the Internet of things.

6   Conclusions

The main conclusion that can be drawn from the study is that a vast majority of students are willing and ready to undertake graduate majoring in computer science in English, and the Lublin software industry needs such graduates. The fields of Computer Science in which students want to be educated and the needs of industry are also very convergent.

The research results show some divergence in interests between students wanting to study in English and the interests of companies: students expect increased wages as a kind of compensation for the extra effort during their studies and the industry is not prepared to pay for it. The industry offers additional advantages, namely work in an international environment, i.e. for customers and partners outside Poland. Taking into account the differences in wage levels and the cost of living in Poland and other countries in which Polish companies implement projects, the ability to work in international teams usually translates into higher wages of their members.

Polish companies implementing projects for foreign customers contribute to the reduction of shortages of ICT professionals indicated at the beginning of the article.

The study has shown a huge demand for software developers generated by companies in the region and the inability to quickly satisfy it by university graduates in the region.

References

1. OECD: OECD digital economy. Outlook 2015, p. 284 (2015)
2. Gareis, K., Hüsing, T., Birov, S., Bludova, I., Schulz, C., Korte, W.B.: E-skills for jobs in Europe: measuring progress and moving ahead. Final report, Empirica Gesellschaft für Kommunikations- und Technologieforschung mbH, Bonn, Germany, February 2014, p. 253 (2014). http://eskills-monitor2013.eu/results/
3. OECD: Skills and jobs in the internet economy. OECD Digital Economy Papers, No. 242, OECD Publishing (2014). http://dx.doi.org/10.1787/5jxvbrjm9bns-en
4. ICT specialists – statistics on hard-to-fill vacancies in enterprises. Eurostat (2015). http://ec.europa.eu/eurostat/statistics-explained/index.php/ICT_specialists_–_statistics_on_hard-to-fill_vacancies_in_enterprises
5. Pratt, M.K.: 10 tech specialties with rising salaries. Computerworld Digit. Mag. 2(9), 18 (2016)
6. Office, I.L.: Offshoring and Working Conditions in Remote Work. ILO, Geneva (2010)
7. Niazi, M., Mahmood, S., Alshayeb, M., Hroub, A.: Empirical investigation of the challenges of the existing tools used in global software development projects. IET Softw. 9(5), 135–143 (2015). doi:10.1049/iet-sen.2014.0130
8. Nylén, D., Holmström, J.: Digital innovation strategy: a framework for diagnosing and improving digital product and service innovation. Bus. Horiz. 58, 57–67 (2015). doi:10.1016/j.bushor.2014.09.001
9. Gaspareniene, L., Remeikiene, R., Schneider, F.G.: The factors of digital shadow consumption. Intellect. Econ. 9, 108–119 (2015). doi:10.1016/j.intele.2016.02.002
10. Alino, N.U., Schneider, G.P.: Consumption taxes on digital products in the European union. J. Leg. Ethical Regul. Issues 15(2), 1–8 (2012)
11. Conchúir, E.Ó., Ågerfalk, P.J., Olsson, H.H., Fitzgerald, B.: Global software development: where are the benefits? Commun. ACM 52(8), 127–131 (2009)

12. Ramasamy, R.: The production of salary profiles of ICT professionals: moving from structured database to big data analytics. Stat. J. IAOS **31**(2), 177–191, doi:10.3233/SJI-150891 (2015)

13. Inklaar, R., O'Mahony, M., Timmer, M.: ICT and Europe's productivity performance: industry-level growth account comparisons with the United States. Rev. Income Wealth **51**(4), pp. 505–536, doi:10.1111/j.1475-4991.2005.00166.x (2005)

14. Plechawska-Wójcik, M., Milosz, M., Borys, M.: Professionalization of computer science studies – experience sharing in EU. In: Chova, L.G., Martinez, A.L., Torres, I.C. (Red:) 7th International Conference of Education, Research and Innovation, ICERI 2014, Valencia, IATED - International Association Technology Education, pp. 328–335 (2014)

15. Miłosz, E., Miłosz, M.: Road map of higher education professionalization. In: EDULEARN 15: 7th International Conference on Education and New Learning Technologies Conference Proceedings, Barcelona, Spain, 6th–8th July 2015, IATED Academy, pp. 1561–1566 (2015)

16. Kozieł, G., Milosz, M.: IT studies and IT industry – a case study. In: Proceedings of the EDULEARN 2014 – 6th International Conference on Education and New Learning Technologies, pp. 5796–5802 (2014)

17. Łukasik, E., Skublewska-Paszkowska, M., Milosz, M.: Meeting the ICT industry needs by universities. In: Proceedings of the INTED 2015 – 9th International Technology, Education and Development Conference, pp. 3135–3140 (2015)

18. Miłosz, M.: Social competencies of graduates in computer science from the employer perspective – study results. In: Chova, L.G., Martinez, A.L., Torres, I.C. (Red:) 7th International Conference of Education, Research and Innovation, Valencia, IATED - International Association of Technology Education, pp. 1666–1672 (2014)

19. Borys, M., Miłosz, M., Plechawska-Wójcik, M.: Using Deming cycle for strengthening cooperation between industry and university in IT engineering education program. In: 15th International Conference on Interactive Collaborative Learning (ICL), 26–28 September 2012, Villach, Austria, pp. 1–4 (2012)

20. Miłosz, M., Plechawska-Wójcik, M., Borys, M., Luján-Mora S.: International seminars as a part of modern master computer science education. In: 6th International Conference of Technology, Education and Development (INTED), Valencia, Spain, 05–07 March 2012, pp. 1494–1500 (2012)

21. Plechawska-Wójcik, M., Milosz, M., Borys, M.: Contribution of international seminars on computer science to education adjustment on European IT industry market. In: Proceedings of the 15th International Conference on Interactive Collaborative Learning (ICL), pp. 1–7 (2012)

22. Miłosz, M., Łukasik, E.: Additional trainings of students as a way to closing the competency gap. In: Torres, I.C., Chova, L.G., Martinez, A.L. (Red:) 10th International Technology, Education and Development Conference, Proceedings, INTED 2016, 6–9 March 2016, Valencia, Spain, IATED Academy, pp. 8590–8596 (2016)

23. Miłosz, E., Miłosz, M.: Small computer enterprise on competitive market – decision simulation game for business training of computer science specialist. In: Chova L.G., Martinez, A.L., Torres, I.C. (Red:) 7th International Conference of Education, Research and Innovation, ICERI 2014, Valencia, pp. 1831–1838 (2014)

Does Human Potentiality Affect IT Professionals' Organizational Behavior? An Experimental Study in Poland and Germany

Jolanta Kowal[1]([✉]), Alicja Keplinger[1], Juho Mäkiö[2],
and Ralph Sonntag[3]

[1] University of Wroclaw, Wroclaw, Poland
{jolanta.kowal,alicja.keplinger}@uwr.edu.pl
[2] Hochschule Emden/Leer, Emden, Germany
juho.maekioe@hs-emden-leer.de
[3] University of Applied Sciences Dresden, Dresden, Germany
sonntag@htw-dresden.de

Abstract. The goal of our paper is to examine if human potentiality (HP) affects IT professionals' organizational citizenship behavior (OCB) in relation to Poland (transition economy) and Germany (developed economy). For the goal of the study the authors elaborated two novel questionnaires: the Human Potentiality Inventory (HPI) and adapted Employee Behavior Questionnaire (EBQ). We investigated seven dimensions of the HP and two dimensions of the OCB. We collected necessary data by random interpersonal network and sequence sampling. We also applied the passive optimal experiment design, conducted among IT professionals, in Germany and Poland. Our findings confirmed the effects of nationality and association between HP and OCB among IT professionals, in Germany and Poland. The novelty of the study is the cross cultural approach, experimental passive design and recognition of association between human potentiality and organizational citizenship behavior.

Keywords: Human potentiality · Organizational citizenship behavior · IT professionals · German · Developed economy · Poland · Transition economy

1 Introduction

This paper presents the model of organizational competencies aspects of human capital (HC) development in information systems (IS) in samples, from developed economy in Germany and transition economy in Poland. The purpose of the study is to test the dependency between human potentiality (HP) and organizational citizenship behavior (OCB) in relation to IT professionals and nationality. In current study nationality is understood - as country of work with its socio-organizational, economic and cultural climate. The development of human capital needed for economic growth requires continuous development of competencies related to the ability to use information technology [18, 22, 23] and ethical approach to the daily job [13, 14]. Poland is a

© Springer International Publishing AG 2016
S. Wrycza (Ed.): SIGSAND/PLAIS 2016, LNBIP 264, pp. 179–194, 2016.
DOI: 10.1007/978-3-319-46642-2_13

transition economy that becomes a knowledge-based economy with its important force – IT professionals [4]. The authors are especially interested in IT professionals' attitudes in the sphere of human potentiality (HP) and organizational citizenship behavior (OCB) because those factors may influence on their well-being, productivity and effectiveness. We define IT professionals as workers who (1) work a minimum of 20 h per week with IS and IT, (2) can skillfully use hardware and software on the highest level, (3) create systems and programs themselves [13]. The authors emphasize that novelty is deepen previous research that related to the model HP and OCB, which is part of the "invisible" components of human capital (HC). One thing is certain, however, that this component exists, interacts and is very important for the effective functioning of the organization as it relates to values which are an important prerequisite for an individual's behavior [16, 17, 33]. In this context we mean the Human Potentiality (HP) and Organizational Citizenship Behavior (OCB). These are two components connected with an ethical context of work approach.

HP is understood in aspects of intentionality and rationality in achieving career goals. OCB means a voluntary organizational behavior, that is not formally included in a job description. OCB support the fulfillment of tasks, increase the efficiency in job and positively impact on IT professionals relations working in the field of information systems (IS). IS are understood here as a human activity system created by factors which belong to five classes: data, methods, information technology, organization, and people [13, 40]. IS are denoted by continuous development [22, 23] concerned with technology and organizational factors, such as human capital. The organization development including IS depends on the technology, infrastructure, knowledge, competence and evolves towards the business environment in relation to market requirements. The development of IS means *a creative effort that comprises the expertise, insights, and skills of employees concerned with the need of improving for business* [14].

The goal of our research is to complement the gap in the scientific literature related to the psychosocial characteristics of IT professionals concerning their human potentiality in terms of achieving career goals and ethical attitudes - OCB components.

The authors prepared two novel research methods. They adapted and elaborated novel questionnaires: Organizational Citizenship Behavior Questionnaire (OCB, Table 1) and Human Potentiality Inventory (HPI, Table 2). The analysis is based on a survey conducted among IT professionals in Poland and German samples, first time in such a context. The authors assumed that: HP of IT professionals affects the manifestation of OCB.

Therefore we presented three research questions:

- Does Human Potentiality (HP) correlate and affect the OCB (OCB-I and OCB-O) of IT professionals?
- Does Nationality of IT professionals have significant effect on HP and OCB and correlations between them?

The results of our study may be addressed to IT professionals, especially to HR staff, managers, and researchers. The conclusions can be applied for organizational climate improving via incentive systems social and economic work results.

The structure of the paper is organized as follows: In the proceeding section the authors review briefly the literature related to HP and OCB. Hypotheses verification is based on the data from a structured survey conducted among 140 IT professionals employed in enterprises located in Poland and Germany. Further, the results of this research are depicted and discussed, with proposition of some ideas for future studies.

2 Literature Review and Hypothesis

The novelty is the analysis of HP and OCB in relation to nationality, together in one research and assumption that HP has an impact on OCB among IT professionals. Employee and employer describe each other. This research approach seems to be more objective than describing himself. The scientific literature contains only few examples of such approach. Moreover, we stated lack of comparison research on this theoretical model in Polish and German research samples.

2.1 Human Potentiality Definition

The authors stated that HP concerns spirituality as a collection of related (specific) skills and abilities, with a direct reference/use in everyday life, used in adaptive problem solving and implementation of purposes (especially in the moral field), which is necessary for the full development in adulthood [7]. Considerations of psychologists [12, 39] about the spirituality show that it concerns the inner life of an individual and usually has positive consequences for organizational behavior.

Based on literature review Kaya [12] argues that it is possible to characterize the phenomenon of spirituality in a few key points that are common to many authors. So spirituality means: (1) inner will and the power of life; (2) intrinsic motivation, life energy, leading people to act; (3) commitment to the common goals of community; (4) will of support of the development and success of others; (5) commitment and affirming the feelings of love, hope, faith, honesty and optimism; (6) developing the spirituality/magic of team; (7) discovering vocation and sense of purpose in life. Such understanding of HP is close to the one that in developmental psychology is called "wisdom" (especially the transcendent wisdom). Attempts to approach spirituality in a way enabling scientific research and measurement have a rich tradition in psychology [8, 30, 31]. Examples include questionnaires on religious attitudes [1, 10, 11, 38] and scales for measuring religiousness - observable behavior associated with religious practices [e.g. 9, 42, 43]. In our study, the variable of the HP is based on the psychological spirituality concept proposed by Straś-Romanowska et al. [44] and Emmons [7]. The following most relevant dimensions of HP were emphasized: 1. holism and harmony, 2. wisdom, consciousness, meaning, 3. religiosity and faith, 4. ethics, morality, conscience, 5. openness to other people, 6. engagement, 7. the aesthetic sensibility. The authors of current paper are interested in how IT professionals and other employees describe the level of HP dimensions, which were pinpointed by Straś-Romanowska et al. [44]. The authors claim that HP may be described by the above-mentioned seven dimensions.

2.2 Organizational Citizenship Behavior (OCB)

Organizational Citizenship Behavior (OCB) has become very popular in psychology and management in developed economies [34, 36]. Organ [32, s.4] stated that *Individual behavior that is not explicitly or indirectly recognized by the formal reward system and that behavior plays a vital role in the effective functioning of the organization.* He termed this behavior as discretionary behavior. By discretionary, we mean that the behavior which is not part of a formal contract or having proposed set of tasks or activities is rather a discretionary choice of an individual to endorse [37]. Podsakoff [36] described OCB as behaviors, which are not covered by the formal job description, but usually facilitate the fulfillment of tasks and support in enhancement of these behaviors in organizational settings. This behavior is voluntary and helpful and it is not required by the individuals role or job description. Employees who display OCB can contribute to improving organizational efficiency and effectiveness [36].

2.2.1 Organizational Citizenship Behavior – Individual (OCBI)
Some researchers have suggested that OCB fits into two categories. Williams and Anderson [46], subdivided OCB into two types: (1) behaviors directed at specific individuals in the organization, such as courtesy and altruism (OCB-I); and (2) behaviors concerned with benefiting the organization as a whole, such as conscientiousness, sportsmanship and civic virtue: Organizational Citizenship Behavior – Organizational oriented (OCB-O). The authors would like to discuss two types of the behaviors revealed by the German and Polish employees, for instance OCBs targeted at individuals (OCB-I) vs. OCBs targeted at organizations (OCB-O). OCB-I helps to maintain a balance in the organization, fostering employee transactions. Proponents of this approach assume that behaviors fall into one of these two categories and that are two higher order dimensions of OCBs that likely have different genesis. For example, OCB-I reflecting helping means that cooperative behaviors are enacted to benefit other people in some way. OCB-I refers to the behaviors that immediately benefit specific individuals within an organization and, thereby, contribute indirectly to organizational effectiveness [36, 46]. Podsakoff [37] labelled this dimension as helping behavior and defined it as voluntarily helping others with work-related problems.

2.2.2 Organizational Citizenship Behaviors - Organizational (OCBO)
The second dimension of OCB includes behaviors benefiting the organization without actions aimed specifically toward any organizational member or members (e.g., adhering to informal rules, volunteering for company). Podsakoff [37] interprets OCBO

as an internalization of a company's rules and policies and standards. Furthermore, Williams and Anderson [46] defined it as behaviors that benefit the organization in general. These behaviors including for instance giving prior notice regarding an absence from work or informally adhering to rules designed to maintain order. Behaviors like conscientiousness, sportsmanship, compliance, and civic virtue are enacted to benefit the larger organization, not specific only for people - are good predictors of OCB-O.

2.3   Human Potentiality and Organizational Citizenship Behavior

Many studies on OCB is focused on discovering potential predictors that are associated with the improvement of the level of tasks [34]. Meanwhile, the phenomenon of HP is a valuable proposal of theoretical and applied psychology, sets a novel perspective for action in achieving organizational success. Empirical studies were conducted by various researchers to establish the relationship between HP and ethical context of the performance of duties and tasks at work, including OCB in management [3, 5, 6, 28, 29]. The present study investigates the relationship between two dimensions: OCB-I and OCB-O as the dependent variables and the seven components of HP and the nationality (Germany or Poland) as the independent variables. In this study, it has been assumed that in the German companies, employees who report high levels of HP in comparison to Polish employees will be more involved in activities such as helping others and defending the organization when others criticize it. On the basis of these assumptions, the following hypotheses have been developed:

- H1: The human potentiality (HP) has significant effect on the OCB of IT professionals.
- H2: The human potentiality (HP) subscales have significant effect on the OCB-I of IT professionals.
- H3: The human potentiality (HP) subscales have significant effect on the OCB-O of IT professionals.
- H4.1: Nationality of IT professionals has significant effect on Human Potentiality (HP) subscales
- H4.2: Nationality of IT professionals has significant effect on OCB subscales.

Figure 1 shows the theoretical model of HP and OCB and nationality relation. The explanation of variables symbols are depicted in Tables 1 and 2. The conceptual model consists of two parts: (1) the measurement model that relates measured observable variables (within rectangles: for example HH1, ..., ES2, OCB-I1, ..., OCB-O8, Nationality) to latent variables (in ellipses: HP, HH, WCM, RF, EMC, OP, E, ES, OCB, OCB-I, OCB-O) and (2) the structural model that relates latent variables to one another (HP, OCB). Variables d1, d2, ... concern residuals.

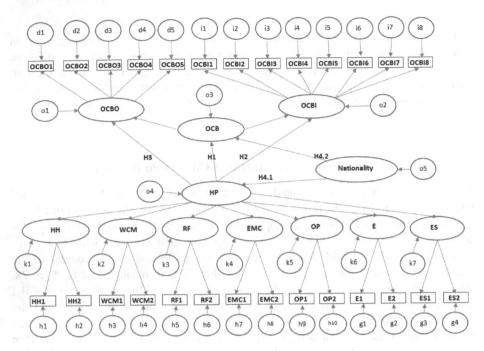

Fig. 1. The model and hypothesis.

3 Methodology

To verify the research hypothesis that guided our research, we applied a random interpersonal network and sequence sampling with the passive optimal experiment design [19, 20]. To measure the dependent variables related to OCB we adopted some dimensions of the Organizational Citizenship Behavior Questionnaire outlined by Konovsky and Organ [14, 21, 33]. To estimate the independent variables related to HP, we adopted some dimensions of the Spirituality Inventory SI [44]. The items of the original OCB test were translated from English to Polish and adapted to Polish cultural conditions. The items of the HP inventory were translated from source tools into branch cultural conditions [25, 26]. The same procedure was applied to prepare German adaptation of the questionnaires.

The adaptation and validation process comprised the following stages [15, 24, 35]: 1. analysis of the initial theoretical positions of the authors; 2. translation of the indications for test operation, the test items, the instructions and the name of the test in the language of the professionals; 3. initial confirmation of the test and verification of the psychometrical characteristics of the items; 4. formulation of the final test version and evaluation of its reliability and validity; 5. verification of the structural relations between the scales comprising the test (only about multifactorial questionnaires); 6. standardization of the test to the respective population; 7. elaboration of methodical indications for application of the test by creating instructions.

The authors used structural equation modelling SEM to verify conceptual model with satisfactory results (Table 6), [2, 41].

Table 1. Items for Organizational Citizenship Behavior (OCB)

Dimensions	Items
OCB-I: Organizational Citizenship Behavior - Individual	OCB-I1: I consult with other employees my activities and decisions
	OCB-I2: I'm helping other employees, although it doesn't belong to my scope or responsibilities
	OCB-I3: I consider the effects of my activities on other employees
	OCB-I4: I focus only on my problems, and not on the problems of others. (R)
	OCB-I5: I respect the rights and privileges of other employees not causing problems for others
OCB-O: Organizational Citizenship Behavior - Organizational	OCB-O1: It is often the case that I carry out more duties than in the scope of my responsibilities
	OCB-O2: I usually trace the causes of failures in the activities of the company
	OCB-O3: I express dissatisfaction with the implemented changes and often complain ever in many trivial situations
	OCB-O4: I am always punctual
	OCB-O5: I manage in tough situations and tolerant occasional inconveniences at work
	OCB-O6: I always do my job on time
	OCB-O7: I suggest improvements at work
	OCB-O8: I care about the image of the company

Imagine a particular person from work and thinking about it to respond to every item in the test, assigning points on a scale of 1 to 4, where the numbers denote: 1 - She/he completely is not like that, 2 - She/he is not like that, 3 - She/he is like that, 4 - She/he is so completely. Source: Own elaboration.

Table 2. Items for Organizational Citizenship Behavior (OCB)

Dimensions	Items
HH: Holism and Harmony	Hh1: My life is a whole spiritual unity with other people
	Hh2: Despite difficulties and adversities, I feel grateful to fate, when I think about my life
WCM: Wisdom, Consciousness, Meaning	Wcm1: I accept that not everything in life is certain, predictable and rational
	Wcm2: I have a strong need to understand the meaning of what happens to me in my life

(Continued)

Table 2. (*Continued*)

Dimensions	Items
RF: Religiosity and Faith	Rf1: I have a sense of community and responsibility towards fellow believers
	Rf2: Thanks to faith I see the meaning of what happens to me in my life
EMC: Ethics, Morality, Conscience	Emc1: I try to live in harmony with the values I hold
	Emc2: What I see around me, makes me feel disappointed, but also encourages to do good
OP: Openness to other people	Op1: I'm certain that doing good pays off
	Op2: I try to forgive those who hurt me although it is sometimes difficult
E: Engagement	E1: My daily activities are accompanied by a sense of realization of universal values (truth, goodness, beauty, etc.)
	E2: I try to organize my time so that I can find a moment to realize spiritual needs on every day basis
ES: The Aesthetic Sensibility	Es1: I'm moved by and admire works of art
	Es2: I can see the inner beauty in other people

Please reply compatible with your ordinary (not: unique) behavior. Respond to every item by selecting one of the five possible answers: 1 - strongly disagree, 2 - rather disagree, 3 - neither yes nor no, 4 - rather disagree, 5 - strongly agree. Source: Own elaboration.

3.1   Participants and Data Collection

The sample construction comprised the methods of random interpersonal network sampling and sequence sampling with the passive optimal experiment design [20, 21, 27]. The trial of 140 (70 from Germany and 70 from Poland) IT professionals was collected via online survey in small and medium-sized companies (SMEs). Polish and German samples were comparable in relation to control variables such as age, gender, levels of education and position within the company (Table 3).

3.2   Statistical Methods. Analysis Results

In our experimental study, for all items measuring the OCB, OCBI and OCBO the variables from the 4-point Likert scale, the numbers meant: "1 - She/he completely is not like that 2 - She/he is not like that 3 - She/he is like that 4 - She/he is so completely". Respondents that valued highly behavior of their boss or subordinate could attribute up to 20 points in OCBI and up to 32 in OBCO categories and up to 52 points in total. For the aim of better comparisons and interpretation we presented means of items and dimensions. In the case of HP - IT professionals responded to every item by selecting one of the five possible answers: "1 - strongly disagree, 2 - rather disagree, 3 - neither yes nor no, 4 - rather disagree, 5 - strongly agree". Respondents that felt spiritually well could gain 10 points in each scale and up to 70 points in global dimension. Again, for the goal of better comparisons and interpretation we presented

Table 3. Sample characteristics

Variables	IT Professionals Germany		IT Professionals Poland	
	Quantity	Percent	Quantity	Percent
Age in years				
24–44	29	41.43	32	45.71
44–64	37	52.86	36	51.43
64 and older	4	5.71	2	2.86
Gender				
Male	29	41.43	24	34.29
Female	41	58.57	46	65.71
Education				
Higher Engineering or Bachelor	16	23	21	30
Master or Postgraduate	54	77	49	70
Position within company				
Employer	36	51.43	32	45.71
Employee	34	48.57	38	54.29

means of items and dimensions. We applied the statistical methods appropriately to measure scales of variables. They comprised the descriptive statistics, the point estimation, the section estimation, the statistical hypotheses verification and multivariate methods like multiple regression, analysis of variance ANOVA, structural equation modeling SEM [15, 21]. Only the most significant results were shown (Table 4).

3.2.1 The Effect of Nationality on the Human Potentiality

In the case of HP the authors didn't observe significant differences concerning the global dimension – HP. IT professionals in Polish group manifested a bit higher level of HP, the mean was higher than the middle point of the scale (HP: $m_{PL} = 3.91$, while the middle point is equal to 3). In German group the mean for HP was a bit less (HP: $m_{GER} = 3.84$), however the difference was not significant. German group of IT professionals was less

Table 4. Descriptive statistics and student's test results concerning comparisons of Polish and German groups ($N_{GER} = 70$, $N_{PL} = 70$).

Codes of variables	Mean PL	Mean GER	Std PL	Std GER
HP	3.91	3.84	0.58	0.47
HH*	3.95	4.22	0.76	0.68
WCM	3.88	3.82	0.78	0.81
RF	3.86	3.71	0.83	0.88
EMC*	4.12	3.88	0.64	0.53
OP	3.98	3.94	0.79	0.67
E	3.62	3.58	0.87	0.93

(Continued)

Table 4. (*Continued*)

Codes of variables	Mean $_{PL}$	Mean $_{GER}$	Std $_{PL}$	Std $_{GER}$
ES*	3.92	3.72	0.81	0.84
OCB	1.71	1.83	0.63	0.80
OCBI*	1.67	1.82	0.67	0.80
OCBO	1.74	1.84	0.62	0.84

* The differences are marked, on the significance level
p < 0.05, Std – standard deviation

differentiated ($Std_{GER} = 0.47$) than Polish group ($Std_{PL} = 0.58$). Similar tendencies concerned WCM (WCM: $m_{PL} = 3.88$, $m_{GER} = 3.82$; n.s.; $Std_{PL} = 0.78$, $Std_{GER} = 0.81$, n.s.), RF (RF: $m_{PL} = 3.86$, $m_{GER} = 3.71$; n.s.; $Std_{PL} = 0.83$, $Std_{GER} = 0.88$, n.s.), OP (OP: $m_{PL} = 3.98$, $m_{GER} = 3.94$; n.s.; $Std_{PL} = 0.79$, $Std_{GER} = 0.67$, n.s.), and E (E: $m_{PL} = 3.62$, $m_{GER} = 3.58$; n.s.; $Std_{PL} = 0.87$, $Std_{GER} = 0.93$, n.s.). In the case of HH, EMC and ES the differences between Polish and German groups were significant. German IT professionals manifested a little higher level of HH (HH: $m_{GER} = 4.22$, $Std_{GER} = 0.68$) than Polish IT professionals (HH: $m_{PL} = 3.95$, $p < 0.05$, $Std_{PL} = 0.76$). In contrast, Polish IT professionals manifested a little higher level of EMC (EMC: $m_{PL} = 4.12$, $Std_{PL} = 0.64$) than German IT professionals (EMC: $m_{GER} = 3.88$, $p < 0.05$, $Std_{GER} = 0.53$). Polish IT professionals presented also a little higher level of ES (ES: $m_{PL} = 4.12$, $Std_{PL} = 0.64$) than German IT professionals (ES: $m_{GER} = 3.88$, $p < 0.05$, $Std_{GER} = 0.53$). In general, we observed that despite of some little differences IT professionals in Poland and in Germany presented high level of Human Potentiality.

Thus, nationality affects HP, what can be perceived by HH, EMC and ES. The hypotheses H4.1 seems to be supported.

3.2.2   The Effect of Nationality on the Organizational Citizenship Behavior

In the case of OCB the authors perceived that IT professionals in Poland evaluated their behaviors not very positively, the mean was a little less than the middle point of the scale (OCB: $m_{PL} = 1.71$, while the middle point is equal to 2). In German group the mean for OCB was a bit higher (OCB: $m_{GER} = 1.83$), but the difference was not significant. German group was more differentiated ($Std_{GER} = 0.80$) than Polish group ($Std_{PL} = 0.63$) of IT professionals. Similar tendency concerned OCBO (OCBO: $m_{PL} = 1.74$, $m_{GER} = 1.84$; n.s.; $Std_{PL} = 0.62$, $Std_{GER} = 0.84$, n.s.). In the case of OCBI the difference between Polish and German groups was significant, German IT professionals used to evaluate better their colleagues (OCBI: $m_{GER} = 1.82$, $Std_{GER} = 0.80$) than Polish IT professionals (OCBI: $m_{PL} = 1.67$, $p < 0.05$, $Std_{PL} = 0.67$). Despite of several differences we observed that Polish and German IT professionals evaluate rather badly their colleagues, the means were less than middle point of the scale. Thus, nationality (in fact place of work with its socio-economic, organizational and cultural climate) affects the OCBI. The Hypotheses H4.2 seems to be supported.

3.2.3 The Effect of Human Potentiality on Organizational Citizenship Behavior

To verify the hypotheses and answer the research questions concerning association between HP and OCB in relation to nationality, the authors applied Pearson's linear correlation coefficients and results were shown in Table 5. The authors interpreted the component dimensions, if the correlations were significant and strong enough.

Table 5. Correlation matrixes (Pearson's correlation coefficients. $N_{PL} = 70$, $N_{GER} = 70$)

PL	HH	WCM	RF	EMC	OP	E	ES	HP
OCB	0.2*	− 0.1	− 0.1	0.1	0.1	0	0	0
OCBI	0.1	− 0.1	− 0.1	0	0	0	0	0
OCBO	0.2*	− 0.1	− 0.1	0.1	0.1	0.1	0	0

GER	HH	WCM	RF	EMC	OP	E	ES	HP
OCB	− 0.2*	− 0.2*	− 0.1	− 0.1	0	0	− 0.1	− 0.1
OCBI	− 0.2*	− 0.2*	− 0.1	− 0.1	0	0	− 0.1	− 0.2*
OCBO	− 0.2*	− 0.2*	− 0.1	− 0.1	0.1	0	− 0.1	− 0.1

COM	Nat	HH	WCM	RF	EMC	OP	E	ES	HP
OCB	− 0.1	0.04	− 0.20*	− 0.1	0	0.04	0.02	− 0.03	− 0.04
OCBI	− 0.1	0.03	− 0.20*	− 0.11	− 0.01	− 0.01	0	− 0.03	− 0.06
OCBO	− 0.1	0.04	− 0.20*	− 0.09	0	0.08	0.04	− 0.02	− 0.03
Nat	1	− 0.2*	0	0.1	0.2*	0	0	0.1	0.1

* The correlations are marked, on the significance level of $p < 0.05$; COM – both nationalities; Nat – nationality; PL – Poland; GER – Germany; symbols of subscales- see Tables 1 and 2

In Polish group only the one dimension of HP – HH was positively correlated with the global dimension of OCB and with OCBO, with a Pearson correlation coefficients of 0.2 for global OCB and for its dimension HH. The strength of correlations was not strong, they related small part of population. It seems that sometimes in the companies where IT professionals higher level of HH, at the same time the OCB were observed.

However, Hypothesis H1 seems to be only partially and not strongly supported.

In German group global HP was negatively, but also not strong correlated with the dimension of OCBI ($r = − 0.2$, $p < 0.05$). Only two dimension of HP – HH and WCM were also negatively correlated with all dimensions of OCB, with a Pearson correlation coefficient of − 0.2 for global OCB and with its dimensions OCBI and OCBO. The strength of correlations was not strong. It seems that sometimes in the enterprises where IT professionals manifest higher level of HH and WCM, at the same time the lower levels of OCB were observed.

Again, hypothesis H1 seems to be only partially and not strongly supported.

This results suggest that sometimes IT professionals who presented higher levels of HP rather don't perceive the ideas of OCB and its subscales. However those relations rarely occurred. The effect of HP on OCB is rather weak in both groups.

3.2.4   The Global View of Results - SEM

In order to examine the hypotheses referring to the conceptual model shown on Fig. 1 -, we performed a series of analyzes using SEM with satisfactory results (Table 6), [2, 41]. The assumed conceptual model is based on the theory and our previous detailed studies, including among others the analysis of correlations, regression models, EFA and CFA [21]. Our experimental conceptual SEM consists of two parts: (1) the measurement model that relates measured observable variables (within rectangles: for example HH1, ..., ES2, OCB-I1, ..., OCB-O8, Nationality) to latent variables (in ellipses: HP, HH, WCM, RF, EMC, OP, E, ES, OCB, OCB-I, OCB-O) and (2) the structural model that relates latent variables to one another (HP, OCB). Variables d1, d2, ... concern residuals. Empirical correlations and the SEM analysis confirmed the

Table 6. The data fit indicators − the results of testing the measurement model for nationality, HP and OCB

Construct	AVE	α	r	χ^2/df	RMSEA	p	GFI	AGFI
The global model	0.7	0.95	0.33	3.1	0.09	0.001	0.95	0.9
HP	0.7	0.9	0.5	2.11	0.08	0.01	0.95	0.9
HH	0.6	0.8	0.4	2.13	0.08	0.01	0.9	0.8
WCM	0.6	0.7	0.4	4.43	0.08	0.001	0.9	0.9
RF	0.7	0.8	0.3	5.99	0.1	0.001	0.9	0.8
E	0.7	0.83	0.5	3.84	0.07	0.002	0.9	0.9
ES	0.7	0.82	0.4	9.35	0.1	0.001	0.9	0.9
OCB	0.8	0.9	0.4	2.24	0.07	0.01	0.8	0.8
OCB-I	0.9	0.8	0.4	3.12	0.1	0.01	0.9	0.9
OCB-O	0.8	0.8	0.32	2.37	0.08	0.01	0.9	0.8

Source: own elaboration; AVE - average variance extracted, α – Cronbach's α, r – mean correlation between items, p – observed probability, χ^2/df RMSEA, GFI, AGFI - indicators of model fit

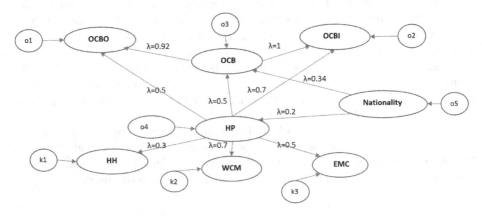

Fig. 2. The empirical confirmed model

influence of the nationality on HP and OCB, and partly the influence of HP on OCB (Tables 5 and 6). The data fit coefficients of conceptual model also confirmed the influence of HP on OCB and its subscales (Table 6). The most important factor loadings (λ) of the best global model related to main hypotheses are depicted on Fig. 2. The data fit coefficients (Table 6) and factor loadings (λ, Fig. 2) show that all hypotheses H1–H4 are supported.

4 Conclusions, Discussion and Future Research

The answer to first research question, that IT professionals' HP has a significant, positive effect on their OCB, implicates the three most important practical suggestion for management. HP is understood in aspect of intentionality and rationality in the implementation of career goals. Supervisors should take into account the subjective level of employee potentiality – like individual way of thinking, intentions of the behavior, specific skills (industry skills, work experience), abilities, social competencies, which comprises the above mentioned OCB components and can be factors of innovative capacity [27]. They should represent the interests of employees and providing opportunities for development, information and communication within the company. The important weight of information and communication as success factors in professional development in Polish companies concerned with IT and IS was also reported by Keplinger et al. [14] and Kowal and Roztocki [23].

HP of IT professionals has a significant, positive effect on their OCB-I. The authors observed a significant impact of nationality on HP and OCB concerning the phenomenon of behavior ethos manifestation. It is important for the IS development to care for the incidence of OCB-I. IT professionals who were mostly satisfied with their jobs more often were directed towards ideas of OCB-I. The processes of globalization makes it harder for building a sense of community in the boundless social space. Probably in the practice the realization of values in global organizations based more on the universalism and pragmatism values, than on the respect for the originality and uniqueness of the life experiences of the individual. That is why the outcome of the research give us the optimistic results, that the variable HP has significantly positive correlation with the OCB-I. People with high levels of HP are interested in creating and initiating OCB-I and transfer them to daily business for the benefit of the achieved economic results.

HP of IT professionals has a significant, positive effect on their OCBO. This result is somehow comparable to the study of Keplinger et al. [14] and Kowal and Keplinger [21]. The results are optimistic and show that IT professionals in both countries obtained high scores in the dimensions of wisdom, morality, conscious (WMC), holism and harmony (HH), and global human potentiality (HP).

However, regarding second question, IT professionals in Polish and in German groups differ sometimes in the spheres of OCBI and OCBO. These phenomena can be implicated by historical, cultural, religious and socio-organizational causes. The differences may be due also to the fact that Poland is transforming the economy from a centrally planned to a market economy. In a centrally planned economies in countries such as Poland dominating authoritarian management style, spirituality and religiosity don't correlate with moral and ethical aspects of socio-economic processes at work. However we observed more positive correlations among younger generations of employees.

Our results show that the higher degree of HP means the higher autonomy of an individual. People with high autonomy can ignore standards and values of organization [12, 30]. Therefore it is important to run process of internalization of organization rules and standards. It can be perceived via positive examples of the leaders' behavior, by training or selection of staff and exchange of work experiences.

The limitations of our experimental study are related to size of samples as the research is limited on the territory of Poland and Germany only. Variables like gender, age, position, or economy sector were not carried out. The authors plan to consider these aspects in future studies.

The conclusions of our research can be addressed to IT professionals or to HR staff. The application of our findings can develop social and economic work effects. The ideas of HP and OCB can be factors of development of IS staff in the context of globalization and cross cultural studies. They can help to develop commitment, efficiency and leads to economic growth.

References

1. Allport, G.: Personal religious orientation and prejudice. J. Pers. Soc. Psychol. **5**, 432–443 (1967)
2. Bagozzi, R.: Specification, evaluation, and interpretation of structural equation models. J. Acad. Mark. Sci. **40**(1), 8–34 (2012)
3. Benefiel, M.: Mapping the terrain of spirituality in organizations research. J. Organ. Change Manage. **16**(4), 367–377 (2003)
4. Brockmann, C., Roztocki, N.:. Topics on knowledge management: an empirical insight into articles published in the international journal of knowledge management. In: 2015 48th Hawaii International Conference on IEEE System Sciences (HICSS), pp. 3834–3840, January 2015
5. Cacioppe, R.: Creating spirit at work: re-visioning organization development and leadership-Part I. Leadersh. Organ. Dev. J. **21**(1), 48–54 (2000)
6. Cochrane, K.: Learning, spirituality and management. J. Hum. Values **6**(1), 1–14 (2000)
7. Emmons, R.: Is spirituality an intelligence? motivation, cognition, and the psychology of ultimate concern. Int. J. Psychol. Relig. **10**, 3–26 (2000)
8. Fry, L.W., Cohen, M.P.: Spiritual leadership as a paradigm for organizational transformation and recovery from extended work hours cultures. J. Bus. Ethics **84**(1), 265–278 (2009)
9. Hill, P., Pargament, K.: Advances in the conceptualization and measurement of religion and spirituality: implications for physical and mental health research. Am. Psychol. **58**, 64–74 (2003)
10. Jung, C.G.: The Spiritual Problem of Modern Man. Civilization in Transition, vol. 10. The Collected Works of Carl G. Jung, tr. R.F.C. Hull. Bollingen Series XX. Princeton University Press (1970)
11. Jung, C.G.: Psychology and Religion: West and East, vol. 11, The Collected Works of Carl G. Jung, tr. R.F.C. Hull. Bollingen Series XX. Princeton University Press (1970)

12. Kaya, A.: The relationship between spiritual leadership and organizational citizenship behaviors: a research on school principals' behaviors. Educ. Sci. Theor. Pract. 15(3), 597–606 (2015)
13. Keplinger A., Frątczak E., Ławecka K., Stokłosa P.: Zachowania etosowe w kontekście pracy zawodowej. Prace Naukowe Uniwersytetu Ekonomicznego we Wrocławiu/ red. nauk. M. Stor, A. Fornalczyk. Nr 35, s. 202–210 (2014)
14. Keplinger, A., Kowal, J., Frątczak, E., Ławecka, K., Stokłosa, P.: Job satisfaction and ethical behavior premises of IT professionals insight from Poland. In: Wrycza, S. (ed.) Information Systems: Education, Applications, Research, vol. 193, pp. 49–64. Springer, Switzerland (2014)
15. Keplinger, A., Kowal, J., Mäkiö, J.: Gender and organizational citizenship behavior of information technology users in Poland and Germany. In: Twenty-second Americas Conference on Information Systems, San Diego, USA (2016, in press)
16. Konovsky, M., Organ, D.: Cognitive versus affective determinants of organizational citizenship behavior. J. Appl. Psychol. 74(1), 157–164 (1989)
17. Konovsky, M.A., Organ, D.W.: Dispositional and contextual determinants of organizational citizenship behavior. J. Organ. Behav. 17, 253–266 (1996)
18. Kowal, J.: Perspectives and directions for professional development in the Lower Silesian Voivodeship compared to Poland and the European Union. In: Despres, C., (ed.) Proceedings of the 7th European Conference on Management Leadership and Governance: SKEMA Business School, Sophia-Antipolis, France, 6–7 October 2011, pp. 206–215. Academic Publishing Limited, Reading (2011)
19. Kowal, J.: Problemy natury praktycznej i teoretycznej a dobór metod badawczych do badań sondażowych rynku, Zeszyty Naukowe AE, Ekonometria 1, 765, (red.) Dziechciarz J., Wydawnictwo AE Wrocław, pp. 66–88 (1998)
20. Kowal, J. (red.): Wybrane zagadnienia weryfikacji reprezentatywności prób w społeczno-ekonomicznych badaniach jakościowych. Metody i oprogramowanie komputerowe, Zeszyty Naukowe nr 12, Wyższa Szkoła Zarządzania Edukacja, Wrocław (2002)
21. Kowal, J., Keplinger, A.: Characteristcs of human potentiality and organizational behavior among IT users in Poland. An exploratory study. Ekonometria Econometrics 3(49), 98–114 (2015). ISSN 1507-3866. http://econometrics.ue.wroc.pl/?lang=pl
22. Kowal, J., Roztocki, N.: Organizational ethics and job satisfaction of information technology professionals in Poland. In: Proceedings of the Nineteenth Americas Conference on Information Systems (AMCIS), Chicago, Illinois, USA, pp. 15–17, August 2013
23. Kowal, J., Roztocki, N.: Information and communication technology management for global competitiveness and economic growth in emerging economies. Electron. J. Inf. Syst. Developing Countries 57, 1–12 (2013). http://www.ejisdc.org/ojs2/index.php/ejisdc/issue/view/117
24. Kowal J., Gurba, A.: Phenomenon of mobbing as IT users burnout premises: insight from Poland. Lecture Notes in Business Information Processing: Business Information Systems, pp. 117–133 (2015). doi:10.1007/978-3-319-24366-5_9
25. Kowal, J., Roztocki, N.: Do organizational ethics improve IT job satisfaction in the Visegrád Group countries? insights from Poland. J. Glob. Inf. Technol. Manage. 18(2), 127–145 (2015). doi:10.1080/1097198X.2015.1052687
26. Kowal, J., Roztocki, N.: Job satisfaction of IT professionals in Poland: does business competence matter? J. Bus. Econ. Manage. 16(5), 995–1012 (2015). doi:10.3846/16111699.2014.924988

27. Kowal, J., Jasińśka-Biliczak, A.: Socio-demographic factors of innovative capacity of IT professionals in small regional enterprises in transition economies. In: European, Mediterranean and Middle Eastern Conference on Information Systems, EMCIS2016, Krakow, Poland (2016)
28. McCormick, D.W.: Spirituality and management. J. Manage. Psychol. **9**(6), 5–8 (1994)
29. Mitroff, I.I., Denton, E.A.: A study of spirituality in the workplace. Sloan Manage. Rev. **40**(4), 83–92 (1999)
30. Nasurdin, A.M., Nejati, M., Mei, Y.K.: Workplace spirituality and organizational citizenship behavior: exploring gender as a moderator. S. Afr. J. Bus. Manage **44**(l), 61 (2013)
31. Neck, C.P., Milliman, J.F.: Thought Self-leadership: finding spiritual fulfilment in organizational life. J. Manage. Psychol. **9**(6), 9–16 (1994)
32. Organ, D.W.: Organizational citizenship behavior: the good soldier syndrome. Lexington Books, Lexington (1988)
33. Organ, D.W.: Organizational citizenship behavior: it's construct clean-up time. Human Perform. **10**(1997), 85–97 (1997)
34. Organ, D.W., Podsakoff, P.M., Mackenzie, S.B.: Organizational citizenship behavior. its nature, antecedents, an consequences. foundation for organizational science. A Sage Publication Series (2006)
35. Peneva, I., Yordzhev, K., Ali, A.S.: The adaptation of translation psychological test as a necessary condition for ensuring the reliability of scientific research. Int. J. Eng. Sci. Innovative Technology (IJESIT) **2**(4), 557–560 (2013)
36. Podsakoff, N.P., Podsakoff, P.M., MacKenzie, S.B., Maynes, T.D., Spoelma, T.M.: Consequences of unit-level organizational citizenship behaviors: a review and recommendations for future research. J. Organ. Behav. **35**, 87–119 (2013)
37. Podsakoff, P.M., MacKenzie, S.B., Paine, J.B., Bachrach, D.G.: Organizational citizenship behavior: a critical review of the theoretical and empirical literature and suggestions for future research. J. Manage. **26**, 513–563 (2000)
38. Prężyna, W.: Skala postaw religijnych. Roczniki Filozoficzne, T. 16, z. 4, pp. 76–89 (1968)
39. Ratnakar, R., Nair, S.: A review of scientific research on spirituality. Bus. Perspect. Res. **1**(1), 1–12 (2012)
40. Roztocki, N., Weistroffer, H.R.: Information technology in transition economies. J. Glob. Inf. Technol. Manage. **11**(4), 2–9 (2008)
41. Sagan, A.: Zastosowanie wielowymiarowych skal czynnikowych i skal Rascha w badaniach marketingowych (na przykładzie oceny efektów komunikacyjnych reklamy), Zeszyty Naukowe nr 605/Akademia Ekonomiczna w Krakowie, Kraków, pp. 73–92 (2002)
42. Socha, P.: Duchowy rozwój człowieka, Kraków: Wyd. UJ. (2000)
43. Socha, P.: Przemiana duchowa jako kluczowe pojęcie psychologii rozwoju człowieka. Psychologia Rozwojowa, tom 19, nr 3, 9–22 (2014)
44. Straś-Romanowska, M., Kowal, J. Kapała, M.: Spiritual Intelligence Inventory(SII). The construction process and method validation. In: The International Conference: The Theory of C.G. Jung. Interdisciplinary Research. University of Wrocław, 12 June 2014
45. Westfall, R.D.: An employment-oriented definition of the information systems field: an educator's view. J. Inf. Syst. Educ. **23**(1), 63–70 (2012). Spring 2012
46. Williams, L.J., Anderson, S.E.: Job satisfaction and organizational commitment as predictors of organizational citizenship and in-role behaviors. J. Manage. **17**, 601–617 (1991)
47. Xia, W., Lee, G.: Complexity of information systems development projects: conceptualization and measurement development. J. Manage. Inf. Syst. **22**(1), 13–43 (2005). Summer 2005

Information Society in Poland - Similarities and Differences in the Perception of ICT Between Generations

Jacek Wachowicz[✉]

BOLS Institute, WSB University in Gdańsk, Gdańsk, Poland
jacek_wachowicz@o2.pl

Abstract. The study takes on the stereotypes associated with the possession of skills related to computer technology tools and information depending on age. It presents a brief review of the literature on the importance of ICT techniques in society. It then presents the results of a survey assessing the usefulness of computers and the Internet to selected characteristics of the information society action in three chosen specific groups - young people (students), mature people who work mentally and seniors who are learning computer science.

Keywords: Internet · Seniors · Information society

1 Introduction

The information society has evoluted due to the unprecedented spread and dissemination of the tools of information and computer technology (ICT), especially of personal computers and the Internet. Now they are regarded as a natural part of reality. Similarly, in a natural way, it is usually assumed that the young generation is the "digital natives" for whom computers and the Internet were "always" there and for whom it is hard to imagine life without them. In contrast, the older generation often has problems with effective use of computers and the Internet. As a result, due to the economic and social importance of skills in the field of ICT, there is often discussion about the threat of digital exclusion. In this chapter, the author undertakes evaluation of these stereotypes by examining the assessment of the suitability of computers and the Internet to selected characteristic fields of use in three chosen specific groups - (1) young people (students), (2) mature elderly people who work and (3) retired seniors who are learning computer science.

2 Importance of ICT Techniques in Society

One of the fastest growing sectors of the economy on a global scale in recent years is electronic markets with both digital products and online services. Its growth is conditioned not only by use of computers, the Internet or electronic means of payment, but also by efficient and seamless communication. One of its important dimensions is the

S. Wrycza (Ed.): SIGSAND/PLAIS 2016, LNBIP 264, pp. 195–204, 2016.
DOI: 10.1007/978-3-319-46642-2_14

possibility to convert offered file formats (or buying multiple format product bundles) [10]. Very essential became also need for building mutual trust between parts, which allows creating proper relations between the client and the vendor [9]. This trust is increasingly crucial. Its main sources might be derived either from a copy of the trust derived from the real world interactions towards virtual services [21] or from online-available comment systems [25]. The first source seemed to be natural and crucial at the beginning as social networking sites and virtual worlds have massively appeared as late as in 2008 [19]. Additionally, Internet and e-markets with its virtual products and services by being a brand new instance with brand new forms of communication brought natural barriers to elderly users.

However, its enormous growth brought electronic worlds towards business and the market economy. As everybody could enter them with relatively small sources and efforts, some saw in electronic markets the potential of being perfectly competitive ones. Therefore, it seems also interesting that in virtual markets, more and more frequently it may be observed the so-called "double jeopardy" phenomenon [5]. This is known from real-world markets and may lead to loss of competitiveness as a result of insufficient recognition. It aptly describes the formula "less known brands lose twice" because not only are they known by a smaller number of buyers, but their buyers seem to be less loyal to them [20].

Another important issue is the constant and rapid evolution and growth of products, markets and services in the e-world. As a result, the present world more and more seems to be supportive towards the importance of the concept of digital citizenship (as presented in Fig. 1). The concept assimilates interactions on different levels and guarantees access to a wider range of online services, without which it brings a serious threat of digital exclusion [1].

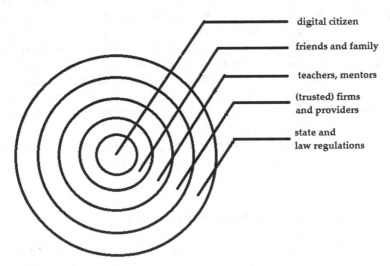

digital citizen
friends and family
teachers, mentors
(trusted) firms
and providers
state and
law regulations

Fig. 1. Levels of digital citizenship [2]

Maintaining competitiveness and the care of the human resources is particularly important in the conditions of globalization of services on the Internet [16]. From the entrepreneurial point of view, the digital revolution has brought a sharp increase in the importance of innovation and intellectual capital in business. This phenomenon was not initially perceived in Poland. Former research showed that Polish SMEs willingly adopted e-commerce solutions (like banking services) but were not eager to set up their own solutions [24]. However, a recent study of the SME sector showed that the situation is changing and has a real influence on SME effectiveness [6, 11].

The awareness of building competitive advantage and innovation potential, just as a necessary mean to compete in the modern economy instead of a low cost strategy, grows. Polish companies are increasingly willing and with bigger success become active players in the market of online services. The most important ways for achieving this goal are human and intellectual resources. In conjunction with the rapid process of a growing population of elderly workers, it urges the necessity of validation of the commonly perceived opposition between so-called "digital natives" and the elderly, who are often perceived as a "digitally lost generation". This is crucial for understanding how online services need to be constructed to be usable for users in all age groups. [4, 7].

Due to the global nature of the Internet, companies and state bodies have to adapt to an ever higher level and standard of services. One can also observe that more and more services provided by the state authorities and local government are transmitted through online services as they are convenient, accessible and cheap to maintain [17]. For having them effective, their construction needs to facilitate factors considered in terms of usability, as described in J. Nielsen's usability methodology [15], meeting consumer needs as in the VIPR model [18], or feelings as in the Kansei Engineering methodology [13, 14]. Kansei basic principles are shown in Fig. 2, which may help in understanding how online services need to be constructed to be usable for users in all age groups. This requires however knowing what are reasons for using electronic media in different age groups. So far there is lack of such comparative (in terms of age structure) studies.

Due to the natural processes occurring in human bodies, psychomotor ability that is essential for effective use of online services changes with age. Another important factor is that new habits are more slowly and not so willingly absorbed by the elderly. On the other hand, mature Internet users have high patience and skills, which replaces enthusiasm and inventiveness of the young generation [22]. To let them find the Internet as a friendly place, providers should be aware of aspects such as avoiding excessive or unusual solutions [23].

3 Study

The study was conducted as an electronic survey, carried out under a grant "Determinants of usability barriers for older people in online services causing the digital divide" (Reg. No. MNiSW N N115 211739), carried out in 2010–2013. The study involved 172 respondents from three groups selected in a targeted manner.

The first group was participants of computer classes at the University of the Third Age, conducted by the University of Gdansk. They represented a specific group of

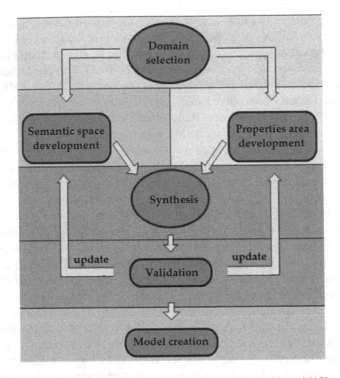

Fig. 2. Design methodology in accordance with the Kansei [12]

seniors already familiar with the computer technology, though still in a beginners' group. This led to focus on the key factors encouraging seniors to get acquainted with computer technology and thus providing the most useful outcomes.

The second group was students of the Faculty of Management and Economics of Gdansk University of Technology, representing the generation for whom computers and the Internet are as natural as the air.

The third group consisted of the employees of the Teachers' Education Centre in Bydgoszcz, which was a "bridge" between the two groups, using the Internet and computers every day in their work (almost as young), at the same time being much more mature (almost as seniors). The age structure is presented in Table 1.

A basic limitation of this research is a relatively small population under investigation. However, the influence of this limitation was minimized by targeted groups' selection. It might be interesting to validate results on a representative population and even further to check the outcomes in different countries.

4   Results

The results of the study showed that in many areas, there were no drastic differences in the perception of the Internet between generations. This is understandable because the Internet has already penetrated the popular consciousness as a natural part of the real

Table 1. Age structure of the respondents (%)

	seniors	workers	students
75–79	2,7	0,0	0,0
70–74	16,2	0,0	0,0
65–69	31,1	5,6	0,0
60–64	28,4	0,0	0,0
55–59	6,8	11,1	0,0
50–54	1,4	55,6	0,0
...	...	...	...
19–24	0,0	0,0	93,8
No answer	13,5	27,8	6,3

world. It is seen as a tool allowing a significant increase in comfort of everyday life and efficiency at work. However, there are interesting differences that the study revealed, i.e. that the groups use this tool differently and emphasize different functionality.

In general, one can say that the young generation, more than the older, draws attention to the possibility of using the Internet and computers in everyday life as a tool to have a good time and given to use in social life. This is in stark contrast to the perception of the Internet by working people and changes with entry into the period of the third age, which is characterized by a greater amount of time available. This can be illustrated by the results shown in Tables 2 and 3.

Table 2. Respondents' answers (%) to the question: "Do you /you think your computer and the Internet are useful for nice spending time and entertainment?"

	Seniors	Workers	Students
Definitely yes	21,6	27,8	43,8
Rather yes	45,9	16,7	41,3
Rather no	21,6	33,3	13,8
Definitely no	6,8	16,7	1,3
No answer	4,1	5,6	0,0

Table 3. Answers (%) of respondents to the question "Do you /you think your computer and the Internet are useful for finding new friends?"

	seniors	workers	Students
Definitely yes	5,4	11,1	25,0
Rather yes	16,2	22,2	38,8
Rather no	37,8	5,6	27,5
Definitely no	31,1	50,0	7,5
No answer	9,5	11,1	0,0

The young generation also recognizes the Internet mostly as a good place to acquire everyday information (Table 4), although the difference is not as visible as in the case of use of the Internet for entertainment. A shift may be observed in emphasis towards a more general answer "rather yes", provided almost twice as often by mature people than young people. In all three groups, the overall negative responses ("definitely no" and "probably not") does not exceed 10 % of the respondents. This leaves no doubt that the Internet is seen as an excellent source of daily news across all age groups.

Table 4. Answers (%) of respondents to the question "Do you /you think your computer and the Internet are useful for checking everyday information - as in the newspapers?"

	seniors	workers	Students
Definitely yes	56,8	50,0	66,3
Rather yes	32,4	44,4	28,8
Rather no	5,4	5,6	3,8
Definitely no	2,7	0,0	1,3
No answer	2,7	0,0	0,0

It is interesting that a similar question concerning the search of useful information (Table 5) was by far the most positively responded by mature, working people. This may indicate that they particularly appreciate the quality of information found, much more than young people looking for more current news. This was confirmed by the results of the next question relating to finding information about current laws and obligations. It definitely proved to be most important for mature people who work (Table 6).

Table 5. Response (%) of respondents to the question "Do you /you think your computer and the Internet are useful for search of useful information?"

	seniors	workers	students
Definitely yes	74,3	88,9	78,8
Rather yes	21,6	11,1	21,3
Rather no	0,0	0,0	0,0
Definitely no	0,0	0,0	0,0
No answer	4,1	0,0	0,0

A specific case was the question on the usefulness of the Internet for contacts with the authorities (Table 7). It was positively responded to only by mature people who work. This may be in part due to the lack of the need for frequent contacts with the authorities in the other two groups, and in part from inadequate (or not satisfactory) functionality of online services available to citizens from authorities and state administration in Poland.

Table 6. Answers (%) of respondents to the question "Do you /you think your computer and the Internet are useful for finding information about current law - rights and obligations?"

	seniors	workers	students
Definitely yes	27,0	66,7	21,3
Rather yes	41,9	27,8	65,0
Rather no	14,9	0,0	12,5
Definitely no	6,8	5,6	1,3
No answer	9,5	0,0	0,0

Table 7. Answers (%) of respondents to the question "Do you /you think your computer and the Internet are useful for contacting with the authorities?"

	seniors	workers	students
Definitely yes	13,5	50,0	6,3
Rather yes	37,8	22,2	41,3
Rather no	23,0	27,8	42,5
Definitely no	16,2	0,0	10,0
No answer	9,5	0,0	0,0

On the other hand, perception of the Internet as a means of helping in finding opportunities to earn (Table 8) was definitively different. This opportunity was seen by the young generation in contrast to the mature persons. This may be due to a lack of knowledge of the sites offering work, the relatively lower demand for seeking earning possibilities and much better developed networks of friends by mature people.

Table 8. Response (%) of respondents to the question "Do you /you think your computer and the Internet are useful for finding opportunities to earn?"

	seniors	workers	students
Definitely yes	4,1	11,1	22,5
Rather yes	28,4	16,7	52,5
Rather no	35,1	55,6	23,8
Definitely no	27,0	11,1	1,3
No answer	5,4	5,6	0,0

A positive approach of seniors was in turn reflected in their assessment of the usefulness of the Internet to acquire new knowledge and learning (Table 9).

Similarly, all respondents recognized the Internet as an excellent medium for keeping in touch with other people including family (Table 10). This is important because the use of the Internet in this field can reduce the sense of isolation and increase socialization

Table 9. Answers (%) of respondents to the question "Do you /you think your computer and the Internet are useful for learning - acquiring new knowledge and skills?"

	seniors	workers	students
Definitely yes	45,9	38,9	37,5
Rather yes	43,2	33,3	52,5
Rather no	5,4	27,8	7,5
Definitely no	2,7	0,0	1,3
No answer	2,7	0,0	0,0

among the elderly [3]. The results showed that the frequency of contacts with the family as well as participation in meetings (except for meetings having a religious character) is significantly correlated positively with the use of the Internet among the generation of 50+ [8]. Awareness of such relationships seems to be evident among all respondents, while definitely revealed in "digital natives" – students.

Table 10. Replies (%) of respondents to the question "Do you /you think your computer and the Internet are useful for keeping in touch with other people - friends, family?"

	seniors	workers	students
Definitely yes	55,4	55,6	71,3
Rather yes	31,1	22,2	25,0
Rather no	8,1	16,7	2,5
Definitely no	0,0	5,6	0,0
No answer	5,4	0,0	0,0

5   Discussion and Future Studies

As a main contribution, the study revealed that, contrary to prevailing stereotypes of so-called "digital natives" as opposed to elderly "who can't and don't want to use computers," there were no diametrical differences in the perception of the usefulness of using computers and the Internet between the characteristic age groups. However, it also showed that there are different accents in the perceived usefulness.

It seems that young people tend to naturally and almost transparently utilize web technology. Therefore, according to the natural inclinations of age, they particularly appreciate it in the social context as a tool for finding entertainment or new daily news or in terms of possibility of finding opportunities to earn.

This may be opposed to mature people who work, who favored the utilitarian use on the first plan of activities such as finding useful information, checking the law or contacting with the authorities.

The third group, retired seniors, particularly appreciated the utilitarian use. However, this included the activities characteristic to retirement age, especially the acquisition of new knowledge and skills, search for information, entertainment and maintaining contacts.

In summary, it can be concluded that the Internet has become part of normal life for all ages and is appreciated especially by utilities that prove to be socially needed for each group, which are different in all age and activity groups.

References

1. Belanger, F., Carter, L.: Trust and risk in e-government adoption. J. Strateg. Inf. Syst. **17**(2), 165–176 (2008)
2. Borcuch, A., Świerczyńska-Kaczor, U.: Serwisy społecznościowe – jednostka i społeczeństwo na pograniczu świata wirtualnego [Eng.: Social Networking Services- the Individual and Society on the Border of the Virtual World]. Zeszyty Naukowe Politechniki Śląskiej. Seria: Organizacja i Zarządzanie, vol. 65, pp. 61–70 (2013)
3. Cotton, S.R., Anderson, W.A., i McCullough, B.M.: Impact of the internet use on loneliness and contact with others among older adults: cross-sectional analysis. J. Med. Internet Res. **15**(2), e39 (2013)
4. Cumbie, B.A., Kar, B.: A study of local government website inclusiveness: the gap between e-government concept and practice. Inf. Technol. Dev. **22**(1), 15–35 (2016)
5. Ehrenberg, A., Goodhardt, G.: Double jeopardy revisited, again - many marketers still don't know about this widely occurring phenomenon. Mark. Res. **14**(1), 40–42 (2002)
6. Ghobakhloo, M., Arias-Aranda, D., Benitez-Amado, J.: Adoption of e-commerce applications in SMEs. Ind. Manage. Data Syst. **111**(8), 1238–1269 (2011)
7. Helbig, N., Gil-Garcia, J.R., Ferro, E.: Understanding the complexity of electronic government: implications from the digital divide literature. Gov. Inf. Q. **26**(1), 89–97 (2009)
8. Hogeboom, D.L., McDermott, R.J., Perrina, K.M., Osman, H., Bell-Ellison, B.A.: The internet use and social networking among middle aged and older adults. Educ. Gerontol. **36**(2), 93–111 (2010)
9. Kossecki, P.: Kreowanie zaufania w handlu elektronicznym – wyniki badań ilościowych [Eng.: Creating Trust in Electronic Commerce - the Results of Quantitative Research]. Problemy Zarządzania, 2/2005 (8): 250–276 (2005)
10. Koukova, N.T., Kannan, P.K., Kirmani, A.: Multiformat digital products: how design attributes interact with usage situations to determine choice. J. Mark. Res. **49**(1), 100–114 (2012)
11. Lopez-Nicolas, C., Soto-Acosta, P.: Analyzing ICT adoption and use effects on knowledge creation: an empirical investigation in SMEs. Int. J. Inf. Manage. **30**(6), 521–528 (2010)
12. Ludwiszewski, B., Redlarski, K., Wachowicz, J.: Możliwości zastosowania metody Kansei Engineering w projektowaniu usług on-line dla osób zagrożonych wykluczeniem cyfrowym [Eng.: The Kansei Engineering Method Application Possibilities in the Design Process of On-line Services for the Digital Exclusion Endangered People]. Sikorski M., Marasek K. (eds.), Interfejs użytkownika. Kansei w praktyce. Warszawa: PJWSTK (2011)
13. Nagamachi, M.: Kansei engineering – a new ergonomic consumer-oriented technology for product development. Int. J. Ind. Ergon. **15**(1), 3–11 (1995)
14. Nagamachi, M.: Kansei engineering as a powerful consumer-oriented technology for product development. Appl. Ergon. **33**(3), 289–294 (2002)
15. Nielsen, J.: Usability 101: Introduction to usability. http://www.nngroup.com/articles/usability-101-introduction-to-usability/. Accessed 21 Sept 2014

16. Popławski, W., Zastempowski, M., Grego-Planer, D.: Niematerialne wartości źródłem ukrytej przewagi konkurencyjnej tajemniczych mistrzów polskiej gospodarki [Eng.: Intangible Values as a Hidden Source of Competitive Advantage of the Mystery Masters of Polish Economy]. UMK, Torun, Poland (2011)
17. Reddick, C.G.: Citizen interaction with e-government: from the streets to servers? Gov. Inf. Q. **22**(1), 38–57 (2005)
18. Sikorski, M., Wachowicz, J.: Towards the value-based design of on-line services. In: Kocak, A., Abimbola, T., Ozer, A., Watkins-Mathys, L. (eds.) Marketing and Entrepreneurship. Proceedings of Ankara University International Conference AUMEC 2009, Belek, Turkey, 20–23 April 2009, pp. 406–413 (2009)
19. Świerczyńska-Kaczor, U.: Wirtualne światy – nowe wyzwania dla menedżerów marketingu [Eng.: Virtual Worlds - New Challenges for Marketing Managers]. Problemy Zarzadzania **6**(4), 179–196 (2008)
20. Świerczyńska-Kaczor, U., Kossecki, P.: Lojalność nabywców wobec marek – jak uwzględniać zjawisko "podwójnej szkody" w zachowaniach internautów? [Eng.: Buyers Loyalty to Brands – How to Take into Consideration the Double Jeopardy Phenomenon in the Behavior of Internet Users?] Problemy Zarządzania, **5**(2): 146–157 (2007)
21. Wachowicz, J., Kossecki, P.: Zaufanie starszych użytkowników Internetu na tle zagrożenia wykluczeniem cyfrowym [Eng.: The Trust of Older InternetUsers vs. The Digital Exclusion Threat. Handel Wewnętrzny, vol. III, pp. 266–276 (2012)
22. Wachowicz, J., Ludwiszewski, B., Redlarski, K.: Factors Disturbing The Internet Usage in Opinion of Elderly Users. Managerial Challenges of the Contemporary Society, Iss. 4, 201–204, Risoprint, Cluj-Napoca, Romania (2012)
23. Wachowicz, J., Redlarski, K., Ludwiszewski, B.: Online services for the elderly towards a better quality of life: what encourages, what discourages? Psychol. Health **28**, 330–331 (2013)
24. Wrycza S., Gajda S.: eBusiness adoption benchmarking for the region, challenges and practices. In: Cunningham P., Cunningham M. (eds.) Exploiting the Knowledge Economy: Issues, Applications and Case Studies, pp. 295–301. IOS Press (2006)
25. Zhou, M., Dresner, M., Windle, R.: Revisiting feedback systems: trust building in digital markets. Inf. Manag. **46**(5), 279–284 (2009)

Author Index

Printed in the United States
By Bookmasters